THE SCOTTISH
MOUNTAINEERING
CLUB JOURNAL

Vol. XL	2007	No. 198

EDITORIAL

THE JOURNAL has not been given to over use of the 'Editorial' – in fact, from perusing back issues, it seems that this device has only hitherto been occasioned by the demise of one editor and the accession of another and, while recognising that tenure may not be solely in the gift of the encumbent, I take solace in the fact that history has shown there to be significantly more job security than that found, for example in the post of football manager. However, complacent I am not, and am only too aware that the 'full support of the committee' may lie just around the corner. Having said that, I have also been aware in recent years, (this year being the worst yet of my tenure) of a great deal of that very complaceny, indeed apathy, among the membership who, judging by the little feedback I do receive, seem all too happy to have the Journal fall through their door every summer but do little or nothing to support it by way of contributions. One does not need to be a demographic statistician to realise that our mainstays, the Smarts, the Slessers, the Campbells, Gribbons, Duttons, Biggars *et. al.* are getting on a bit and there are very few coming to replace them, and that does not bode well for the future.

There are a number of reasons for this and, apart from the obvious lack of literacy in the young, one of the main ones, I would suggest, is 'The Lure of The Mags.' I happened to be in Borders bookshop recently, tempted to 'consider my position' over worry about where this year's Journal was going to come from, when, after a triple shot latté from Costa, I sought further solace in a quick browse through these very 'Mags'. The fact that I picked up three, one after the other, and in each found major articles on Scottish climbing, two by our members and one by a recent W. H. Murray prize-winner, only served to take me a bit closer to the edge. I can understand that there are economics involved here and that the Journal cannot compete at that level, nor would I wish it do so. I only tell the tale, not as a criticism of those involved, who contribute greatly to the Journal, but to point up a reality that, unlike in days gone by, the outlets for writers are many and the Journal, for a number of reasons, is not necessarily the first port of call.

It should also be noted that I see the rise and rise of the 'Mags' as being directly responsible for our decline, both in circulation and in advertising revenue. Unlike the former, I don't think that the Club should be overly

Dave McLeod on Rhapsody E11, Dumbarton Rock. Photo: Steven Gordon.

concerned about this and seek in any way to change our focus or to compete in order to raise revenue because, put quite simply, we are in the hands of the market in this and what was a bonus – selling a few copies to defray costs – was simply that and its time has passed.

We are a club Journal first and foremost and that is what our focus should continue to be. That said, I would wish us to retain a position in the forefront of such publications and this can only be done if members – across the board – will contribute. Your president voiced the opinion to me of late (in a phone call after hearing reports of my fragile state of mind following the 'Borders Incident' sounds very Le Carré does that!) that he felt perhaps the high standard of writing intimidated would be contributors – nice thought – but personally I'm more inclined towards the 'lazy buggers' theory myself.

Please guys it's your Journal, it has a good reputation, it has enjoyed 116 years of unbroken publication – Let's all get involved and keep it up there.

Charlie J. Orr, Hon. Ed.

THE LAST OF THE GRAND OLD MASTERS
(Tom Patey, a personal memoir)

By Dennis Gray

"You're a long time dead," as Don Whillans often observed. But if it is true that, as the ancients believed, one lives on while anyone still remembers you, then Tom Patey is still with us in spirit. Along with Don he was the most unforgettable character in my five decades plus of climbing. He was a doctor, musician, writer, raconteur and mountaineer of the highest ability. I have never met anyone else in the climbing world with such an array of talents. And to give some indication of this versatility I would like to record some of my own experiences in his company.

In 1951, as a 15-year-old, I hitch-hiked on my own from West Yorkshire to Skye, and there, in the MacRaes' barn, I first met Tom and his fellow Aberdonian Bill Brooker. They were older than I was and Patey, though himself still a teenager, had started training as a doctor. Bill decided I was a "cheeky little bugger" but from that first meeting I remained friends with both of them and enjoyed many memorable 'excursions' with Tom until his tragic death in 1970.

His climbing record bears comparison with most, recording a myriad of first ascents in Scotland, particularly in the Cairngorms and the Northern Highlands; outstanding new routes in the Alps, and the first ascents of the Mustagh Tower and Rakaposhi. Plus some early pioneering in the south-west of England on the Shale Cliffs, Chudleigh and the Dewerstone. Most of which was achieved when he had to meet the demands of his work as a doctor – with a huge geographic area to cover – and in being a family man. But above all, a fact making him unique, was the marrying together of so many high-standard abilities into what can only be termed the mountain scene. Anyone not familiar with Tom's writings and climbs, and the spirit in which they were carried out should read his posthumously published book of articles and songs, *One Man's Mountains* (Gollancz). Many of these had previously been published in the *Scottish Mountaineering Club Journal* or in magazines such as *Mountain*.

I climbed in several different locations with him, and even on one occasion accompanied him to one of my local outcrops Almscliff, where his highly unorthodox techniques were tested to the limit. Somehow he climbed the *Bird's Nest Crack* (HS), a smooth crack climb without jamming but with lots of judicious use of his knees! But it was in the high mountains that he came into his own, and on mixed ground of snow, ice and rock I never saw anyone to equal his ability at picking a line and moving fast. However, my own most memorable outing with him was when I lived in Scotland and, in March 1966, we visited Applecross together.

We stayed in the inn near the Bealach na Ba pass, where Tom had once been based while working as a locum for the local doctor. When we arrived, old friendships were renewed, and that evening – and subsequent evenings – after a fine meal and a few drams, the music began to flow. A heartening feature of these outposts in the Highlands is that people can still make their own entertainment.

The next day we solo climbed three routes, including the famous *Cioch Nose* of Sgurr a' Chaorachain, a fine climb and then a long rambling Hard Severe, which, when I suggested that it looked a bit loose and vegetated before we set out Tom admonished me with: "Good god mon it has some of the finest vegetation in Applecross!"

Our final route was for me an epic. Much shorter than the other two it was nonetheless 350ft. in length; *The Sword of Gideon,* pioneered in 1961 by Tom, climbing solo. It lies on a buttress a few minutes up from the Bealach na Ba road, on the north side of the pass. The crux is 5a and in the guide the route is graded HVS. Tom climbed in front of me, this being something he was enthusiastic about, climbing what he called "solo together". By the time we reached the 5a pitch I had lost my enthusiasm for this, and needed a rope, especially as we were climbing in boots and carrying light sacks. Tom had his old 'for emergency only' light rope in his, but by that time he was so far ahead I had to grit my teeth and keep battling upwards on my own. We ended the climb in the dark – with Tom a good day's climbing always finished at the day's end – and descending, we came down on the wrong side of the buttress. We escaped swinging down on Tom's old rope, descending in the darkness. My head torch had packed in and Patey did not have one, claiming to be able to see in the dark. I have never been so relieved to set foot back on a road in my life.

With Tom every outing was an adventure. This was the spirit in which he approached his climbing, but do not misunderstand this, for although he often had to climb solo for lack of companions, and despite his unorthodox climbing style, he was an extremely safe climber. As he pointed out, the habitual solo climber has to be competent, otherwise he will soon be dead, and Tom did not die during such a climb. He was killed while abseiling in the company of experienced companions after an ascent of The Maiden, a sea-stack in Sutherland.

Tom was the most unlikely looking doctor I have yet come across. Powerfully built, of medium height and with bushy dark hair, he had a face which looked as if it had been hewn from the granite of his native county. Spontaneity played a large part in his climbing activities, and he often made do with a minimum of equipment, enjoyed travelling light and would think nothing of climbing all day without a rest or a stop for food. He had built up an incredible bodily stamina over the years and he could manage on a minimum of sleep for days on end.

On one occasion we based ourselves in Jimmie Ross's hotel, The

Rowanlea in the Cairngorms for five nights. Each night there was a ceilidh in the bar, and each day we roved far and wide into the hills. One day to Braeriach, another a route in Glen Avon. Our party was made up of Jim McCartney, Eric Beard, Tom and myself, and by the fourth day I had to insist on climbing in Coire an Lochan which is easily reached from off the ski road. I just could not stand the pace of the other three who moved at great speed on the long walks in and out again. Eric held just about every worthwhile fell record in the UK, including the Skye Ridge, when he was killed in a car crash in 1969. And Jim, a fellow Aberdonian, could have been Tom's natural successor on the northern Bens in winter, for he was one the most powerful ice climbers of his generation, but cruelly, he was to die in an avalanche on Ben Nevis in January 1970.

News spread about the evening ceilidhs and more and more climbers and skiers turned up for the event. Jimmie was one of the outstanding exponents of the Highland fiddle and with Tom backing him on the accordion or piano they were an unforgettable duo. Patey had the finest repertoire of tunes and ballads of anyone I have met, and his own songs, poking fun at our sport and its institutions and personalities, were masterpieces of subtlety.

When I lived in Scotland in the mid-Sixties I worked for a Glasgow printing and publishing firm and I had a roving commission over the whole of Scotland. We printed the Aberdeen bus tickets, the Cairngorm chair lift passes, and the timetable for the Orkney and Shetland shipping line. On the back of the latter there was, on one occasion, a picture of the Old Man of Hoy. Shortly after this came out I visited Ullapool, where Tom was the doctor, to meet representatives of the Council for they wished to have a tourist brochure published to promote the delights of their picturesque town. I stayed with Tom and his wife, Betty, and I showed him the picture of the Old Man of Hoy and asked him if it had ever been climbed. He thought not and took the brochure from me and the rest, as they say, is history. He went on from the ascent of Hoy to climb several other sea-stacks; The Old Man of Stoer, Am Buachaille, Handa etc. which earned him the nickname of Dr Stack!

Tom kept a set of scrapbooks and you were very privileged if he showed them to you. In them he kept photographs and magazine cuttings, particularly about the Alps and on these he had traced many new route possibilities. It was from this source that many of the new climbs he pioneered around Chamonix in the Sixties were gleaned. First ascents such as the West Face of the Plan, the North-west Face of the Aiguille Sans Nom, the North Face of the Point Migot and several others, usually in the company of the 'uman fly, Joe Brown.

The Bailie of Ullapool went by the nickname of 'The Giant', and he was a great friend of the Doctor's. I expected him to be a huge Highlander like the man on the Scott's porridge oats packet, and was surprised at our first meeting to find that he was a wee fellow and that his nickname was obviously given in jest.

Behind Tom's house in Ullapool was a bothy, which he had caused to be set up for any visiting climber to stay, and from which a vast swathe of the Northern Highlands were accessible. There was also, adjacent to this, a small operating facility, for sometimes in winter the road to Inverness became blocked with snow. Amazingly, word of his bothy had reached as far as Munich. Once when I was visiting, some climbers from that city were in residence and they had brought Tom a record entitled *Hitler's inferno*. Tom could hardly wait to play it to me when I arrived and I was surprised that this included a selection of wartime Wermacht marching songs. In his youth Tom's initial Salvationist approach to the hills, had been eroded. Gordon Leslie, one of his early companions, cultivated a distinctly Teutonic brand of humour, which had left its mark on him. It was with Gordon that, in December 1950, Tom pioneered the first Grade V winter route in the Cairngorms, *Douglas-Gibson's Gully* on Lochnagar. One of Tom's earliest songs contained the following verse:

Two tiny figures on the ghastly north wall
And a hungry great bergschrund just right for a fall
Let the Valkyries howl in the pitiless sky
But the two tiny climbers must 'Conquer or die!'

It was in Tom's bothy that the Alpine Club song *Red Pique* was written. I was with him on that occasion and my prior task had been to visit the pub and obtain a bottle of the Doctor's usual 'Morangie'. The original of the Alpine Club song was too trenchant for general release and so a watered down version was subsequently prepared and this is what appears in *One Man's Mountains*. I kept the original under lock and key for more than 30 years and then, deeming it alright to do so, passed it over to the Club's Secretary for safe keeping. Perhaps some day the original can be published and I will make the suggestion that the Alpine Club arranges for this song to be performed on a suitable occasion. Perhaps at an Annual Dinner? Meanwhile, it would still, I am sure, be rewarding to hear sung in good voice a verse such as that below which is from the version which is published in Tom's book:

The noble blood of an English Peer
Adapts to a rarefied atmosphere
And that is why the Old School Tie
May be expected to go high
Up they go, Damn good show
Kicking steps in the virgin snow
Hey nonny No! Fol de rol
Jolly John Hunt and the Old South Col.

And before the editor is tempted to reach for a red pen, I can assure the reader Tom's intention was always to have fun and not to jeer. He was happy that I kept the original out of circulation pointing out that such whisky-fuelled rhyming might be construed as libellous. He wrote a song about myself, not as good but in a similar vein to his outstanding, *The Legend of Joe Brown*. But as it included reference to a young lady with whom I was having what is now referred to as an 'affair Blunkett', and it all ended rather sadly, he was happy that this too never saw a wide circulation. The chorus line was:

Dennis Dillon Gray she has taken him away
And he'll never climb on Cloggy any more!
He'll be fitter he'll be fatter, but still full of bleeding patter
That poor old Yorkshire Pudding Dennis Gray
(Sung to the tune of 'Keep your feet still Geordie Hinnie').

Tom's songs such as *Onward Christian Bonington*, *The Legend of Joe Brown*, *The Last of the Grand Old Masters*, and a spurious Teutonic version of the SMC club song *Oh My Big Hobnailers*, but tranposed by him into *Ach Mein Grossenbotten* were satirical masterpieces. No one so lampooned ever, to the best of my knowledge, took offence. But to understand just how effective these were you had to have heard Patey sing these parodies in person. Such songs and singing have a long historical tradition in these Islands. When I was studying in Leeds I organised, a folk and poetry club at the Grove Inn, with five other students. One night at a party I sang and played a couple of Tom's songs for them and everyone then wanted to meet him. One of my acquaintances was Bob Pegg who, with his wife, Carol, had their own club and, with another friend Nick Strutt went on to form 'Mr Fox', the first folk rock band which was the forerunner of the subsequently famous 'Fairport Convention'. They asked on the strength of this if I could bring Tom to their club in Kirkstall.

By diverse means, on our way back from a trip to Wales where we had been the guests at a Pinnacle Club dinner, and after a failed winter attempt on *The Slanting Gully* of Lliewedd, subsequently *en route* for Lochnagar, I managed to persuade him to stop off. Tom played and sang for them as they wished, and afterwards Bob and Nick agreed that as a lyricist his word play was outstanding. No mean accolade for Bob Pegg held the first Doctorate in Folk Music.

In 1967 I persuaded Tom and Joe Brown to do a lecture tour on their Mustagh Tower expedition. Joe will not normally undertake such activities, and the only other occasion I have known him take this on was when Don Whillans died and a group of his friends came together to raise funds for a suitable memorial to him. Climbers in England had never then heard Tom or Joe lecture and the three events I organised were all well attended despite it being 11 years after the expedition had taken place. The first lecture took place in the Holdsworth Hall, Manchester, Joe's hometown, and it was a sell-out. Afterwards, Joe went home to his mother's, while Tom and I went out on the town with some of the city's climbing fraternity. We ended up in the Riverboat Club in Salford where we were gobsmacked to find on entering, that there was a strip contest in progress. Tom the son of an episcopal minister observed that: "Nothing like this ever takes place in Ullapool!"

The second night was in Liverpool in the Mountford Hall and again it was well supported. Both Joe and Tom were excellent speakers, and the crowd loved it. Joe was already a legend in climbing circles by this time, while Tom was also a mythical figure. Afterwards, Joe again went off home to spend the night at his mother's in Manchester, leaving Tom and I to be the guests at an after lecture party in a large house in the Sefton Park area of Liverpool. Tom was, in such company, extremely sociable and he loved mixing with fellow climbers. Out came the accordion and he sang and played the night away. I remember Pete Minks, Tony Stead, and a young Al Rouse were among those present and I think it was because of such meetings that Tom eventually agreed to take on the Presidency of the Alpine Climbing Group in 1969. But then I lost him, he just disappeared and I was in a blind panic.

The following night the final lecture was at the St George's Hall in Bradford. In an absolute sweat I arrived there early hoping Tom would appear out of the ether, for he was driving himself around in his Skoda car. On arriving at the Hall I pushed open the door and walked in. All was darkness except on the stage where someone was playing a Steinway grand piano. A part of the first movement of the Grieg Concerto rang out as I walked down the darkened aisles of that huge hall and I realised it was Tom. He was no Ashkenazy, but then few people are, however, he really could play and as in the past I had only heard him playing jazz, climbing songs or folk music. I sat down in the front row and listened quietly until he had finished. It was obvious that the music meant a lot to him, and as I enthusiastically shouted out when he finished playing he looked sheepishly back at me and dismissed this by saying he needed more practice. But as I knew already that it had been a toss up when he was young as to whether he would follow a career in classical music or medicine, I was not as surprised by this performance as I might otherwise have been.

Tom had to drive enormous distances in carrying out his medical duties in the Highlands and because of this, like his stamina for climbing, he had developed an impressive facility for driving long distances. He would occasionally phone me in the middle of the night at my flat in Edinburgh. "Would yea be available for a climb?" he would demand. If the reply was: "Err...err... yes", I would then receive an instruction to rendezvous somewhere near to Fort William, at the Laggan Bridge or in Rothiemurchus with the admonition: "Do not to be late or I'll go without you!" Usually, this meant being there by dawn, and if you protested that the roads were icy and that it might take some time, he would point out that it was only 3am. and: "Good god mon yea have at least three hours to get there!" For someone who drove such amazing distances, often in inclement weather, it was surprising he had so little mechanical knowledge. A glib salesman had talked him in to purchasing a Skoda car, back in the bad old days when they were a joke. I write this tongue in cheek for I later drove a Moskovich, but he was stuck with them. No other dealer would take it in part exchange and he needed to buy a new one nearly every year. I drove his car on several occasions, and once we crashed when Tom was driving due to experimenting with the adaptation of the O. G. Jones climbing grading system, to the road bends. I shouted out a Severe when it should have been Extreme on the old acute Z-bends at the Ingleton Bridge. He merely shrugged his shoulders and said: "Is it serious?" There was water and oil pouring out all over the road.

From 1957 to 1961 Tom served in the Royal Navy as the medical officer on attachment with 42 Marine Commando. Like all of us in the Fifties he was called to do National Service and took on a three-year short service Commission. Unfortunately, as he later told me, there was a mistake in his pay and emoluments at the Navy pay office, and they grossly overpaid him. He was thus forced into paying this back and the only way he could do this was by serving an extra year. His opinion of pay clerks was not very high, and I kept from him the news that as a non-combatant, my two years of forced service were spent at the Army Pay Office in Manchester and my task there had been to prepare the pay and emoluments of Officers!

At the end of the Sixties I did some lecturing for Exeter University to HM Forces units and many of Tom's commando climbing acquaintances were still in the area. Dickie Grant who had been with him on Rakaposhi was Colonel in charge at the training depot of the Royal Marines at Lympstone. Mike Banks was still around, and he had reached the summit of Rakaposhi with Patey on the Services expedition in 1958 of which he had been the leader. And Vin Stevenson, an old mate of mine from our Langdale days in the early Fifties, had been the leader of the Cliff Assault Wing. They all had stories about Tom; on Marine training trips to the Cairngorms, forays to Norway during which he had made a winter ascent of the Romsdalhorn with the legendary Arn Randers Heen, and climbing at Chudleigh (of which he was an original pioneer), on the Dewerstone, at Morwell etc. The story I liked best (and one that Tom told me himself) was 'The buggering of Brigadier Billy's boots'.

Tom was in the Cairngorms in the winter with a group of trainee Royal Marine commandos. By the end of the first week all he had taught them was how to find Karl Fuch's hostelry at Struan House in Carrbridge, but then he received a signal to report that Brigadier Billy was going to visit them to inspect their training. "Bloody hell this was serious!" So he sent his men up onto Cairngorm, in the command of a Sergeant and told them to dig into snow holes in Coire Raibert. The Brigadier duly arrived that evening and, after spending the night sharing quarters with Tom, decided early next morning to go up personally to see the men on the hill. But Tom in a panic could not find his boots. Mercifully, he found a new looking pair under a bed and surprisingly they fitted him.

Off they went up the hill and found the men all happily dug into snow holes. "Well done Patey," was the Brigadier's verdict but, on returning to the valley, and as he was preparing to leave he was ransacking the billet. He was looking for his best boots, which had been bulled and bulled by his batman until you could see your face in the toes. Of course these were the boots Tom had worn, and by then they looked like something even Charlie Chaplin would have discarded. Patey discreetly made himself scarce.

Academically gifted, Tom won the gold medal for Physiology while at Aberdeen University, and if the mountains had not held him in thrall all his life he might have followed two or three other brilliant careers. I think now we were fortunate that it was climbing which turned out to be his leitmotif. In the British mountain world during the 50-plus years I have been climbing, only three personalities known to me have, I believe, earned the status of being 'A Legend' – namely, Joe Brown, Don Whillans and, of course, Tom. To hear him play and sing *Dark Lochnagar,* a mountain on which he had writ his name large into its long climbing history, was a magical experience. He was truly one of the last of the Grand Old Masters who represented more than anyone else I have known the freedom to be found in the hills.

BRIEF HISTORY OF THE 'IAS' HILL-WALKING CLUB

By Graham E. Little

IT SEEMS that the European Union (EU), formally the European Community, is forever expanding with an enthusiastic queue of aspirant members. There are clearly strong attractions to being a member of this big club with all the economic and social benefits it offers. In homage to the pleasures of being a member of a much smaller club, I had the idea in 2002 of visiting all the mountainous countries in Europe with names ending in 'ia' before they joined the EU (in the comforting knowledge that my club would operate in a rapidly-changing environment with no hope of permanence). As the founding member, I immediately gave myself permission for a little bit of retrospective ticking, instantly claiming Slovakia, even though I'd visited in 1991 when it was still part of Czechoslovakia. This was essentially a rock climbing trip to the Tatra Mountains and the fantastic sandstone towers of Teplice and Adrspach. However, it did include an ascent of Lomnicky Stit, 2635m., not to mention saying goodbye to the last Russian General to leave the country – somewhat bizarrely at a pop concert in Prague (with a guest appearance from Frank Zappa). Slovakia joined the EU in 2004.

The true beginnings of the 'ias' hill-walking club coincided with a change in lifestyle, with family holidays taking over from climbing trips with the boys (although the bi-annual expeditions still linger on!). With an impressive membership of three – including my wife and son – the club's first outing was to Slovenia in July 2003. This small country at the eastern extension of the Western Alps, where if the guidebooks are to be believed, every citizen has a genetic desire to ascend Triglav, 2864m., the country's highest peak, is many times blessed. With the magnificent Julian Alps in the north, fertile plains to the south, a little section of Adriatic coastline and a healthy national identity, it is as close to an ideal country as one can imagine. Surprisingly, considering the mayhem that was later to engulf the Balkans, Slovenia achieved its independence from the former Yugoslavia in 1991 with only a 10 -day near bloodless war.

Armed only with the expression 'Dobra Dan' (often shortened to 'Dan') we booked a package deal and established our base at the Bellevue Hotel on the shore of Lake Bohinj (where Agatha Christie wrote a number of her detective stories). We ranged across the stunning limestone peaks, limited only by what a six-year-old boy was capable of doing (at a push!). Avoiding Triglav, the highest peak, for logistical reasons (it's a two-three day outing), we tackled several of the more accessible peaks, largely following way-marked routes, with the steel cables and ladders giving reassurance on the more exposed sections. After a hard day on the hill, it was a delight to walk through the flower decked meadows and to swim in the surprisingly warm waters of Lake Bohinj. The mountaineering highlight was an ascent of the mighty Prisank, 2547m., from the high Vrsic Pass, via the East Ridge route, with a descent down the South-west face. Roped adults were somewhat taken aback at the sight of a small boy picnicking on the summit! A couple of days later, I left the other club members to enjoy a canoe outing on Lake Bohinj and climbed the excellent Razor, 2601m., to the south of Prisank, finding the name of Terry Isles in the summit log book. Trying not to sound like a hyperbolic member of the Slovenian Tourist Board, I have to say that Slovenia is a really brilliant country with a day in the capital Ljubljana a must. Slovenia joined the EU in 2004.

Given the political and economic restrictions on foreign travel, it's not surprising that hillwalking and climbing on home ground or in immediately adjacent countries was the only real holiday option for the vast majority of people in the Soviet block countries. The breakdown of the Soviet Union in 1991 heralded a slow increase in holidays abroad for the locals and an influx of Western Europeans keen to sample the delights of hitherto unknown mountain ranges, using the fine network of paths and huts and enjoying the favourable exchange rates. Bulgaria well illustrates these changes. Bulgaria holds two main mountain ranges, the Perin and the Rila, both with peaks close to the 3000m. mark. Although the Black Sea coast has long attracted tourists of a certain persuasion, the mountains, with the exception of the winter ski resorts, have been largely neglected by Western mountaineers. Bulgaria is now easy to get to, good value to stay in and, with the exception of some truly terrible roads – erratic driving is mandatory – a pleasure to visit. The road signs are mostly in Cyrillic script and the maps pretty hopeless but this all adds to the sense of adventure.

In July 2005 we flew to Sophia and, from a base in Bansko, enjoyed several great days in the Perin Mountains. This fine range is composed of granite in the east, limestone in the west. At the interface is the shining marble peak of Vihren, 2914m. (the second highest peak in Bulgaria) which together with its fine neighbour Kutelo, 2908m., gave us a splendid outing from the carpark at Hizha Vihren, descending over shrinking snowfields below the shovel–shaped North-west face. Another excellent day was had, again starting from the same car park, when we hiked past Frog Lake and Long Lake to scramble over great granite blocks up the narrow East Ridge of Bunderishki Chukar, 2731m.

A very hot day in the Rila Mountains proved too much for my wife and son who mellowed out at the magnificent Rila Monastery (a UNESCO World Heritage Site), deep in the valley. I struggled to the summit of Maljovica (Malyovista), 2729m, under a basting sun and under constant attack from huge cleg-like flies with bulging green eyes and a well developed blood lust.

Lost in the heart of Sofia, on our way back to the airport at the end of the holiday, in desperation my wife accosted some Bulgarian police – in mid arrest! – to ask directions. Bundling their suspects into the back of their car and with blaring sirens, they guided us through the city centre at high speed to gain the route out to the airport. I can't imagine that happening back home.

In May 2006 I managed a short rock climbing trip to Croatia with the boys, encouraged by my wife who realised that I needed to get to grips with some serious rock. Although bolt protected and therefore relatively safe, the solid mountain limestone in Paklenika National Park is a joy to climb on which is qualification enough in my book for Croatia joining the EU immediately. There is something for everyone, from single pitch top-roping exercises to multi-pitch classics on the highest rock wall in Croatia. For me, the highlight of the trip was the magnificent *Velebitaski*, a 12-pitch 6+ route (climbed with Phil Ebert) leading to the summit of Anika Kuk, 712m. The superb fish restaurant, appropriately called Dalmatia, in the nearby village of Starigrad was definitely a bonus. Croatia is currently an EU 'candidate country'.

In July 2006, having recently watched a daft, but rather entertaining, film about Transylvanian vampirism, we flew to Bucharest in Romania to pick up a hire car and embark upon our grand tour of the South Western Carpathians. Arranging accommodation as we travelled and enjoying daytime temperatures ranging from 7° to 37° centigrade, we climbed in five mountain groups, and visited the stunning medieval centres of towns like Brasov, Sighisoara and Sibiu. The evidence of the Ceausescu regime was everywhere with crumbling concrete factories standing witness to misguided attempts to industrialise the countryside. However, Romania proved a captivating country with much to enthral the mountain lover.

Starting in the verdant Ciucas, with its strange conglomerate towers, we progressed to the limestone spine of Piatra Craiului, to the great schist mountains of the Fagaras and the Parang to finish on the excellent fine grey granite peaks of the Retezat range. My son was delighted to realise that a month's pocket money made him a Romanian millionaire and we thought nothing about blowing two million lei on a night's accommodation. The cabanas (mountain huts) ranged from very run down to the well maintained and from road accessible to those requiring a two-three hour walk to reach. We climbed over a dozen peaks with the highlights being an ascent of Parangule Mare, 2519m., in the Parang from the excellent roadside Groapa Seaca Cabana and an eleven round in the Retezat, including Custura, 2457m., Papusa, 2508m. and Peleaga, 2509m., (the latter two in Romania's top 10) from the Buta Cabana. We even took the tourist soft option by staying in the modern Balea Lac Cabana (the only accommodation we stayed in that would accept Euros), near the highest point of the spectacular trans-Fagaras highway. From this high point, the main Fagaras ridge is easily accessible, with the rocky summit of Vanatoarea lui Buteanu, 2507m., less than an hour away.

Climbing days were interspersed with cultural pursuits and sampling the local produce, especially the wine. Romanians love eating al-fresco, often to blaring music, but have the unfortunate habit of leaving all their rubbish at the picnic site – there are some strange contradictions in the national psyche. Both Bulgaria and Romania are lined up to join the EU in 2007, although certain governance concerns are outstanding.

So where to next? The only other 'candidate country' that I haven't visited is Macedonia, having been refused entry from Bulgaria because we couldn't provide the required car hire documentation. However, as it definitely has some mountains we will no doubt make a second attempt some time soon. After that there are only the longer shots of Bosnia, Serbia and Albania who's EU membership aspirations will no doubt grow. Sadly, we missed the boat with Estonia, Latvia and Lithuania, although I guess they can hardly be classed as mountainous. Another option would be to change the club constitution at the next AGM and climb a hill or two in Austria!

BOULDERING WITH GHOSTS

By John Watson

GHOSTS have different solutions to things, they bring you different gifts. Nonchalantly, they walk through the walls of time, in swirls of out-moded language and kit, often dressed absurdly, sometimes in tweed or wartime surplus, sometimes in lycra, recently with strange beds attached to their backs like colourful hermit crabs. Each one has a different approach, a different piece of rock in mind, a different way of saying the same thing.

Here I was thinking I'd have the boulders to myself – I'd squeezed the boulder kit into the Dropzone mat, hauled the beast onto my back and stomped off up the new path to The Cobbler, intent on the clean schist swirls of the Narnain boulders. Out of nostalgia, I turned right up the old pipe-walk, steeper but quicker, stopping at the water-cup cistern on the flat bit before entering the corrie under the horns of The Cobbler. Maybe that diversion is what started it all. It was a fine summer's day, the sweat stung my eyes and a pleasant breeze whispered stolen conversations through the deer grass. I dumped my boulder mat by the first boulder and took off my top letting it dry in the breeze. I pulled a Sigg bottle out and glugged down the cool contents.

Then I heard the voices…a party of folk on the other side of the North boulder, but there was something odd about them, like the words inside a church meeting, they seemed deeper, differently inflected, sterner, but also light and relieved with the joy of a summer's day in the high corries. Normally no boulderers up here, I thought. Maybe walkers? I threw on a fresh T-Shirt (www.scottishclimbs.com – a fetching blue with orange logo, I seem to recall) and stepped round the corner. The shaded north face sported a stand-out arête on which a flat-capped climber in ragged short-cut pantaloons was fully stretched. He seemed to be wearing walking boots, loosely laced about his ankles, I was quite impressed, for I knew the problem was British 6a and steep, with tiny footholds and surely too technical for a pair of old leathers. There was a posse of similarly dressed lads around him, from teens through to bristled looking industrial types in flat caps or double-rolled beanies, old woollen sweaters and army surplus trousers, odd fashion I thought as I nodded at one or two of them who glanced my way.

"Go oan John!" shouted one. "Show them SMC boys how it's done!" and he winked at me for some reason.

"Don't look at me," I whispered and looked up at the climber, while peeling a banana.

"Where'd you get that?" said one of the younger boys.

"Sainsbury's," I said. "...organic." He seemed to be fixated on the banana. I pointed the banana at the problem: "That's at least an E3 crux," I added. He blinked. I decided to say no more. Our attention turned back to the boulderer.

A high hand-hold allowed him to pull down powerfully and get his feet high on the arête and then a steady leaning-back, studying the next holds, showed he was a poised 'trad-man', though I had the oddest feeling he'd done this before and that this was for effect. Indeed, all the other lads looked humbled – the greatest sign of this being a communal burying of hands deep in the pockets and the hunch-backed stance like a heron, which either means: "Yeah, it's easy, I could do it if I was bothered," or it could mean: "No way I'm trying that!" I wasn't sure which way it was with this group, but I felt I was witnessing something a little special, the gentle banter surrounding an event of some significance being treated as casually insignificant, the trademark of all great moments. The climber topped out, turned round, leaned over and put his hands on his knees.

"Right lads, who's next?"

Uproarious laughter and a dismissive waving of hands. Smiles all round. I found myself smiling too.

"Grand bit of climbing, John, just grand!" said somebody.

"Aye, no bad," I piped up. "What about the sit start though?"

John Cunningham stared down from on high.

"The whit?"

I swallowed as the posse all turned and looked blankly towards me. I had the acute feeling that I'd just stepped into a welder's yard with a tray of Tiffin.

Other ghosts can leave you furious, despite their reputation. Here's what happened. I was busy tending the handholds and footholds of a Font 8a, smacking them vigorously with a chalky beer mat. Clouds of carbonate dust made me choke and step back, then return to flog away again, hoping to squeak the holds dry enough to allow some sort of friction. I was thinking of using 'pof', but demurred and thought the rag would do, I'd be pilloried anyway, my shame would be all over the forums. There was a polite cough behind me as I applied the finishing touch of the toothbrush to the extra carbonate slick. I stepped back from the overhanging crack I was busy cleaning, defensively dipping my hands in a large chalk-bag like it was one of those film-star's hand-muffs. I raised my eyebrows.

"Alright?" I said.

The man was dressed head to toe in tweed, plus-foured at the bottom with puttees spiralling into the top of two brown leather boots. A fringe of hob-nails winked along the lip of the soles like shark-teeth. He wore a nifty trilby-style hat and he was smoking a fat pipe which was wedged heavily into a moustachioed mouth. Very camp, I thought.

"A stumbling block, eh?" he inquired, running his pipe up the line of the crack. "Mind awfully if I give it a jolly?"

It was a rhetorical question. He put the pipe back in his mouth, rummaged through a bulging hip pocket and pulled out a stubby hammer. From his left pocket he pulled some ironmongery, stepped up to the crack and, before I could offer him my toothbrush or chalk-bag, began to bang in an iron piton. The echoing clangs sank the peg deep into the crack and he expertly fiddled a short cord through the eyelet, tied it off, then, giving it one tug, he hauled himself up, hobnails scrabbling on my 'poffed' little ledge. He reached the big flange, explored it experimentally for a few seconds, then dropped back down to the ground. He was reaching in his pocket for another peg before I touched him on the elbow…

"Hey, what the hell do you think you are doing?"

I recognised him now…it was Harold Raeburn, he'd soloed *Observatory Ridge* in this outfit at the turn of a previous century. I liked the guy in his books, with his earnest instructional photos from *Mountaineering Art*. But hell, he was no boulderer, he had no ethics at all…abominable approach! I scolded him: Hobnails? Pitons? Did he know the damage he was doing? I had to ask him to leave, politely of course, put his hammer away. He pocketed his ironmongery, walked off sulking with his pipe and stood under the crag a while, gazing up at a long snaking crack which withered away before the apex of the cliff.

After I wiggled the peg out, I went back to working my project, shaking my head occasionally, brushing and re-chalking all the scratched and muddy holds. When I looked round after a while he had gone. I felt the pang of unexpected sadness.

"Dammit," I said to myself, dipping my hands back into the chalk sack, "I meant to say cheerio."

Other times the ghosts are not climbers, they appear as souls and people who, despite any rational rigour, invade your emotions in certain landscapes at certain times. They can leave you invigorated with a sense of the great wheel of life, or they can leave you angry, embittered and sad at the random swipe of history and its cruel tantrums of indifference.

My bouldering was interrupted by my own ignorance one day. I'd escaped to the Trossachs, to a special bouldering spot known as 'An Garradh', or 'The Garden' – a jumble of boulders under a wooded copse

Andy Nisbet on Still Game (VI,7), upper tier of West Buttress, Coire Mhic Fhearchair. Photo: Dave McGimpsey.

on the flanks of Loch Katrine. I was aware of a curious ghost following me through the boulders in the copse. I didn't see her until I'd gained some height and could see the shadowed grass of her family's run-rigs, the melted rubble of her shieling.

It is the late spring sun which brings her out to play, away from the stern retributions and privations of her home. She is dressed in a filthy linen smock which barely covers her driftwood frame, but despite that she is happily singing away among the boulders, occasionally chewing wild garlic leaves and spitting them out in disgust: "Yechhh..."

Suddenly, she's at the top of the boulder I am climbing.

"You can see for miles here... aw the way to France." She clutches her skinny raw legs and bites her knees, soaking up the glory of her Highland home, tranquil in the sun, a lookout at the junction of these perpendicular lochs, watching the smoke of her house rise into the still air of a clear Scottish day. She frowns at me. "What are you doing? You should be working, the cattle need shiftin', does your father know you're here?"

I gain the top of the boulder but she is gone again. I clasp my own knees and stare out over the landscape for a while, looking for clues to something I don't quite apprehend. When I look carefully, hold my gaze longer than a few seconds, the blunted outline of the ruined shieling rebuilds itself like the internal magic of salt crystals, the run-rigs sprout with crops, the detail sharpens and there she is, running over the tufted grass, through the sucking sphagnum up to the boulders where her favourite spot is, where she gains reflection, where she comes to claim this land as her own. This is her view, these are her stones. Her mother will call her down, but for the moment she is queen of the rocks in this hardened place. I am a curious visitor, like a coloured bird from the woods, or a strange beetle she might poke with a snapped reed.

Then the vision wipes as a cloud passes over. The smoke fades in swirls of nothing, the shieling sags down under the grass like a fugitive hiding under a cloak, there is the sound of schist rock calving and blocks of stone heaving to the bluebelled earth. Erosion. Time. Deer collapse and shrink into their bones, flies buzz their furious dot-to-dot pictures and flesh dissolves into the ground. These are Clearance lands, I must remind myself. These are not necessarily pleasant visions and it is right and proper I get things in perspective.

I pack up my boulder mat for another day, closing the book on another landscape and head back to the city, all the ghosts stuffed back into the mountains – layers in the rock, one on top of the other, assuming the geology of silence, the end of all our brief skeins of time on this earth and I am happy in my own way. Indeed, it seems to me that bouldering can be a form of listening...to deeper histories, to voices that ring like struck stones and too easily vanish into the clear air.

Heather Morning with trainee SARDA dog, Milly, looking south towards The Devil's Point. Photo: Carl Haberl.

Niall McNair throws for a hold on the second ascent of Spitfire 8a, The Anvil, Loch Goil.

CLOSE ENCOUNTERS WITH TOM WEIR

By Ken Crocket

My first real encounter with the free spirit that was Tom Weir took place around 1985; I had finished the manuscript of my Ben Nevis history and before I had approached any publisher the Scottish Mountaineering Trust asked me if I would consider them. They gave the MS to Tom to read, and following this he invited me to his home in Gartocharn.

As just about everyone who has visited Tom will know, a pair of boots or wellies is advisable. He whisked you off for a walk through the neighbouring Nature Reserve betwixt Loch Lomond and the Endrick Water, where his gimlet eyes, trained by a lifetime of animal watching, would pick out small birds, made microscopic by distance but obvious to the maestro. Although I remained appreciative, I could never remember one small bird from another, but he never showed any annoyance.

Before our first walk, he stopped me in my tracks with a question about the book: "Who is it written for?" In my blinkered enthusiasm for the subject, this crucial commercial point had never entered my mind.

"For climbers I suppose," was the only answer I could give. He gave a non-committal grunt and the walk began.

The book went ahead and Tom, with typical generosity, wrote the Foreword. Our paths met from time to time, and I was a Vice-President during his time as President. I even received the honour of having a cover photograph of The Ben for the Scots Magazine, thanks, no doubt, to a friendly word from Tom. This was in 1986.

Tom was by now in his mid-70s, when most climbers would be content to wind down a little, ease off on the grades, and certainly lose interest in the latest bit of shiny, tinkling gear. Not this man. I received a telephone call one night. He was curious about this "front-pointing thingy", and would I possibly be able to show him what it was all about? My brain began to go over the potential outcomes, good, bad, and disastrous. So I asked him whether he had any particular route in mind, thinking he might suggest some easy snow gully. Would I mind *Crowberry Gully* was the answer, he quite fancied doing it again using the new methods. I said yes, all the while wondering quite what I had gotten into.

We agreed to wait for a good spell of weather and conditions, and go for a mid-week date when presumably the hill would be quieter. February came and so did the day, so off up to Glen Coe we headed. Neither of us had children, and we had not reckoned with school holidays, especially English school holidays. The gully was lined with teachers from down south, all slowly and deliberately stepping up the wonderful line that is *Crowberry Gully* in good condition.

I tied Tom into a spare Whillans harness, gave him a two-minute basic primer in the use of two banana picks, and off we went. We moved steadily until we reached the belay below the Junction Pitch, where the inevitable traffic jam was waiting. Having climbed Crowberry four or five times previously, I knew how much time we needed. I also knew how much daylight was left, and, at the pace of the slowest rope above, it would be a night finish. Climbing with such a senior statesman as Tom I was in an awkward position; I was going to leapfrog several ropes by traversing hard right onto steeper ice then climb straight up parallel to the more normal line – there was no other way. I could do it without interfering with any of the other teams – who were paragons of good manners I must add – but I had to run the plan past Tom. He was perfectly content to let me do what I felt had to be done if we were to finish the gully.

The traverse right and the climb up led to a steep belay on deep snow. A deadman and an indifferent foot ledge had me sweating blood. The embarrassment of a fall here was one I would never live down – assuming I lived that is. Tom came up like a trooper of course, admitting to being impressed by the ambience. And all the while I was leading, the gully was echoing with conversations between this rope and that rope with Tom, lecture dates were arranged, names exchanged and friends made.

Apologies were made as I passed climbers, but no feathers were ruffled as we made the belay at the foot of the last real pitch, the icy Cave Pitch. Another apology to a pair of teachers and I set off up the bouncy ice. I belayed above and watched Tom closely here. He was by now showing signs of tiredness, unsurprisingly. Most novices at front-pointing expend too much energy at first, until they gain some experience. Tom had been a pensioner for some years now. As he made the last moves over the ice bulge his picks were bouncing gently, but his legs were as good as they had been at the start and we were soon up, out, and standing on the summit. He was happy and I was happily relieved. In Lagangarbh Coire we indulged in a monster bum slide, both of us whooping like the two children we were. The teachers, well some of them anyway, were far away in the gully, but we were free!

Like many a day with Tom, it ended sitting in front of his coal fire, admiring the flames from a deep armchair with a healthy dram. The glow we both had went deeper than the skin on our flushed faces.

I had thought that would be the end of it, but not with a human dynamo like Tom. The next winter he decided he would like to try it again. This time we chose the Cobbler, a mountain which for both of us held an almost mystic hold. What to do? Four years earlier, in 1983, Alastair Walker and myself had found a surprising gully on the lower tier of the North Buttress. It was unrecorded and gave us *Chockstone Gully*, an unusual Grade II, finishing by a pot-hole like squeeze below Great Gully. So Tom and myself headed for that on St Valentine's Day, 1987.

I led the first easy pitch then handed over to the old reprobate. I watched as he led the crux pitch, shuffling up a rocky ridge *a cheval* in grand old style. There's a photograph of Tom leading this pitch in the 1988 SMCJ, (facing p.64). He has a huge grin on his face. Once out of *Chockstone Gully* ahead rose Great Gully Buttress. Tom had experienced his first front-pointing gully, now it looked like he would discover the joys of frozen turf.

For a few minutes I examined the North face of South Peak – *North Wall Traverse* looked to be in excellent condition. However, at IV, 5 this was a fairly serious proposition, with long, traversing pitches above a steep wall. I turned instead to the rocks ahead. There was a blank stretch of buttress, turfy ledges and short, icy walls zig-zagging up the buttress. That would do. A few moments explaining to Tom that frozen turf was easily the best climbing material in the known universe and off we went. It was as if our ages had been reversed and I was the father, he the child, as he discovered that a pick in turf would hold an elephant. He romped up the route and soon enough we had a new Grade III in the bag. On the summit we watched enthralled as snow crystals, caught in the sun, glittered as they drifted in the air over the col.

As it was St Valentine's Day I called the route *Heart Buttress*, but privately I also intended it as a tribute to the wee man with the big heart. We did a few summer routes as well over the years, including *Spartan Slab* on the Trilleachan Slabs, but it was those two magical days in his company which stand out. Like others who knew him, I have been truly privileged.

WE NEVER KNEW HER NAME

By Gavin Anderson

IT was just a matter of time.

"There it is!" The other three leapt forward running through the snow to the head of the corrie, little white puff balls spurting off their heels. I had no illusions about what lay ahead, so bracing myself I walked slowly and deliberately.

They were standing around the body in a dither of indecision. It didn't need more than a glance to tell me that whoever it was, he or she was dead.

"It's a woman." Brian broke the silence, and I realised, I knew who it was. This was a long time ago. How different climbing was then. We were all disciples of W. H. Murray, whose two volumes arrived as if with our mothers' milk. Rock climbing, ice climbing, and hill walking were all building blocks, all of equal weight in the grand collective experience we called mountaineering which had a lot to do with the romance and poetry of the outdoors and nothing to do with the world of designer labels. Isolation was the ideal, the frenetic proximity of the gym anathema. If there were any who didn't take off their PAs in September to pad around the brilliant coloured hills in bendy boots, I had never heard of them. As to the affair itself, nowadays you would call it a learning experience like Whymper's descent of the Matterhorn was a learning experience.

Our base this weekend was the freezing squalor of Jean's Hut, at that time located somewhere in the bog land below Coire Cas on the Rothiemurchus side of the Cairngorms. The door couldn't be shut as, uninvited, a whale-back of snow had pushed its way into the centre of the room bringing with it unseasonal air-conditioning. However, we must have managed some sleep in this frozen midden, for the skier banging at the door complained he had been knocking some time.

"Have you seen a women in here?"

"No?" Still baffled by sleep, I couldn't figure out what he seemed to be hinting at, this not being the sort of question generally asked of climbers huddled in an igloo, hardly your ideal assignation location. Then, when he told us that a women had been wandering about all night looking for her companion, we cottoned on.

"There's a search party out here looking for her."

"Do you need our help, then?" This came in the tone used for unwanted doorstep salesmen. There was a blizzard outside and I had no interest in swapping it for my warm pit.

"You seem to have loads of volunteers." Outside I could see a long queue of skiers lined up earnestly prodding the snow with their poles. Although, for all the good they were doing, they might as well be searching for Roman coins, as the terrain was flat.

Robertson leaped out of bed as if scalded.

"Of course we're going," chiding me for my chicken-heartedness and him representing the selfless tradition of the hillman.

Outside the skiers were still there, patiently pricking out needles in haystacks on the gentle slope of Coire Cas. Adding to their number was pointless, so we crossed the ridge into Coire an t-Sneachda where there were real cliffs to fall over. On our way we picked up two English lads, plodding through the porridge towards some route on Aladdin's Buttress, who immediately volunteered to join the search.

Both Robertson and I were still pretty green. Most of our experience was second-hand, a combination of reading *Mountaineering in Scotland* and *Nanga Parbat Pilgrimage,* making for a volatile mixture. We were still boys really, products of Edinburgh public schools, with the arrogance of callow youths who thought we were God's gift to wherever we might presume to donate our talents. That weekend was to give our presumptions a stinging rebuke no schoolmaster could deliver.

It was to be our first excursion into the realm of the ice climb. We had howked our way up Ben Lui's *Central Gully* and other venerated snow bound classics in the canon, religiously following in the footsteps of the Grand Old Masters, even to the extent of wearing tricouni nailed boots. This was different. The Cairngorm climate was far less hospitable than the West, with its frigid gales whipping across the Arctic plateau, added to which vertical ice was a particularly unyielding medium.

We were tackling *The Vent*, a Grade III winter climb tucked into the left-hand fold of Stob Coire an Lochan. Its ice-pitch, elementary to the expert, was furnished with traps for the neophyte. The rock that looked as if it was sporting an accommodating jughandle was ice-coated, and that snow patch luring you on to a safe haven was just a sugar coating sprinkled on ice.

It was also the first time on crampons. The man in Lillywhites assured me they were a perfect fit, despite the two front drop spikes sticking out a good half-inch from the toe of my boot, and they had the habit of falling off on any excursion exceeding 10 yards. My fault in not strapping them on properly, the salesman told me, like he knew and I was an idiot. To prevent loss, I should pull the straps tight enough to get frostbite, then wrap two old tent guys round boot and crampon.

The only way up ice was by step-cutting, every upward move invested with labour and craftsmanship. Try skipping a few steps, hoping to levitate to the top of the pitch, then expect trouble. The belays weren't too hot either, a belief in prayer as effective as an ice-axe stuck in the snow, and as for running belays, good luck. Measured against the march of technology, we were at the rubbing two sticks together stage. Ice pegs were superannuated tent pegs from Bertram Mills Circus, hard to insert, requiring a dentist's tenacity to extract, and they didn't come with a guarantee of arresting a fall. Over spiky rocks we could drape a sling, and that was that. Stories, filtering up from down south, of nuts purloined from railway sleepers jammed in cracks as runners, were taken as another example of the Sassenach's insidious ways. Flodden and all that.

Real security only came when you were on *terra firma*, and sometimes not even then in the ferocious blizzards that passed for the norm hereabouts. Better say safe when that first pint is slithering down your throat in the boozer. Whymper wouldn't have blinked if he could have seen us, attired splendidly for grouse shooting with Prince Albert, in our hairy breeches, which when wet gave off an aroma redolent of Highland cow pastures. Harnesses were not yet a gleam in Whillans's eye, a rope round the waist tied off with a bowline sufficed, and slow strangulation after a fall was guaranteed, so peeling was no fun. But we saw sunsets to set your heart afire and heard our boots scrunching crisply over the snow on lonely Bens in a Scotland as quiet as of long ago, where only ghosts remained in the ruined sheilings in the glens.

So there I was struggling slowly upwards, bodily heat, unrestrained by any thermostat, pulsating to every corner of my being. I was gasping from excitement and effort, picking away at the ice like a mad pointillist painter. Way up above, the gully exit was hidden in the quickening murk with now and again a patch of blue flickering across the cornice, gone in the blink of an eyelid. I glanced up. Two women were standing on the cornice, waving at us! "Jesus!" I about jumped out of my britches.

"For Christ's sake get back," I shouted. That cornice didn't need much of a push to tumble. Their washing the windows wave told me they were women, men would give a half-hearted Neronian salute, or point out what a coo's erse I was making of the step-cutting. They retreated. The blizzard redoubled its efforts, throwing chunks of ice upwards through the funnel, freezing my face and hands, so I returned to chopping with extra vim.

A short trudge up a snow slope, and I rolled over onto the plateau, plonked my axe into the snow, tossing my rope round it and called it a belay. Euphoria charged through my veins in a surge of glorious voltage, which not even wet breeches freeze-welding onto the neve could dampen. Robertson came up breathing rapidly, so I assumed he was suitably impressed.

"Jeez, man, You spaced these holds out for a ffff…lipping giant!"

"Oh. I forgot you're the dwarf wi' the plastic heid!"

These pleasantries dispensed with, we stuffed our snow covered gear into our sacks, not bothering to sort out the frozen spaghetti of ropes, but after a few steps we reluctantly pulled them out again as we were navigating blind. The wind knocked us back and forth into each other, making steering akin to riding a bucking bronco. With the rope between us now arched like a bow, now whirring like a crazy skipping rope, we stumbled over the ice-speckled frozen tundra, back down to our frozen slum.

The weather was so miserable that night we went to bed early, but the cold forced us up to make a brew, the stove and the hot drinks managing to drive the temperature fractionally upwards. Eventually, we returned to the chill embrace of our sleeping bags, managing to fall asleep till the agitated skier knocked us up early the next morning.

The four of us were now spread out into a line along the corrie basin. I thought it was more realistic to fix on the crest not on the soft snowy slopes far below, and sure enough there was a neat V snipped out of the cornice bisecting its graceful arabesque.

Directly below scuffed up snow, a red snowball the size of a football, and what looked like a log laid awkwardly across the slope told all. A curious thing now happened. Approaching the body, I felt I was stepping out of reality, and watching events unfolding as on a screen. The mind's defence mechanism to cope with the dreadful? Or was our own existence so tediously insignificant that reality only exists through the medium of the small screen? It was the first time I had seen death up close. It could only have been one of the women we saw yesterday.

We stood around. Nobody wanted to go near to touch the body. The face was totally smothered in ice, obviously dead, but I felt somebody should check for any vital signs.

"Suppose we should check for a pulse and that." They all nodded, but no one moved, so I knelt down in the snow, pulled back the anorak, a thin jumper and lifted the corner of her blouse, feeling weird and intrusive, as if I were a necrophiliac. If she had been alive I don't know what we would have done, but she was stone cold dead.

My initiative with the corpse somehow put me in charge of the operation. Next thing was to get help. I asked who was the fastest, and this English lad in the middle of a Cairngorm blizzard standing over a recently dead woman, gave me a stride-for-stride account of his prowess as a cross-country runner, filling me in on all the cups and honours won as corroboration. He paused in his eulogy, giving me time to say: "You're the man for the job. Run like the bleedin' wind, and get help. There's 200 skiers in the next corrie piddling around on a slope that couldn't harm a fly. Go get 'em!"

He was off like a rocket, ably demonstrating his resumé, leaving the three of us standing guard over the girl's body, with time on our hands. Anticipating a long wait, we passed the time as if we had just missed the bus and the last one was a long way away. With the gale blowing we had to stand with our mitts against our faces to protect us against the snow pellets stinging our cheeks. We talked about climbing. And, as in any situation where you are not called upon to perform, we bragged. We've all done it. Holds recede, slabs are tilted up just a wee bit and the second is hauled up on a fishing line unable to follow our awesome leads. We did the hand ballet familiar in every climber's pub, a lay-back here, a hand jam there, here a jug there a jug. A few minutes of this usually palls for anyone of voting age, but we hadn't established anything else in common so we kept at it, slapping the air for virtual handholds, while taking breaks to scour the intermittently visible skyline for succour.

When the rescue team emerged from the white-out they were treated to the incongruous sight of the three of us, hand jiving over a woman's dead body. Without fuss the body was bundled onto the stretcher, the legs bouncing on the canvas with the stilted gesticulations of a marionette. The fact that none of us knew her name added to the impression that this was just a shell left on the hillside the person inside, whoever she was, long gone.

The clouds parted for the cliff to take a final curtain call, then they drifted away like smoke unfurling until the last particles of mist were nibbled up by Strath Spey. Framed by a suddenly enormous blue sky the snow glistened and sparkled where the light hit the slope, while the crags, now red, now pink for that moment appeared friendly, making for a scene of beauty, capable of holding anyone for as long as visibility allowed. But to me it was a hideous kind of beauty, a sterile wasteland of indifference, lacking even the pitilessness of the diabolical, more depressing than frightening. I thought then that Mallory was wrong. Nothing is 'There'.

We were driven down to Aviemore to report to the police. In retrospect this seemed hardly worthwhile as by a process akin to Chinese Whispers our account was mangled by the Press unrecognisably the next day. Fortunately, the Mountain Rescue waited and gave Brian and myself a lift back up to the road end so we could retrieve our gear. We collected it, swore never to return to this dump and trudged back to the van through the snow. As we were loading up, the sun dropped over the horizon in a sunset you might wait for a whole lifetime, as if in dying it had thrown a challenge at all the colours of the spectrum. Beautiful, but for me it pricked the heart with melancholy.

Just 24 hours ago another could have shared these feelings. I began wondering about the woman, and not knowing who she was, I felt free to ad lib. I imagined her enjoying simple things like going to the pictures, throwing clay about in a pottery workshop and having her pals round for a coffee and a blether. She liked to laugh a lot with her own little circle. She had a gift for friendship and was loving and loved in return. Now that self-contained little world was switched off. I wished I had been nicer when I shouted at her to stand back. The last words she heard from a stranger were not kind. But then if wishes were horses... I never knew how that saying ended.

"Hurry up, Jimmy, We're freezin!"

"Okay."

The door was shut, the engine chugged ponderously into life, and off we went down into the gloom.

THROUGH THE EYES OF THE OWL

By Ian Mitchell

Joy of my heart Creag Uanaich, where I spent my youth
Crag of hinds and stags, a refreshing, joyful, bird-filled crag
A crag where the hunt went frequently and which I loved to frequent
Sweet was the baying of the hounds, driving the herd into the narrows

THE verbal memory of the old Gaelic poets was legendary. Duncan MacIntyre, for example, could recite all his 7000 verses of poetry by heart. In centuries before, this faculty must have been at least as well developed. But what about visual memory? The Bards of the Bens, I think, had this faculty developed almost as well.

I took the train to Corrour a wee while ago, with a mission to fulfil. When, 10 years ago, I was researching my book *Scotland's Mountains before the Mountaineers*, I had come across a poem, written probably around 1590, by a Gaelic poet, Domnhall mac Fhionnlaigh nan Dan. This described the poet taking refuge in the area around Craig Uanaich because "there was much fighting and raiding in Lochaber at that time". There, according to the poem, he lived off hunting the deer as he roamed an area about 10 to 15 miles in radius from the hill. From a study of the poem I was able to argue that Domnhall probably made the first ascents of several mountains in that region of Lochaber, including Sgor Ghaibre and Carn Dearg (Mountaineers, p14-16). Time subsequently allowed me to work more on the poem, and its place names, and to go from the text and maps to Craig Uanaich. My aim was to ascend the little mountain and, taking in the view from its summit, to see if I could identify more of the places mentioned in the poem. The results were surprising.

At Craiguanaich Lodge I observed the increasing decay of the building which had still housed a family when I first came here 25 years ago, but which is now only used for occasional sheep shearing and dipping. The hill, a Graham, which gave the lodge its name, towered above it. The first thing I noticed was it was very steep, the second that it was very craggy, and also heavily vegetated on the crags. Ascent from the south being problematic, I skirted the mountain through a little 'Khyber Pass' and waterfall to its eastern flank and there began an ascent. Its cragginess had protected it from grazing, and allowed a splendid mixed wood to flourish on the hill, and this was certainly, as it had been 400 years ago, 'bird filled' as I ascended. Large amounts of animal droppings also showed that it hosted a varied fauna, and near the top I came upon some deer grazing, on a grassy summit endowed with natural pools of drinking water, where the poet, Domnhall, probably refreshed himself after the hunt.

From the summit I was able to compare the poem with what I could see, and found that mountains mentioned with the rider 'I see' (chi mi) were all visible, while those which were mentioned without it, were not. Domnhall wrote this poem long after he had left the sanctuary of the Loch Treig area where he had gone around 1560, and was composing the song from his visual memory, which proved astonishingly accurate.

I sit on the fairy knoll and look towards Loch Treig
From Creag Uanach the sunny high ground of the deer
I see distant Coire Rath, the Cruach and Beinn Bhreac
I see Strath Ossian of the Warriors, and the sun shining on Meall nan Leac
I see Ben Nevis above, and Carn Dearg below
Past another little corrie is distant moor and the sea
Splendid is Coire Dearg where we loved to hunt
Corry of heathery knolls and the great stags
I see the summit of Bidean nan Dos on the near side of Sgurra Lith
I see Sgurr Choinnich of the slender stags
I see the wide strath of the cattle and the Corry of Maim Ban
I love today all that I can see
I see Garbh-Bheinn of the red stags and Lap Bheinn of the hillocks
And Leitir Dubh where I often spilt the deers' blood
Farewell from me to Ben Alder, the most eminent of bens
And also to Loch Erricht, where I loved to be
I shall drink my fill from Loch Treig and that will lift my spirits
Farewell to Coire nan Cloich and to the Usige Labhar
And to Bac nan Craobh and both sides of the Bealach nan Sgurr
And the Eadar-Bhealach where the Lowland tongue was unheard
I shall now take my leave of you
The most miserable farewell I shall ever take
No more shall I carry a bow under my arm.
And not till the world's end will I release the hounds

The ascent on the hill from Corrour is done in an easy couple of hours. There was still plenty of time between trains, so I decided to return to Corrour by way of Lap Beinn, and add it to my second round of Munros. From here I looked down on Strath Ossian of the Heroes, where Fingal, Ossian and Diarmid had supposedly fought in centuries before our own poet arrived.

BACK IN GEAR

By Carl J. Schaschke

WHEN the discovery was broadcast of Mallory's sun-bleached body, which had lain undisturbed for the best part of three-quarters of a century, I paid barely more than a passing interest. 'Snickers at 10', the so-called code used by top US big wall climber, Conrad Anker, over the airwaves was intended to throw others in the vicinity off the scent. Now I was fully engaged. A member of the North Face Team, Conrad had almost by chance found Mallory's body on the north side of Everest. Photographs of Mallory's corpse made the front pages of newspapers around the world.

Conrad and I had once been members of an international expedition to the impressive granite spires of Kalidaha in the Dharlang Nullah of the Kishtwar Himalaya. Back in those carefree days of the late 1980s we had shared just about everything and got to know each other better than we ought to admit. I had a reasonable measure of everyone on the trip, yet I never quite got my head around Conrad's *raison d'être*. "You see", offered fellow US big wall climber Kev Gheen, also on the trip, by some way of explanation: "He's not American, he's Californian."

Years later, I met up with Conrad again, this time in Glasgow. He was on tour from the US, and I'd spotted a larger-than-life poster of the career climber in Tiso's announcing a lecture that evening at the Mitchell Theatre. I popped along and was pleased that he remembered me without prompting or reminding. Tall and lean as ever, his fine golden locks were shorn but otherwise it was the same old Conrad. After his well-attended show in which he didn't even mention our trip – clearly it didn't appear on his radar of impressive places he's climbed – he suggested we go for a beer. Catch up on the news, that kind of thing.

"You still climbing there, Carl?" He still rolled those r's with that West Coast burr. Conrad seemed genuinely interested. I avoided the answer. Breaking the awkward pause, he began to reminisce and told tales that suggested to me that our trip had, for him, been some kind of kindergarten outing. It didn't seem like that to me. It was an unclimbed set of granite spires which soared skywards. Damn it, I'd put my life on the line.

Again: "You still climbing?" Ouch! It made me wince. The ensuing silence afforded me a false air of equality. With such an impressive accrued portfolio of mountaineering achievements into which I could casually dip, where should I start? Oh, the dilemma of picking and choosing from those bulging filing cabinets of outrageous routes and mountaineering escapades lodged inside my skull. Where to begin? Truth is, I was struggling to think of anything at all, let alone anything even vaguely comparable. My CV in recent years was blank. And I knew it.

Perhaps I should mention that I finished the Munros? Would he know what a Munro is? Would he even care? What about Auchinstarry? It's a great place to climb but it's not really in the same league as the walls of the Big Ditch for which Conrad holds numerous speed records on El Capitan.

"Sure, I've been to…" My mind drew a blank and the words trailed off into nothingness. I cursed myself. Yes, it was great to meet Conrad again that evening but I had to content myself with the fact that our lives which had once so closely crossed, had gone off in diametrically opposite directions. While he is actively living the NFTs 'Never Stop Exploring' and is now running the Khumbu Climbing School in Nepal, I pass my days locked away in an office in Glasgow. The closest I now get to a Himalayan mountain is the one made of paper. Not quite the same, really.

Persistently, racked by thoughts of what could have or should have been, but never was, I have searched long and hard for answers. I'd long lifted the foot off the pedal running trips to the planet's bigger ranges. I'd once put teams of twinkies together, and I could do it again. I'd been the one to raise the finances, sort out the administration, do the peak booking, travel arrangements, organising food, seeing the expedition through to its conclusion, braving life in a thousand ways and still coming home unscathed. People relied on me to do it. To hell with the weekend over-climbed over-rated guidebook routes. I needed to light that fire again; something big; something abroad; a team effort. A real focus, something different.

Was it a blindfold decision, the proverbial pinning the tail-on-the-donkey, that had somehow picked out Mount Lassen as the target? Well, it seemed to fit the bill nicely – a big dormant Californian volcano. And in Conrad's own backyard, too. Before the 1980 eruption of Mount St Helens in Washington, Mount Lassen was the most recent volcanic outburst in the contiguous 48 American states. The volcano sits at the southern-most end of the Cascade Range which thrusts up into British Columbia, Canada. Characterised by its great lava pinnacles, jagged crater and steaming sulphur vents, it is surrounded by forestation, steep valleys and meadows. Yes, Mount Lassen would do nicely.

The dream was alive again. The team of four had bought into the idea and flew out to the US. Arriving in the small hours, we went to pick up the hire car at San Francisco International Airport.

"You looking for an upgrade on this occasion, Sir?" It was very late and we were very tired. "No, just give us the car we ordered."

"I'm sorry, we haven't got one available right now, Sir. But we do have a van."

We'd been dropped off at Glasgow airport in a van, uncomfortably squeezed in among a set of tool boxes. I was not in the mood to negotiate with this over-cheery rep for the prospect of driving around the searing Californian heat as White Van Man. She could forget it.

Reading the situation well, and looking to rapidly defuse a near international incident, the rep twisted her VDU to allow us to see what was being offered. "This, Sir, is a van."

So apart from the four wheels and steering wheel, vans in the US bare little resemblance to vans in the UK. So a van it was. What a monster! It was more like a bus – and a luxury bus at that. What does it cost to run a bus like this? With US fuel prices a fraction of those anywhere else, it wasn't an issue. Fuel in the US is well worth abusing. Who cares about CO^2 emissions when it's this cheap? The gas-guzzling monster with its essential air-conditioning served perfectly as a mobile beer chiller. We took turns at sitting in every seat. Hell, this was fun.

The team were of mixed ages, capabilities and experience. Well balanced, I thought. Collectively, we could claim a reasonable list of achievements with a few volcanos chucked in including Kilimanjaro and Mount Bromo in Indonesia. We'd all been up Mount Toro (where?) Mount Lassen was ideal and unless it was going to erupt again, it was well within our capabilities.

Peter Lassen, for whom the peak and its National Park are named, was a Dane who'd pioneered trails way back in 1848 as routes to the west during California's gold rush. Lassen had guided settlers and tried to establish a city. Mining, power development projects, ranching and timbering were all attempted. American Indians – Atsugewi, Yana, Yahi and Maidu – lurking in the pine forests are a thing of the past; the last, a Yahi Indian named Ishi, being flushed out around a century ago. Only bears now remain a threat.

As required in the Park, we made base in a designated camp site which came complete with camp fire bin. The Ranger tediously lectured us on the Park's rules: the don'ts and the don'ts. Strictly forbidden was the use of collected wood for fires which lay temptingly all about. All logs were required to be purchased from the Ranger. Sounded like a nice little earner. The group in the site next to us merrily burned their purchased logs in a oner, impressively creating flames licking a good 10ft. into air with the sort of burn NASA uses to launch space rockets. The scorching radiative flux was either going to melt the synthetic fabric of our nearby tents, or the shower of embers was going to pepper the fabric with burn holes. With the flames equally perilously close to the surrounding tinder-dry pines, I contemplated how it was that devastating forest fires should ravage California on an annual basis. Creating insanely over-sized infernos are, strangely, not against the rules.

Although tantalisingly close by, the big peak remained out of sight being obscured by the canopy of pines. Near the tent lay the fresh water lake of Manzanita. From the far shores, the snowy summit could be viewed. We all took a dip in the somewhat refreshingly cool waters. The Ranger was on our case again. Surely, not another rule? No. In his 30 years he'd never seen anyone swim in the icy waters. But then he obviously hadn't met anyone from Scotland. We eat porridge.

Time to go. How was it done again? A route carefully planned and executed with plenty of contingencies along the way and strong leadership. Clearing the forest, Mount Lassen was straight ahead. Wow! Was this the surrogate unexplored steep granite with tasty bonatius hand cracks with occasional pitches of hooking detacho flakes, copperheading kitty litter, dicey runout friction or big ugly chimneys with verglas in 'em? Should I pull rank and take the driver's seat and steer the team in the right direction? It was my idea, after all, wasn't it? Onwards and upwards. It was steep. First gear and power up all the way. No heroics: just follow the line of least resistance. Keep the wheels on the road. I knew how it was done.

Passing features such as Hot Rock and Devastation Area, we climbed up through King's Creek close to Bunpass Hell. It was now within launching distance of the summit. This had been good progress. We were still all together. Surely, another push would do it. Up here it was cold and the air thin. It was a strange world of volcanic rock, snow and ice. But the mood had changed. I sensed there were thoughts of no longer reaching the summit. The focus had shifted.

It seems I was right. The two youngest members were overcome by the nauseous vapours of sulphur percolating from hidden underground fumaroles all around. In places the ground was so hot, our Vibram soles melted on the hot rocks. They'd had enough. Together with the third member, they opted to remain by the frozen and aptly named Summit Lake – their high point. What were they thinking about? We'd only just begun, hadn't we? Had I picked a weak team? Too young and inexperienced? So it was down to me to finish the job. I would meet them again on the descent.

How far, how long from here to push alone to the summit? A team of Cheese-Eating Surrender Monkeys were ahead, caught up and rudely overtaken, plumes of ochre cinders kicked up and spat out. And there, at last, was the rarefied atmosphere. The lungs could feel it. This is what I'd come for. Like a child with a toy at Christmas, I was excited. Not far now. I carved my way past a couple of Americans making heavy weather of the ascent. There was an exchange of unpleasantness and gone. Less burgers, boys.

No more up, this was the caldera – a rim of jagged volcanic rock. Snow lay in the crater. To the north Mount Shasta was clear above a heavy haze. Result!

Barely half-an-hour after threading the summit, the mix of snow and cinder ash allowed swift descent. Fast approaching the frozen turquoise lake below, I could make out the three far distant dots of the other team members. Were they going to be disappointed? Would they even talk to me? So near yet so far for them. It was their choice, wasn't it?

The team had tracked my descent and seemed pleased to see my return. "Look! We've made a snowman with Mum. What do you think of him, Dad?"

The little darlings. We climbed aboard the van parked by the lake. Back in gear again and back off down the long mountain road. Mission Mount Lassen complete. I wondered what Conrad would have made of it. Frankly, I no longer cared.

RED FLY THE BANNERS OH!

By Iain Smart

We CLIMB in the spirit of our times. At present, we live in a Golden Age. Climbing shops are Aladdin's Caves full of shining metal and brightly coloured nylon. Climbing gear, camping gear, and clothing are wonders of intelligent design. Climbing standards have reached stratospheric heights of excellence. The whole world is accessible to people of modest incomes. I once heard some of our members discussing the possibility of climbing Mount Kenya in a long weekend from Edinburgh. I remember leaving my home in Glen Shee about lunchtime and the next evening standing on a remote peak in East Greenland watching the sun set briefly behind a jagged row of northern peaks with my ski tracks leading to a comfortable camp on a snowfield far below. My friend Phil Todd standing beside me had also flown over the day before from his home in Oregon on the far Pacific shore. Nearer home my grand-daughter has to have all her gear, ropes, slings, karabiners etc. in matching colours.

It was not always so. I write of the years of the mid-1940s spanning the last years of the Second World War and the beginning of the Cold War. During this time Russia became morally dominant and the extension of Communism seemed imminent. Russia and its leader, Stalin, were idolised and idealised by many in the industrialised West and in the emerging post-colonial countries of Asia and Africa. The great fear was that the Americans might use 'The Bomb' if Russia attempted to overthrow Capitalism in the small part of Europe west of the Iron Curtain. I remember people saying with fearful awe that the Communists had learned how to 'change human nature'. Top of the Pops was the Red Army Choir singing loud and vigorous renderings of stirring songs. In comparison the Rolling Stones would register less than the half droop on the virility indicator and the Beatles would seem soft and self-indulgent and ideologically immature, if not, frankly decadent. It is only against this backdrop that the events described below are plausible.

Glencoe by lamplight:
This episode must have taken place in the middle of the war. We were in Glencoe Youth Hostel. It was a winter night. About a dozen and a half young boys were in the common room; we were all below military age. The smell of beans and dried egg still lingered after the frugal supper. The room was lit by tilley lamps; electric light was not yet with us. A group of seven or eight lads sat together at one end. They were engaged in serious talk. The rest of the room gradually fell silent as the group broadcast their earnest conversation to engage our attention. They told of the new world to come after the war. They were members of a Young Workers Club from somewhere in the Glasgow area. I remember watching with the fearful awe of an outsider in the presence of dedicated believers. They had hope

and a frightening idealism. They talked of the dictatorship of the proletariat that would be established after the war and how the working class would be released from bondage; their vision was of education, intellectual advance and high endeavour, not booze and free-loading on the broo. They were not unfriendly, far from it. But they did glance at the rest of us, implying that this was the new reality; it was coming and we had better adapt to it. Stalin and the USSR were models of a workers' republic. They would liberate the whole of Europe and after the war there would be a Soviet world of working class unity in which the nation state would wither away.

They sang a lot of songs. One I can still remember. Instead of *Green Grow the Rashes* it was a rousing, *Red Fly the Banners-oh.*

Five for the years of the five-year plan
And four for the four years taken,
Three, three the rights of man,
Two, two a man's own hands,
Working for his living-oh,
One is workers' unity
And ever more shall be so.

Another had the chorus line:

With every propeller
Roarrrrring 'Red Front!'
In defence of the USSR!

We crouched behind our paper-thin copies of RLS and Frank Smythe as these songs were followed by the inspiring sound of the *Internationale* and the *Red Flag* passing over our heads. I knew that if the workers' republic ever came to pass I was doomed. Not because I was against a fair society – an educated population was what civilization was all about – but, in the one they offered there would be no room for solitary seekers; individualism would be classified as deviationism and suppressed for the good of the community. It was this need to conform that struck an icicle into the heart.

The next morning we climbed up the path to Binnein nam Bian in shabby clothes and sub-standard hobnailed boots. We clumped through the snow on the final slope without rope or ice axe. At one time we saw the vanguard of the proletariat silhouetted against the skyline of the Aonach Eagach on the opposite side of the glen. As far as dress and equipment were concerned we and they were indistinguishable. We were all shabby, under-equipped mountaineers. They were, if anything, more affluent than we were; they had jobs and an income however small; we were still at school and dependent on our cash-strapped parents. Even so, between us there was a deep glen of incompatibility. If only we could have suppressed our desire to explore by ourselves we could have joined their band of hope and marched in the vanguard of a reforming movement singing rousing songs. People who won't follow a leader have always been a problem in any well regulated society.

Ben Alder Cottage:
Also during the war as a schoolboy on a visit to Ben Alder cottage, as reported in SMCJ, 1991,xxxiv, 182, pp 593-596, I encountered Communists who were more intellectually sober. They had guns and one had fought in the Spanish Civil War. In their conversation there were quotes from Marx and Lenin. I felt an empathy with these robust exponents of the great ideal; they were worldly wise and serious but this was tempered by oblique, dead-pan humour and an agreeable gallusness. I felt at home with them, perhaps because they went out on the hill in ones and twos and fished by the lochside alone. Their type of Soviet Scotland might not have been at all bad.

Playboy of the Western World:
My first visit to the Alps was with early versions of Malcolm Slesser and Geoff Dutton who were even then bright stars in the firmament. It was just after the war, probably in the summer of 1947. We were inexperienced and overawed by the scale of the Swiss Alps. It was quite a challenge even to get to Switzerland. Money was short, tickets were hard to get; they had to be bought in advance in London. Malcolm's sister who lived there queued for them. They were the size of a pamphlet printed on low-quality brown paper. After the dinginess and frugality of war-ravaged Britain and France we entered undamaged Switzerland where food was abundant – except we didn't have money to buy much of it. We climbed the Fiescherhorn and the Wetterhorn and then ran out of Swiss francs and we had to return.

I stopped off in Paris and stayed at something called a Camp Volant – about a dozen old army tents pitched on a dusty bombed site. The address I remember was 8 Rue Barbet de Jouy, somewhere near the Musee Rodin. For a very small sum you got a camp bed, a well-used blanket and breakfast of a single tin cup of curious flat coffee and a piece of dry bread. In the evening a simple one-plate meal was served. We sat around trestle tables lit by hanging kerosene lanterns and ate beans and bread and cheese. I think you could buy 'coffee' as an extra.

The other people at my table that night were young intellectual communists; they were students; none were working class. They, too, assumed that Capitalism was doomed; it was just a matter of knocking away a few rotting props and the whole shoddy edifice would come tumbling down and socialist republics modelled on the Soviet Union would bring, justice, education, self-respect and honourable employment to all. It was here I first heard the word 'dialectic' used in discussion. I did not understand what it meant.

The man opposite me was a young Englishman complete with beard and spectacles who exuded moral superiority with a quiet matter-of-fact scholarliness. He had practical experience; he had spent the summer working on the Yugoslav Youth Railway. In this project young idealists from all over Europe had assembled to help build a rail track somewhere in Bosnia. Each morning they marched off to work singing rousing songs. (Those members old enough to remember Len Lovat singing *La Banda Rossa* will recall how rousing these songs were.) From such seeds a new socialist Europe would grow, the man opposite me declared. I kept quiet. I felt like a spoiled brat, a playboy who had been scrambling in the Alps while European youth were resisting the re-establishment of the yolk of monopoly capitalism and the tyranny of the military-industrial complex. The group of Left Wing intellectuals at the table came from half-a-dozen countries. They seemed less abrasive, less aggressive than the bright-eyed singers in Glencoe or the practical working men of the Ben Alder Soviet; they were intellectual by-standers who were witnessing the inevitable; they felt no need to man the barricades. But once again I felt out of it. I could have climbed the Fiescherhorn any old year, but the Yugoslav Youth Railway was an unrepeatable moment in history. A few years ago I met by chance in a bothy someone who had actually worked on the railway. He had shared a barrack with Austrians and Palestinians. On the wall he distinctly remembered a slogan reading: "Long Live Arab-Jewish Anti-Imperialist Unity."

The spirit didn't last. The professional priests and politicians couldn't allow power to slip out of their hands and they had to re-exert religious and political differences; their futures depended on exploiting these divisions. The politicians were on a loser since they promised heaven on earth. The religious authoritarians won because they were more astute; they very sensibly promised heaven after death and, unlike the politicians, have yet to be proved wrong.

The sunny side of the street:
About the same time I encountered idealists working from the other side of the social order. I was an instructor one Easter in one of the first mountaineering courses run by the Central Council of Physical Recreation. Its acronym CCPR was not too different from USSR in Cyrillic lettering, but there the similarity ended. We were based in the luxury of the Cairngorm Hotel in Aviemore – war-worn Glenmore Lodge had yet to be renovated. We went by lorry each morning along the dirt road from Coylum Bridge to Loch Morlich, then by footpath to Coire an t-Sneachda or Craig Calaman. Many luminaries graced the course. Frank Spencer Chapman of Arctic and Malayan war fame spoke of facing down adversity by sheer force of character. Prunella Stack an attractive, athletic, up-market lady who was a leader in the Health and Beauty movement spoke of a healthy mind in a healthy body; I have experienced this combination myself from time to time although only for short periods and she was quite right, it

really is a very agreeable state. Norman Odell, the last man to see Mallory and Irvine on their way up Everest was there and I had the honour of climbing a route in a corrie of Braeriach with him. He cut the most enormous steps even on relatively easy ground, obviously mindful of the train of porters coming up behind. One day I went out with Lord Malcolm Douglas-Hamilton. He feared Britain was in imminent danger of becoming a Left Wing dictatorship. As we trudged up the path through the old Caledonian forest, he explained how it was quite likely that within the next few weeks Aneurin Bevan would mastermind a coup, seize parliament and the radio stations and declare a Socialist Republic. The *Daily Worker* would replace *The Times* and public schooling would mean just that. It was all maybe a little paranoid but in the context of the time not entirely implausible.

Epilogue:
In the event it was the *Sun* and the *Mail* that replaced the *Daily Worker* and *The Times* as the most widely read and influential papers in the land. The *Internationale* that united the human race and caused the nation state to wither away was a global market in which everything was for sale and international boundaries were archaic impediments to maximising profit. Nevertheless, feral Capitalism, for all its faults, encouraged inventiveness and individuality. Inventiveness in the mountaineering market has generated affordable equipment of astonishing ingenuity and sophistication beyond the wildest dreams of the gas-cape-clad denizens of the mid-1940s, carrying their cotton tents with separate groundsheets in heavy ex-army Bergen rucksacks. Individualism has flourished as never before as is evident in the pages of our Journal.

Under a Soviet system an off-beat organisation like the SMC, full of difficult people who won't do what they are told and don't like being led, would not have been allowed; the present membership would have been sent off to the Gulag for re-education. Ironically, we would probably have found the Creag Dhu already there as even worse examples of incorrigible individualism. Unless, of course, as is not unlikely, they had finessed the situation and were actually running the place, in which case they might extend a kindly tolerance to those of us who could climb above HVS.

One day runaway Capitalism will collapse under the weight of its internal contradictions and drown in its own excrement. Before this unhappy terminal event we have great opportunities for travel to the world's remotest mountain ranges. There is even a railway to the fabled Forbidden City of Lhasa where you can erect your tent in the municipal campsite. We can also do it all in greater safety than before. With our GPSs we can now find out exactly where we are and, if we do get into difficulties, we can use our mobile phones to summon a helicopter. If we ever get lost, now we can be found. Truly an Amazing Grace! It's all too good to miss. Let's get on with surfing the present wave of prosperity with all the originality we can muster… before it hits the beach.

DEATH BY MISADVENTURE

By Alan Mullin

Alan died in tragic circumstances earlier this year. He wrote this article after his ground-breaking ascent of Rolling Thunder *on Lochnagar and it is offered here as a tribute to a climber of exceptional ability – a complex character, never far from controversy, who climbed as he lived – giving his all. (Ed.)*

I ARRIVED back from the Accident and Emergency unit three hours ago and my eye is till excruciatingly painful. I should have known better than to sharpen my crampons with the angle grinder without wearing goggles, well I paid the price for my stupidity, a shard of steel straight in to the old ocular. I don't yet know what is more painful, the shard that was lodged in my eye or the needle used to remove it. I am lying in my darkened living room looking like black patch straight out of *Treasure Island.* I still intend to go climbing though, as I can use one eye to climb with, of that I am sure. I only have one problem! No bloody partner to climb with. I had my heart set on *Rolling Thunder* on Lochnagar having looked at it with my binoculars the previous summer. It is an E1 rock route and to my knowledge no one had yet repeated it since its first ascent in 1982. It was an ideal target for a winter ascent being very grassy, wet and foul in summer and, surprisingly, it looked to me to be quite easy from the ground. I was sure it was climbable.

I had called various people about doing this route, but sadly, I had been let down again as usual, with promises of "I will call you back, honest Alan". As was the case on so many occasions, the phone call never materialised and I resigned myself to another missed opportunity. The weather was looking fine – albeit a bit stormy. I guess it was the thought of on-sighting this unrepeated E1 on a cliff notorious for its few weak spots that put partners off. I believe now that if I had known how tough its armour really was I would not have embarked on my appointment with fear. I don't consciously know what made me want to solo it. I guess it just popped into my head and seemed the right thing to do, but in retrospect, there were probably subconscious factors at work as well.

Firstly, I had climbed *The Steeple* a month before and I felt confident in my ability. Secondly, I had been having a particularly bad time of late, much criticism in the media and by other climbers of my ability and a fair amount of personal problems had turned me into someone even my wife could not comprehend. I truly felt I had come so far in life, yet people who did not know me on a personal level could not help but put me down. I really felt that my life was one big bloody mess. I've had to fight so hard all my life just to achieve the smallest goals and I've suffered many set backs, such as losing my beloved job in the Army and at the same time losing some of my lower spine. This, consequently, resulted in my addiction to painkillers and alcohol sending me spiralling into depression. I had to fight so hard to overcome all these things, and more, and now this shite about me being a crap climber had really taken its toll on me, even though I had worked so hard to achieve my goals.

I made my mind up there and then lying in the dark alone with my thoughts – I was going to solo *Rolling Thunder*, and what better time than right bloody now.

It is 10pm and my eye still hurts but as I say goodbye to my wife I can sense she is not happy with yet another one of my insane ideas. I reassure her that my eye will be fine by the morning and that if it still hurts I can always come home. I know this is a lie and even if it feels painful I will still climb. I know deep down inside that she worries intensely about me, but I am selfish at heart and always have to get my own way. Perhaps that's why I love her so much, because I guess she understands me better than anyone else and does not hold my selfishness against me.

The weather forecast is crap and the roads are almost blocked but that does not deter me, I simply take the long road towards Aberdeen and even this main route is quite hazardous. I am missing out the road through Tomintoul as everything is blocked over that way. I am struggling slightly with the driving as one eye is not as good as two and when I arrive at the Loch Muick car park it is still dark. I sort myself out, and although I have not slept since the previous night, I feel OK. I see a car arrive just after me and I think it looks like Pete Benson, but I don't bother to go and speak to him as I am in a world of my own right now and don't feel very sociable. I have to wear my goggles for most of the walk in and with deep snow underfoot it is tough going with a heavy sack that soon starts to make my shoulders ache. I have no other thoughts in my mind except for *Rolling Thunder*. I can feel the wind pick up as I reach the Meikle Pap Col, but I don't worry too much as cols are often blustery places due to the channelling of the wind. I can't quite see the Tough Brown face yet, as it is shrouded by low cloud cover, but I can feel the chill in the air. This is definitely going to be a full-on winter ascent and no mistake. I carry on humping my load through the now thigh-deep snow in the Corrie and am beginning to feel slightly tired, but one bonus is that my eye no longer hurts so badly and I can now remove my goggles which have been misted over for the past three hours.

I eventually reached the First Aid box and can now see clearly my objective up on the right of the Tough Brown face: "Jesus, it is wintry alright." I witness an airborne avalanche sweep over the top of *Parallel Gully B*. I still have to negotiate the slopes and the deep snow that lies in the bowl formed just below the Tough Brown face. It is hard work, and as I approach the foot of the route I can see other climbers over at the First Aid box. I am sure they are wondering what the idiot over here is up to. I finally get this monkey off my back and have a well-earned rest. I survey my route above, a series of steep slabs and grooves finally ending at a big roof. I am sure I can climb this route on-sight, but I have no idea what gear I will need. I have just brought my normal soloing rack which consists of four pegs which are all I own, along with my trusty hexentrics, a few nuts, quick draws and a few cams. I have come to rely heavily on my hexentrics as they can be hammered into icy cracks where nothing else will suffice.

I sort out a peg belay and anchor one end of the rope to it with the free end running through my soloist and am now ready and start climbing up the initial overhanging roof that is harder than it looks. I clear the snow from the groove on the left side of the roof only to be confronted with a horrible blind crack. "Damn." This is quite confusing as it looks just like the cracks normally found in Cairngorm granite, in other words quite accommodating. Sadly, this was not the case here, as the cracks seemed to be horrible, blind and misleading. I hope this is not normal on this cliff otherwise I could be in trouble. I manage to get a semi hook in the groove which allows me to reach a little higher and get some turf and strenuously pull over the roof. I am now on a nice terrace. I go right under a small roof and climb another unprotected blind groove right of it and immediately above. After 10m. climbing on reasonable ground I eventually find somewhere to place a decent hex. I thank God for this as I am beginning to get seriously worried here. I make a small traverse out left and pull up right onto a half decent ledge below what looks like a hard slab with two cracks running up it. I am sure this will certainly constitute the lower crux as it is steep, and as it leans left I can't seem to get straight on it without doing a barn door out leftwards, which is throwing me off balance. I have now searched for half-an-hour in vain looking for protection. I finally get a small nut at the base of the slab in a very icy crack that I know is shite but it is better than nothing.

I survey the slab above, a horizontal crack runs up the middle of it with a smaller corner crack on the right edge of the slab. I try to convince myself that they will be nice deep Cairngorm cracks! "Wrong," they are bloody useless, shallow and crap. I now know that when I attempt to climb the slab I will not be able to stop and place pro as there is no possibility in this blind rubbish, and anyway it is way too strenuous and looks technically awkward. I eventually manage to place a lousy copperhead at the base of the corner crack. I dare not test it as it has fallen out twice already. However, it does allow me to work a few moves up the slab.

"Jesus", it is technical and there is nothing much for my feet but, more worryingly, there is nothing in the way of protection to stop me hitting the ground should I fall. This makes for a very hard decision. I have calculated a ground fall as my hex is 10m. below and if I fall I will go 10m. past it. Obviously, this means a ground fall and I must give it my all if I am to commit to the moves above. I focus on the moves, remembering everything

I have ever learned about technique. I make my mind up and take the gamble.

"OK" – get psyched and go! Left tool hook in the crack, flag left foot out on the slab and hook the right tool in a small corner up right, bring the right foot up for a mono in the crack. Now high step up, left tool up above head and crap hook in the crack, right tool again in the corner, now quickly heel hook with my left foot on the ledge above.

"Man this is bloody mad!" No gear and well mad. I remove my right tool and thwack into turf and mantle on the heel hook. I feel great! I am amazed! That took total concentration and I did it. I actually climbed that in a trance, I really felt no fear – nothing but the moves coming together.

I can sort myself out now and calm down a bit. I feel happiness like no other, a sense of elation even. I look up at the next section, and a small groove leading to a ledge.

"No problem." Or so I think. I manage to place a decent nut at the base of the groove but it's choked with ice above so I know I won't get gear there. I get a hook for my left tool and move up, get a thin one for the right in the ice above but as I try to pull up into the groove my hook rips sending me flying backwards and partially down the slab I have just climbed. I am also upside down. I pull myself upwards and immediately check myself for movement of all limbs.

"Phew, I am OK." No injuries and I can now pull myself back on to the ledge. "Well that will teach you to be so cocky you dick head!"

"OK." This time I get a slightly better hook that allows me to pull onto the ledge above. The guidebook description, which is firmly implanted in my memory, says go out right on a grassy ramp, but I can see a better alternative directly above. I look up and can see that it's a thin groove leading to another slab. I manage to get another nut at the base of this groove, albeit it's small but it's better than nothing. I start up the overhung groove and, bridging out, I can at least maintain balance on this one. I really wish there was some pro here but it's all blind shite, only good enough for small hooks and little else. I pull on to the slab above and just as I get a decent hook my feet come off.

I fall all the way back down to the ledge somersaulting in the process. I am very lucky that the back-up knot stops on my Soloist and, unbelievably, the nut has held – just!

I don't feel scared just annoyed and even manage a deranged sort of laugh to myself. I stand up and go again as there really is no time like the present and this time I am successful. I climb the thin groove up the slab and reach a really nice ledge above, thank God!

I am really hoping for something bomber here as I need to go down and pull my rope up, I manage to get a good thread and half-decent cam, I sort myself out and rap back to the base and get ready to remove the bottom belay. I can't believe what I am seeing here. The bloody peg that I have been belayed on has fractured and as I hammer it outwards it snaps off.

"Well, once again that was bloody lucky Alan."

The weather has now turned really bad with strong winds and a chill that's eating away at my very bones. However, I am more determined than that as I know deep down inside I am a good climber and I can deal with this and refuse to give in despite the atrocious conditions now prevailing. I re-ascend to the belay above. I have a 60m. rope so it should be enough to link the next two final pitches together.

This section looks hard as it's a 20m. slab problem and I am now guessing that I will be getting no protection due to this totally unaccommodating bloody granite. I climb up a shallow groove and look at my problem. There is a bulging arête to my left with a shallow crack running up it's right side. I scrape away at the crack in the hope of finding just one deep weakness but, predictably, it's another useless shallow load of pants. I can see some small clumps of turf higher up the arête and if I could just reach them then I am sure I can link the moves above to the ledge which is tantalisingly close now. I can just put my left foot on a sloper on the arête. As I try to stand high on it my foot comes off and I have no bloody tool placements. I am catapulted backwards through the air and the next thing I know I am dangling upside down on the slab below the ledge.

Once again I am only stopped by my back-up knot. Sadly, the Soloist does not work on upside down falls so I have to rely on back-up knots which can be difficult to tie or untie *in extremis* but they are my only fail safe. I have one tool in my hand and cannot see the other, is it on the ledge above? or has it gone to the bottom of the cliff? I really hope not, this is all that concerns me at this point. All I can think about is where my other tool is. If I lose it I will have to retreat and there is no bloody way I am giving up on this route for anything.

I pull back onto the ledge only to break out in the loudest fit of insane laughter I have known. I see my tool lying on the ledge and thank God once again for his kindness. Predictably, I can't believe my luck. "What a jammy bastard Alan." Not a scratch or a mark in sight. I quickly sort myself out and I am now fully confident that I at least have a totally bomber belay. This time I stick to the foothold on the arête and precariously reach up high to get the moss and some more turf which allows me to climb the arête and mantel onto the ledge above. I now arrange some rubbish runners under the slanting roof which is the junction with the route *Crazy Sorrow.*

The guidebook says you carry on straight up, but the weather is really foul and I don't like the look of the way ahead or what little of it I can see through this horrible blizzard. Instead, I opt for the other guidebook hint at 'escape out right.'

"Jesus, it looks no better." A large roof blocks the way with yet another slab below it. I am fed up with this slab climbing as I find it all rather thin and more to do with good footwork than strong arms. I traverse up right to below the left side of the roof and look below. "Cool," there is a load of ice under the roof but I can't see anyway of protecting it and the ice only means that there is not even the chance of a psychological runner. I manage to place a spectre hook in the turf on the left side of the roof and now I can step down to reach the slab. It feels steep and a fall here will send me smashing down left for a bad landing. I really need to focus my attention and stay nice and calm. I traverse under the roof delicately, no room for mistakes here, I am now climbing with my feet and I am grateful that they are sticking for now.

Finally, after much heart in mouth I reach the right-hand end of the slab and can get a torque under the roof, which allows me to reach high with my right tool and get some turf and thankfully reach a ledge above. "Phew." That felt weird but only after I climbed it, not during – quite bizarre this climbing game. The weather has really taken a turn for the worse and I am being blinded by spindrift and the wind feels fiercely strong. I carry on for a while traversing, the ground is friendlier here and I am getting better gear at last, albeit not where I really need it. I traverse along at first but I am forced to make a slight descent and then more climbing straight up which takes me to the crest of the Tough Brown Ridge – or what I believe is the ridge anyway. Sadly, I can't see where the hell you are supposed to abseil from. Something in the description about a block with a sling around it – but as I can hardly see my hands, I don't think I am going to find it now.

I switch my head torch on and look again. Bloody nothing but spindrift blasted in my face. I think I'm going to panic, but wait – what about reason. And for me that's the way I have just come. I know where everything is and I have belays that will allow me to descend. I mean, what's the difference? Descend here, providing I find said block, which is looking more unlikely by the minute, or go back there, which I have to anyway, then descend. I have made my mind up and it's back the way I came and descent for me.

I pull my way across my rope, and eventually, I am back at the roof. I am not keen on this traverse but it's this or, in my mind, confusion over on the ridge, trying to find a lousy block in this shite. I manage to place my tools on the turf and step back down to below the roof. I know the ice is good enough so I just have to remember that. I traverse again tenuously and thinly but my feet are doing all the work and they're sticking to the thin ice here. I seem to be willing my mono points to stick and they are doing it. It feels like the longest traverse of my life, almost being blown off several times, I begin to feel sick. I can now get at the turf on the other side of the roof and pull onto the ledge. I throw up all over the ledge the retching has made my eyes water and my tears are freezing straight onto my cheeks. I also discover the spectre hook has completely ripped out the turf. "I am so lucky it's not real." Or so I think. I rap from the roof junction but as the gear consists of two nuts sideways under a roof I decide I would be better rapping from the *in situ* thread lower down. Well I have tested the thread fully and at least I know it's bomber. I rap from the thread to the ledges below, finally another rappel and now I am safely on *terra firma.*

I have problems seeing my hands in front of me and know it's far from over yet. I put away my frozen rope but can't remove my harness as the webbing buckles are totally frozen stiff. I put my sack on and try to get out of this nightmare, I am having a horrendous time descending as I can't see my compass properly and the snow is waist deep in the Corrie. I don't know if I can carry on, my body is exhausted and with no sleep for two days or decent food I am at breaking point, literally.

I am not even at the First Aid box yet and I have been floundering here for more than an hour. I sit down blasted by spindrift and freezing, I start to cry and panic, it's hopeless. So this is how it ends for those stupid enough to defy common sense and all that goes with it in the mountains. I drift off to sleep; somehow it no longer seems important to move. I think I am dreaming, remembering my time in the Army. I seem to remember how many times I had feelings just like this, but when I was at my lowest ebb, tired, starved and feeling hopeless I never ever gave up. I always managed to keep going, that was my spirit and I needed that resolve right now. After all, I had everything to live for, a great wife, lovely kids, and an insatiable lust for life.

I open my snow-encrusted eyes, get up and start moving. I am thinking: "As long as I don't go down or descend I will get out of here." Up and right was the way home and that's where I put my head. Four hours later I eventually reached the Meikle Pap Col after what can only be described as the basic struggle for survival in the mountains when they are venting their fury. I am weary of body and mind but I keep moving with the enduring thought that I must get home foremost in my mind. I reach the track going towards Glen Muick and I can rest now.

"Thank God." It's finally over, and with just a walk down a long track I will be there. I rest my aching body and have the strangest feeling. I start to shake uncontrollably and break down in tears, I am filled with unknown emotions. "Wait a minute." I know what they are now. They are the feelings of remorse and fear. I am remorseful because I could have easily killed myself and that would have been selfish, as I know my wife deserves better of me. "That's it." The feelings I should have been having on the route were those that I had repressed. That's why I felt a profound sense of calm after falling so many times, but now all the feelings of fear and common sense that I had ignored are suddenly filling my mind, flooding back like waves. It feels like a wake-up call and I am suddenly intensely aware of my own selfishness and yet it feels too late. I pull myself together and carry on down the track, I get the frozen clothing off and get in the car anxious to get back home and see my wife. I feel content and am slowly warming up. I feel a strange kind of satisfaction and now I know that I no longer have to worry about what people will undoubtedly say about me.

"I can climb." Of that I am now certain.

TIME FOR TEA

By Phil Gribbon

FRAGILE fragments shimmered through my heat-saturated brain. With limbs limp we lay flat on the rock close to the edge and in love with the sun. We were comfortably warm but thirst husked.

Somehow, the long traverse to the summit had given adequate difficulties. All nicely exposed; it gave a string of short slabs crisp with lichens that stopped by dropping into space, a sequence of uncomfortable straddles along painful sharp edges and open chimneys with downward views. The solitary gendarme had been seduced in a delicate skirting girdle around its waist.

By getting the pitch sequence right I was rewarded with the final pitch. It was all pleasurable, a pull on the edge and a layback onto a slab. Just go on tiptoe, then reach for the top.

Summited, as they say!

Already the day had seemed timeless and endless. Hours had slipped away since we had stood in the early dawn light with mist seeping and eddying in the corrie and a cool dankness creeping off the quiet lochan, and had supped a last brew to salute the virgin mountain looming above us. We had been shocked awake by a chill grasping swirl of the current as we crossed the river and schrunched on to the initial frozen snowfield. Somewhere up there was our objective, an extraordinary rock feature that marked the apex of the ridge.

Now listless and content, we were drooped over this apex. We had perched ourselves on a quirk of nature. It was a gigantic blocky tower, bluntly eroded and tilted askew, that pitched its eaves over a glacier far below. Its whole structure mimicked an improbably ridiculous architecture. Perhaps mystical eons ago the mysterious hand of a marauding giant toupidek had surpassed itself in artistic cleverness and carved out a celebratory fistful of stone. It appeared both secure and immutable but perhaps on some stormy night, in the fury of the elements raging over the broken landscape of southern Greenland, the whole edifice might tumble off in an awesome trundle and crash into the icy depths. Statistically improbable but still possible, and it could happen any time.

I heard and felt a deep rumble. Was this sensation coming from within the earth or did it have a much closer origin? Of course, it was just a hunger pang that fed my fantasy. Try a piece of gum to stifle any inner complaints. Chew on it and dream on.

"I'm off! I want a brew."

Thus spoke Freefall. This was his own chosen sobriquet that he had adopted proudly after having endured several involuntary backward plunges in Glen Clova and elsewhere, but we preferred to ignore such glib self advertisment. It seemed too tempting to Fate in our remote world to hark back to his past exploits on local crags. So there he was bracing himself back on the abseil ropes, his silhouette dark against the blue sky. He put more tension on his ropes, and with his voice emphatic and decisive he paused and sniffed disdainfully,

"C'mon now, I want my drink."

"What's the rush? It's taken hours to get here." I pleaded in an attempt to keep my sun-warmed indolence intact, "I'm in need of a good rest."

Meanwhile, our third member aka MacFrenzy was staring concernedly and hypnotically at the abseil sling and listening to the crinkling stress as it pulled taut round its anchor block. He refrained from comment but asked tentatively: "How long will it take to get back?"

"We'll say seven hours. but it doesn't really matter 'cos we'll never make it today."

Although we didn't wish to scamper after the fleeing Freefall there seemed little benefit in malingering, but if I hesitated long enough I would win the satisfaction of being the last person to quit the summit.

"You're next," and I handed the loose ropes to MacFrenzy. "Let's follow the guy who longs for his drink."

He went down cautiously, trying to ignore the blankness behind his back but unable to avoid a downward glance at the criss-crossing network of open crevasses on the glacier.

There was the wild world in all directions around the horizon. Silence held its sway on every peak. The sharpest spires were dark in shadow and etched against the dazzling brilliance of the sunlit sea fog and to the north the jagged ridges, bleached of colour, were stretched in rough waves into the distant haze. Gentle cloud shadows had settled tentatively on the adjacent cliffs and in the fjord the lost icebergs that had forsaken the moving pack ice drifting round the coast lay becalmed. I heard a soft whisper of distant white water raging down another valley, while close by the twin ropes creaked in their tension to offset the companionable sounds of Freefall and MacFrenzy drifting up from the hidden under-belly of the summit boulder.

We joined the ropes together. The peak was abandoned and we began our retreat along the ridge, two to move and one to belay. We threaded through the black teeth rotten with rock tripe and over fissures cutting across our route. Any initial uncertainties turned quickly to casual competence. We moved steadily with the rich light of the gathering evening deepening and staining the rocks of the high ridge while the darkening shroud of the dusk spread throughout the valley below.

Sheltering in a niche and bathed in golden glow we shed the token ropes. Unsuccessfully, I tried to stuff a rope elsewhere in the hope of finding its home in another rucksack. However, Freefall had claimed one rope and started his dash towards the other lower summit while MacFrenzy had closed his pack tightly and was looking the other way. All right, I'll be public-spirited and take my share, even if it lasts all night. There was soon no doubt that Freefall had the proverbial passion and fitness edge on us. In our jaded state we were soon lagging farther and farther behind our leader of the boundless energy. When we caught him up at our objective he was huddled out of a nippy wind and munching his ration.

"What is keeping you both?"

I ignored the obvious slur on our competence because I had a more important matter to consider.

"Now, where is that tin of beans I cached on the way? I'm starving, and even managing to salivatate."

I retrieved the can, ran the wee opener round the edge, flicked back the lid, sniffed my elixir and spooned in my beautiful chilli beans. MacFrenzy was still stacking jam on his biscuits as Freefall shouldered his sack and left, announcing with ambiguous optimism: "We'll make it before the day is done."

In his trail we scuffed our boots down a gravelly steep scree towards a snow saddle and gingerly trod in the icy pits melted and refrozen from our earlier footprints. All around the snow glowed with an alpenrosen pinkness spread out over its white creamy surface, while below the valley depths were darkening imperceptibly. Under the coffee-stained hills and squeezing out a green flash in a twinkle of crimson fire the sun irrevocably dropped under the horizon. On we went, until another icy problem presented itself.

"Put on your crimpons, folks!" Freefall declared in his twisted vernacular, and sidled off across the hardened surface.

Speed was of the essence. No time except the present. We played the crampon game: on an off, and on and off. We crossed little gendarmes with their broken ribs visible in the faint glimmerings of night. We backmarkers in our exertions were breathing hard, but he was racing still further ahead. He skipped daintily in a dance over shifting rattling stones and pushed them into a cascade toppling into the void and then he flitted feline-like on to another pinnacle.

We were glad that he was testing and working out our route. We found him waiting at the lip of a shadowed northerly wall.

"It's down here," he claimed.

In agreement, but with a note of caution: "Sure. Move together, and watch it."

Our numbed minds were losing a detailed recollection of the many foibles of the ridge. We had forgotten about this wall, but we had to move and keep watching every step. Down, and up again on a rising traverse back to the ridge. We emerged from a cleft where, imbedded inside the mountain, we struggled for minutes with our jammed sacks.

"My honour," he assumed.

Out of balance and thrust from the rock I followed, sidling down an airy gangway where treacherous gravel lurked under moss cushions. Waiting in a tiny amphitheatre I realised the reason for his choice. Underneath was an irreversible wall of which my memory was only of excessive difficulty and constant terror. We had no pegs, so we used a single rope loop to bind a fragmented nest of thin splinters into an abseil point.

MacFrenzy peered shortsightedly at the projected take-off point and kicked it gently.

"May the Good Lord preserve us, and we'll need the length of the ropes to reach the ledge."

Freefall expressed some skepticism of its unseen existence somewhere down the wall, but I insisted: "Aye, there's a ledge, a projecting shelf near the bottom of the rope." We hadn't any other options.

"The first man down finds it."

"Okay, I'll believe you," declared Freefall, and his insubstantial shadow faded into the gloom of the wall. Luckily, the ledge was more substantial than we had remembered and for the moment we could relax.

Across the western sea a wan orange moon sliver cast an unruffled reflection while, in the sunset glimmer, a clearcut outline of twin figures were busy untangling the ropes. They hurried at their task impatient to get to the next problem.

Freefall set off across the face. Suddenly, there was a grating crash as his footholds fell away, but somehow he remained on the rock as the fragments bounded off towards the glacier. This wasn't the moment to live up to his name. It needed some serious self-appraisal to convince myself that what I had traversed in the morning I would now be able to manage in the dark. I moved off with slow trepidation first crossing an icy tongue hanging down from a breche in the ridge, and soon I was crawling up the shelves of a pinnacle and traveling by touch rather than by sight.

"Jings, I'm knackered," I confided to MacFrenzy as we sat below the ultimate pinnacle. Rising up in front of us was a smooth wall down which we had abseiled without a care in the early morning sunshine.

"We'll have to kip here."

All the world around knew it was time to sleep, but I had spoken too soon because, as he loomed up through the darkness, Freefall had overheard my hopeful wish and now he was to reject any plea for rest. More importantly he would never have considered a bivouac was a good substitute to a warm pit in a snug tent.

"No, I'm not stopping here. If you like I'll go ahead."

"Well, if you insist…"

It was an offer I couldn't refuse. I looked in the direction of the indistinct slabs where dark recesses hid the seemingly impossible nature of a ladder of overlapping upward steps. He realised that I wanted to shirk the horrors of those slabs. So Freefall led. I followed a line dictated by a nut. It was pretty desperate stuff up the virgin flank where a recent rockfall had exposed unweathered slab sheets devoid of features save for a few tottering blocks and some sparse incut holds behind an unstable flake. I climbed in pursuit of my mocking moonshadow, pushing up on tiptoes and clawing with my fingernails. Overhead an auroral curtain bundled itself into applegreen sheaves and a satellite tracked behind a still figure sitting on the skyline. It had been his lead through midnight and into tomorrow.

We went downhill in giant strides with the snow crust grabbing at our crampon straps. The familiar hills began to grow in stature round the cirque. Chill and invigorating blew the night wind. The morning star was on our backs and the stones were brightening for another day. We saw from afar the glimmer of a candle still flickering its welcome to our camp. We waded hotfoot and without hesitation across the river. Refreshing? Yes, but after seven hours a-waiting, the brew was an unfathomable sweet strong pleasure of epicurean simplicity. We raised our mugs in our cupped hands.

"Ah, me…" Freefall spoke in hushed tones of reverence. A careful refined sip.

"Great...great." Slurp.

"Quite a trip!"

Steven Gordon approaching the South Peak of The Cobbler: Photo Dave MacLeod.

WHO NEEDS THE HIMALAYAS?

By Brian Davison

ANOTHER night of reading through guidebook manuscripts loomed ahead of me. It was the Ben Nevis guide this time. I've never been a fan of the Ben. Far too crowded and far too pawed over were my feelings, there just weren't any good new obvious lines left.

Simon Richardson, the author, had produced a flawless text as you'd expect from someone so organised. After several hours I was nearly at the end, I'd reached the traverses. The summer girdle by Bell took a natural line of terraces. The grass and scree covered ledges seemed an obvious choice for winter and I read on wondering what the grade would be. At the end of the chapter I went back, had I missed it, was it re-named? I still couldn't find it. Surely, such an obvious winter line hadn't been overlooked, unless people were put off by the 4km. of traversing. A traverse of Alpine or even Himalayan proportions would require a competent and trustworthy partner and they can be difficult to find.

Simon would know if it had been climbed but if I asked him it would alert him to the line, if he didn't know about it already. But what better partner to choose than the guidebook author, he'd have an excellent knowledge of the mountain. A phone call soon sorted it. We'd wait until late in the season when there was more daylight, and a good firm snow covering was necessary for rapid progress. For good snow cover we had to wait several years. In late March 2006 I was sitting in a snow-covered field in Switzerland. It was supposed to have been ploughed two weeks earlier but a metre of overnight snow dump had stopped that and my work there. Browsing through the Internet I noticed Scotland appeared to be suffering the same fate. If that consolidates and hardens it could be good in a few weeks I thought as I typed an e-mail to Simon.

A few weeks later and still there were reports of avalanches on the Ben. Conditions weren't certain but we could wait no longer as it was getting increasingly warmer. I woke at 3am. from a night spent folded round the seats of my car. I envied Simon in his large estate. A quick breakfast while packing a rack, we were both eager to set off so I decide to leave making up more drink and left with just my flask of coffee, relying on there being water on route. Soon we were there, wandering through damp snow as we climbed *North Gully*. At half-height we reached the freezing level and by the top it was nicely frozen. I looked at the snow at the top of Castle Corrie and wondered about its stability, the first rays of the sun just glinting on it, better to test it now than later, at least I was at the top to test it out. A traverse under the cornice and a few probing stabs and nothing had gone so I headed on a downward traverse under Raeburn's Buttress. I didn't know this area of cliff so just followed my nose which lead to *Ledge Route*. The sun was up and I was overheating, I took a jacket off and Simon passed me, obviously pleased with our progress. I plodded on

Dave McLeod on the first ascent of Apollo 8a+, Tighnabruaich Viewpoint Crags, Cowal.

Simon Jenkins on Yammy, Upper Great Gully Buttress, Glen Coe. Photo: Peter Wilson.

in his footsteps until we reached *Thompson's Route* and tied onto our one rope and grabbed the rack. After 10m. I hit a large piece of ice in the chimney, it lifted and fell nearly knocking me with it. I looked around and found some protection, this late in the season the ice was rotten so I was forced to make some mixed moves on the sidewalls. Progress was slowing but once belayed, Simon soon followed and traversed over Number Three Gully Buttress and down. I passed his belay and the first water I'd seen, I drank as much as I could before traversing across to *Green Gully*.

Simon took us down *Hesperides Ledge* to the base of *Comb Gully* and another belay with running water, he had all the luck to be static at the belays with copious supplies of drinks. We unroped and headed across to *Glovers Chimney*. The going was easier here until just short of Tower Gap were the rope came out again for the final few moves and soon we were across the gap and tucked into an outcrop for lunch. Simon had brought several isotonic drinks, which I greedily drank trying to rehydrate myself as we looked at the way ahead. We'd covered half the route in six hours but I knew that what lay ahead looked more precarious, traverses along ledges with large drops below, not as friendly as the first section. Simon told me of his retreat from *Point Five Gully* along a shelf system through the Indicator Wall section of the cliff so we were hoping to travel this in the opposite direction.

As we headed across, the snow started to feel less secure under foot. It was time for the rope. Simon led off with me hoping he'd reach *Point Five Gully* in one pitch. My optimism was short lived as he ran out of rope and direction and constructed a disintegrating belay by an outcrop. I could see the gully tantalisingly close. A careful traverse down and round some suspect rock led me into the gully just above the Rogue Pitch and a poor belay above. Simon was soon with me and he headed off up the steep Left-Hand Finish to *Point Five Gully*. I passed him on the belay and led up the continuation of the snow runnel looking for a belay rather than the line of the route. After several metres of climbing together I gave up and wedged myself across the runnel until Simon joined me, after which we down-climbed to a line he'd spotted crossing *Observatory Ridge*. This lead to a belay overlooking *Zero Gully* where we debated the line of the route, the options being to down-climb *Zero Gully* to reach a natural line of weakness crossing the *Minus Face* or to follow a gentle rising traverse over *Orion Face* to finish on top of *North-East Buttress*.

The aesthetics of finishing on top of the mountain won the day and I headed off, popping in the odd runner with no intention of stopping until I reached the top and an excellent belay around the cairn. Simon joined me and we looked across the snow-covered peaks, we'd taken just more than 12 hours and there was still several hours of daylight.

The 250-mile drive home felt longer than usual and I was looking forward to some sleep as I pulled in at 3:30am. just more than 24 hours after getting up. Looking round I couldn't find my keys. Oh! well, looks like another night spent curled up in the car.

UNTRODDEN WAYS

By P. J. Biggar

PATRICK O'Dwyer and George Reddle sat in the hut while the warm drizzle crept along the stony hillsides and the effects of a violent midging slowly receded. Both men were still afflicted by that dreadful burning, itching sensation. They had lingered too long in the little pub by the sea-loch where the locals huddled under dripping umbrellas for a quick smoke. By the time it came to make the short walk to the hut, the summer breeze had died away and the curse had risen in visible grey clouds.

"They're a bit like bloody terrorists," ventured O'Dwyer pouring more tea. "Cause mayhem and vanish."

"An' ye can't beat them." Reddle's flat Yorkshire accent came from behind the paper.

O'Dwyer smiled ruefully. The reference to terrorists made him uneasy. From little things they had said it seemed that he and his companion disagreed radically about the recent wars and the violence which had followed them. One might have thought that the dour, old Yorkshireman would take the side of pragmatism and see the allies' point of view, but it was the other way round. O'Dwyer, the younger man, a Scot of Celtic extraction, held that military intervention was necessary to protect western interests. He had half guessed a long time ago that Reddle might have had a background as a pacifist, might even have suffered for it. He had never asked him about it and he never would: Reddle was notoriously secretive about his past and O'Dwyer had always respected that. O'Dwyer pushed his whisky flask across the table.

"Help yourself." Reddle grunted non-committally but eventually, though he seemed absorbed in what he was reading, his hand strayed towards the flask and he poured himself a dram. O'Dwyer studied the guidebooks and topos which cluttered the table. Choice of crag was important. Reddle had always been by far the better rock climber, but now, with the onset of old age, he had some obscure complaint which meant he no longer wanted to lead the harder pitches. Reddle poured himself another drop of O'Dwyer's whisky and pushed the paper away with a contemptuous snort.

"We'll end up having t'negotiate," he said. "Why not start now, 'stead of years down the line?"

"Who do we negotiate with?"

"These so-called terrorists."

"They won't talk."

"They will if we show we're serious. It's a question of finding the right gesture – release a prisoner, send an envoy."

"But there are so many different groups."

"Send lots of envoys. Give the buggers something to do." Reddle poured the remains of the tea into his mug.

"What's the alternative?"

"I don't think it's as simple as that," said O'Dwyer.

"Nobody said it was simple, lad," said Reddle with one of his strange, infrequent smiles. "What's simple is dropping bombs, but every one you drop makes things worse not better."

"They make things worse every time they blow up innocent civilians."

" No-one would deny it," said Reddle. O'Dwyer finished his whisky and got up.

"I think it's time to put the tatties on," he said.

"If you're putting a pan on…" said Reddle, never stirring from where he sat leaning up against the wall under the map of the North-West.

Smiling to himself O'Dwyer washed the potatoes and got the pan boiling. When he returned to the other room, Reddle was occupied in making a pencil sketch of the old ruin which could be seen in the overgrown meadow in front of the hut. O'Dwyer admired the delicate impression of peaceful crumbling stonework and blowing grasses, with its suggestion of a vanished way of life.

"You've caught that well," he said. "I like the atmosphere."

Reddle shrugged.

"It's a rough attempt," he muttered, sounding pleased nonetheless.

"It's a pity I left that bottle of wine in the car," he went on, "the midges just got to me. I couldn't think what I needed."

"Is this it?" asked O'Dwyer with a gentle smile, producing both bottle and corkscrew. "I found it rolling about in the boot."

Reddle pushed back his empty plate, groaned with satisfaction and stretched himself out comfortably on the long wooden bench.

"How's old Mac these days?" he inquired. "Still getting out with little Harvey?"

"Not so much," said O'Dwyer. "Mac's a bit like me, not so good on rock. Harvey needed someone to push him up the grades a bit. He does quite a lot with Rab Auldburn these days. Mac and he still go walking."

"Rab's got his work cut out," muttered Reddle. "Th'only time I did a long route with Harvey, he got us way off line. I had the devil of a job." He yawned noisily. "Partnerships, partnerships," he murmured drowsily, "they come and go..."

"They're not like friendships are they?" said O'Dwyer, but there was no answer. Reddle seemed to have drifted off to sleep. By the time O'Dwyer had done the dishes, he'd come round again and was sitting by the window sketching the same scene by the changing evening light.

"Tha surely hasn't done the dishes?" he inquired. "That were my job."

"Och, no problem," said O'Dwyer tolerantly. "What's the plan for tomorrow, then?"

The crag they chose for the last day of their little holiday was about half-an-hour's walk from the road, through scattered birch trees at first and then out on rolling heather moorland dotted with lochans. The sun came and went behind high clouds. The great North-Western peaks stood up clear and proud.

From uncertain beginnings on wet sandstone, O'Dwyer had felt his form steadily improve during the week. Reddle too was climbing more confidently than he had for some time, indeed his chief problem seemed to be lack of practice: when one was nearer 80 than 70, partners were hard to come by. O'Dwyer thought that, if all went well, there was a route they might just be able to tackle – he stored it away at the back of his mind.

Their first climb was a delightful rough slab, just full of holds.

"Tha made that look easy," said Reddle.

Then they chose something longer: a steeper crack line which O'Dwyer had seconded before. He remembered the crack with some trepidation, but found he had climbed it before he had even started to think about it. He turned round just before making the crucial move: "This is good!" he shouted.

Reddle led through, exclaiming over the excellence of the rock. Ahead was a choice of ways. Reddle moved up slowly, placing protection with care. To his right was a steep slab devoid of obvious holds, and to his left an easier traverse into a corner. Reddle hesitated. Watching from below, O'Dwyer could sense the temptation of the steeper way tugging at the older man. He remembered many times watching the soles of Reddle's boots vanishing upwards, remembered also how Reddle would pause before making the vital move and make some light-hearted remark. Now, he hesitated, then made a rather tentative move towards the steeper ground. O'Dwyer could sense a tremble in the rope he was holding.

"George," he shouted up, "it looks much easier to the left." Reddle looked down at him: "Don't you fancy going right, eh?" It was like a wasp sting from the past. O'Dwyer winced. "Mind you, y'might be right – it is a bit steep is this. T'ud be all right wi' a few holds." With some regret he took the easier option.

O'Dwyer lay back partially at peace in the heather at the base of the crag. Reddle got out his sketch pad: he seemed completely relaxed. Away over the moor in a mystical light the great peaks seemed closer than they were. He put down the water bottle, stretched, and came over to see how Reddle's sketch was progressing.

"Almost an Arctic light isn't it?"

"Aye, it is a bit," Reddle agreed. "Sharp spires above the tundra and all that, eh?"

O'Dwyer paused.

"Do you remember canoeing back across the fjord after walking down that long valley?" Reddle looked up from his drawing

"Aye," he said. "Like yesterday." O'Dwyer nodded. He couldn't easily put it into words, but it had been on that specific occasion that he had felt

Reddle's attitude towards him undergo a subtle change. They had been carrying the canoe up the rough shore and he had stumbled clumsily and dropped his end. They were both tired and Reddle had inclined to be snappish, but O'Dwyer had apologised at once and he had sensed a softening in Reddle's attitude towards him. Afterwards, at dinner, he had felt that Reddle was making a special effort to be nice to him – praising his contribution to the meal. Reddle had been a senior member of the expedition and O'Dwyer a mere rookie, but it seemed to him that a relationship which had lasted more than 30 years had its roots in that trivial incident. He was going to try to say something, but Reddle had shut his sketch book and was getting stiffly to his feet.

"I s'pose if we're going t'do owt more, we'd best make a move."

They coiled the rope, picked up the discarded gear and moved round to the main face of the crag. O'Dwyer felt apprehension stir. This was the time to do that route, if only he could make out its wandering, elegant line. They walked to and fro at the base of the crag. The light had dulled a little as the freshening breeze brought cloud from the Inner Hebrides. The gneiss seemed to hang in grey armour plates and reveal nothing. Then a solitary beam of sunlight illuminated the rock.

"That's it!" said O'Dwyer pointing. A sinuous way crossed the crag from top to bottom; it was the longest route and the classic line; it followed slabs and cracks and ever so gradually thinning ledges, steepening as it went.

Although he was eager to be on the rock and doing the only thing which could truly relieve the anxiety he felt, O'Dwyer forced himself to make sure that every bit of gear was in its proper place. Then he stepped up the first few moves and wiped the soles of his brightly coloured rock boots. The rock was abrasive and secure to the touch. Confidence flooding through him, he moved on smoothly up the steepening slab. At the top of the slab he paused. The route went leftwards up a narrow shelf. He slotted a nut into a perfect crack. That would keep the rope right for George. O'Dwyer clipped in and tip-toed upwards. He could sense the rock sticking like sand-paper to his feet.

Gradually, as he moved higher up the receding edgeway O'Dwyer felt something like a brake being applied to his ease of movement. He breathed deeply and made a conscious effort to stand out from the rock, but he still couldn't quite see where the next section of the route went. He looked down. The heather was a long way and Reddle a mere face and shoulders looking calmly up. A few moves more brought him to a narrow bay where two could stand in reasonable comfort.

"I'll bring you up to here, George," O'Dwyer heard himself shout as his hands tied the knots as if of their own volition. Reddle waved an arm in acknowledgement. When all was ready he climbed the pitch steadily, having to make only one longer pause to free an embedded nut. He paused for a moment before stepping up to the ledge and O'Dwyer could see him assessing the route ahead.

"Tha'd best go on."

"No problem," said O'Dwyer. He noticed that he must have partly expected this outcome because he had not started passing the gear to his partner. Perhaps some tiny part of him would have been relieved if Reddle had been determined to lead the crux, but he knew in himself that this would have been like going back in time. Things were different now. It was up to him: he felt pleased. With careful deliberation he arranged the gear which Reddle passed him.

 Leaning back against the rock, Reddle prepared to pay out the rope. His hands looked oddly frail; his forearms, once so muscular, had lanked with age. He glanced sideways at the younger man:

"Dance away, Patrick!" Partly a compliment, partly a challenge: O'Dwyer rubbed his shoes against his trouser legs and started upwards.

The route was like a compelling argument: all men are mortal; Socrates is a man… it was pushing O'Dwyer farther and farther to his left. For all things, if that thing is a man, that thing is mortal. O'Dwyer's hands and feet sought places to go and they became fewer and fewer. A beak of grey rock was approaching – it jutted out over nothing. He didn't want to go there, but the logic of the rock forced him nearer and nearer. He felt little drops of sweat trickling across his ribs and a little tremble began in his legs. He paused, breathed deeply several times and straightened himself up to look. Far below, the breeze ruffled the surface of the lochans. He partly heard a bee buzz across the rocks collecting nectar from the heather which bulged from the ledges. Now out of sight, Reddle cleared his throat. Then he saw it. Just to the right of the grey beak, and hidden until he was almost touching it, was a steep crack in the abutting wall. To left and right were ways he couldn't go: the crack was the last figure of the dance, the conclusion of the argument. O'Dwyer felt very mortal, but he knew he wanted to do it, and he wanted to do it well.

At the base of the crack was another much narrower parallel fissure. After several moments of anxious effort he placed just the right nut. He looked up, the holds were all there. He looked down and then scolded himself:

"No point in looking down, we're not going there." Exposure had always been his bugbear, but now he felt calmer, more in control. He took another couple of deep breaths.

"That weren't too bad at all," said Reddle, as he made the final step up. "Y'did quite well, lad."

"Good rock, wasn't it," said O'Dwyer grinning but trying to conceal the deep sense of exultation he felt.

As they coiled the ropes on the heathery brow of the crag, they could feel the evening breeze starting to drop. Tiffany, O'Dwyer's wife, would have a meal waiting for them on the far side of the country. They ambled down to the path in amicable silence. Reddle paused to admire the last view of the great peaks.

"You were saying summat t'other night about partnerships and friendships an' that…" O'Dwyer wondered what was coming. Effusiveness was not Reddle's style.

"I've been thinking," Reddle went on. "Y'know we've been climbing for a good number of years now, and," he added generously, "your rock climbing's not quite so bad as it used to be. I reckon we could just about get you in. D'yer fancy joining t'Club?"

O'Dwyer was so surprised he hardly knew what to say. He'd never considered himself anywhere near Club standard, but now that the possibility arose it seemed somehow right.

"Why thank you, George," he said. "I'd like that very much."

"Ay, right," said Reddle, "I'll get t'Secretary t'send you a form. I can't promise owt, mind. Tha knows what committees are like."

"It certainly won't affect our friendship if it doesn't work out," said O'Dwyer. For a moment their eyes met.

"Nay, lad," said Reddle slowly. "Nowt'll affect that." And he turned away down the path. "We'd best shift before this breeze drops altogether."

NEW CLIMBS SECTION

Corrections and comments on descriptions and diagrams in the new Scottish Rock Climbs guidebook are to be found on the SMC web site at: http://www.smc.org.uk/books/books_scottish_rockclimbs.htm. Opinions on grades are not necessarily in the majority as further opinions were collected in preparation of the book and these are not reproduced. Further corrections and comments are welcome to anisbe@globalnet.co.uk.

OUTER ISLES

HARRIS, Sron Ulladale, North-East Face:
Note: J.Preston and G.Ettle climbed *Inversion* on 11th June 2006. Pitch grades 5a, 4c, 5a, 4c, 4b, 4c. "Exposed and amazing positions throughout, but really very dirty. The rock is completely covered in lichen and there are some steep moves on grass and various other types of vegetation. I suppose you could give yourself one star if you get to the top alive."

Variation: 15m   E1 5b. S.Gillies, G.Gavell. May 1997.
From the belay at the top of pitch 2, instead of "traversing left round a corner…etc" climb an obvious crack above the belay to emerge on the "edge" as described on pitch 4, thereby cutting out the traverse left and up then down and right.

LEWIS, Beannan a' Deas (NB 055 290):
A south facing crag reaching a height of about 30m on the south side of Beannan a' Deas (252m). The best climbs lie on the right side on excellent rock, generally well protected. Numerous smaller crags are passed on the described approach, with many potential 15 to 30m routes. Routes are 25 to 30m.
Approach: Park up a short hill 200m west of the weir at the end of Loch Suaneabhal. Follow a faint path following a buried pipeline marked by occasional posts and man holes. The path skirts the east side of two unnamed lochs and then goes to the north of Loch a' Bheannain. 400m past the loch the path heads south up an unnamed valley to the west of Beannan a' Deas. Continue to the next unnamed loch and take the east side to near the end of the loch. Head due east for about 200m along the north side of a shallow valley and some small walled enclosures. Head due north up the hill and the cliff appears in 50m. It is easily identified by a prominent triangular niche in the upper centre, 35 to 45 mins.

Wandering Zig Zag   E1 5a *. K.Neal, A.van Lopik. 8th June 2006.
Take a left-trending diagonal crack for 4m, step right on the slab and follow a right-trending crack up and right to a hanging arête. Hand traverse left to the top (quite bold).

Crunch   E3 5b *. K.Neal, A.van Lopik. 10th June 2006.
Climbs directly up the highest part of the crag with some suspect rock and poor protection until half-height. Pull onto a hanging ramp and make a couple of moves rightwards before pulling through onto the main wall. Follow faint grooves bearing

slightly leftwards to gain the left side of the triangular niche. From here follow shallow cracks to the top of the crag.

Diagonal   HVS 5b **. K.Neal, A.van Lopik. 10th June 2006.
Takes a right to left line. Climb a short thin crack in the slab leading to the overhang. Make a stiff pull over this and follow a continuation crack to gain the triangular niche. Bridge steeply up the corner-crack to the top.

Commitment   E3 5b/c ****. K.Neal, A.van Lopik. 10th June 2006.
An absolute classic pitch of climbing, taking the stunning roof on the right-hand of the crag. Start at the right-hand crack system just below the roof. Climb up to the roof and hand traverse left. Gain the holds above the roof to a hanging semi rest. Finish out right.

What a Day   E2/5b **. K.Neal, A.van Lopik. 10th June 2006.
Starts on the same crack line as for Pump Master, and then traverses right around the arête to finish up a lovely crack to the top. (small gear)

The Neb   VS 5a **. K.Neal, A.van Lopik. 10th June 2006.
Climb up to the prominent flake at the right side of the crag and gain a standing position on it. Continue to the top via cracks.

Note: Grade opinions from K. Neal:
Mangersta Slabs: *Moscow Mule* – HVS 5b **.
Singapore Sling – E2 5c ** , grade right, quality route.
Aurora: Star of the Sea – HVS 5a.
Red Wall: *Limka* – E2 5b.

LEWIS SEA-CLIFFS, Torasgeo:
These routes lie on the usually sheltered west (east facing) wall and are all non-tidal, described from left to right as looking at the crag, starting with the obvious south facing slab of *Argonaut*. The first three routes are approached by a 55m abseil from a convenient boulder down a vegetated corner to a large boulder cove exposed at all states of the tide (about 30m north of the obvious decaying stack/fin).

Argonaut   55m HVS **. P.Donnithorne, E.Alsford. 4th June 2006.
Start below the slab.
1. 35m 5a Trend up and right across broken grooves, then back up left, and up a short groove abutting the main slab. Follow the obvious red quartz seam up right, to the right edge of the slab, and follow this to a slabby ledge.
2. 20m 5a Follow the tapering ramp up rightwards to its end, then steeply up into a groove which leads past a bulge to the top.

Triton   55m E1 ***. E.Alsford, P.Donnithorne. 7th June 2006.
Takes the groove-line just right of the arête right of the previous route. Start immediately to its right by the largest boulder.
1. 30m 5b Traverse right just above high water mark for 3m to an obvious shallow slabby groove. Ascend this until forced right on big holds to beneath a steep corner. Go up this past a bulge to a large sloping ledge.

2. 25m 5b The corner above leads to another slabby ledge (the belay of Argonaut). Launch up the orange wall above slightly leftwards to finish up a short groove in the arête.

Palace of Colchis 80m E1 ****. E.Alsford, P.Donnithorne. 7th June 2006.
A spectacular traverse of the west wall starting up Triton.
1. 40m 5b Follow Triton for 13m to below the steep corner. Follow an obvious white juggy line up steeply rightwards, with good positions, until it is possible to step down right onto brown slabs. Continue traversing horizontally right to a small vegetated stance.
2. 30m 5b Continue in the same line across an orange wall, above the large roof, to a spike on the arête. Continue traversing, crossing The Black Carrot, to belay on a ledge in the obvious corner of Bosphorus Groove.
3. 10m 5b Step left and follow a fine thin crack in the streaky wall above (between The Black Carrot and Bosphorus Groove).

Below the right-hand end of the west wall is a commodious non-tidal ledge with a short chimney at its left end. The next two routes start at the bottom of the chimney. Abseil approach.

The Black Carrot 45m E3 5c ***. P.Donnithorne, E.Alsford. 8th June 2006.
Move left onto a ledge and pull onto a pink slab. Move left along this, under small roofs, and up with difficulty to quartz footholds on the arête. A small groove leads to big flakes. Trend up and left more easily to reach the Black Carrot and climb the crack forming its left side to a small ledge. Go up a short groove leftwards to finish over blocks.

Bosphorus Groove 45m HVS 5a *. E.Alsford, P.Donnithorne. 7th June 2006.
From the top of the chimney move left to climb the obvious left slanting groove-line. Move left under steep ground and pull up into a corner. (optional belay, common with belay at end of second pitch on Palace Of Colchis). Continue up the twin cracks in the right wall to an easier angled finish.

Symplagades 45m E1 5b *. P.Donnithorne, E.Alsford. 8th June 2006.
Based on the right edge of the wall, approach from the commodious ledge by scrambling rightwards along a thin ledge to a slabby corner. Climb the corner for 10m, then make a rising rightwards traverse to some gigantic flakes. Step right and climb the arête to the top.

Ein Schiff voller Narren 30m E5/6 6b **. P.Thorburn, B.Fyffe. June 2005.
There is a large wall to the right of 42nd Street. This route takes the crack in the wall to the right of a left-leaning corner. Climb a left-slanting crack to ledges. Then climb up a vague block rib, then up a crack just right of the arête above.

Moac Wall:
Fullminate 25m E4 6a *. P.Thorburn, B.Fyffe. June 2005.
Climbs the right side of the pink intrusion.Climb the left-hand side of a wide groove to the pink intrusion. Gain the projecting ledge in the black wall and continue steeply up rightwards to easier ground.

Wedge on a Ledge   30m   E2 6a. B.Fyffe, P.Thorburn. June 2005.
The wall just before Black Wall. Climb a thin crack above the apex of the wedge to ledges (crux).Continue up the wall to the left of the wide crack/fault.

Black Wall:
The obvious black wall facing Moac Wall.
Vital Spark   35m   E4 6a ***. P.Thorburn, B.Fyffe. June 2005.
Climbs the black wall at its highest point. Start on the ramp just left of the slime streak. Climb up to a roof, and traverse rightwards into The Black Cat. Go up this to stand on a flake. Climb slightly left and up to the first diagonal break. Boldly climb the wall just left of the pink intrusion to a second diagonal break. Continue more easily being wary of the odd loose hold.

The Black Cat   35m   E3 5c *. B.Fyffe, P.Thorburn. June 2005.
An attempt on the groove just to the right of the previous route. Climb up a short wall just to the right of the slime streak. Trend up and left into a shallow groove. Climb this to the first hollow blocks. Move rightwards to gain a notch on the arête. Continue up the left side of the arête past another notch to the top.

Parahandy   35m   E4 6a *. P.Thorburn, B.Fyffe. June 2005.
Climbs the hanging corner system in the centre of the cliff. Start at the seaward end of the ramp. Climb up rightward leaning black grooves to ledges (possible belay as the starting point is threatened by the sea). Climb a flake, step left and pull over the roof into the corner system. Continue more easily up this.

Dark Shadows Rising   30m   E3 5c **. P.Thorburn, B.Fyffe. June 2005.
To the right of the previuos route, past a blank corner system is a right slanting intrusion. Abseil to small ledges near the base of the next corner system to the right. Follow a short crack into the corner. Pull left onto the wall above. Follow pink band exiting by a large block on the arête.

Little Broomstick Route   20m   VS 4a *. B.Fyffe, P.Thorburn. June 2005.
This route is on the wall to the right of the right-hand corner system. Start as for the previous route. Climb rightwards up a small ramp and then straight up the wall above on good holds.

LEWIS SEA-CLIFFS, Aird Uig Area, Chapel Head:
G.Ettle and J.Preston freed Sallie's Dilemma at 5c on the Black Wall, 12th June 2006; this has already been freed by Groove Armada (2002). Chapel Crack is **, not ***. Three routes left of Colonel Huff were were in fact Severe to Hard Severe instead of VS to HVS.
Dalbeg Area: Dilithium Crystals, Tea for Two, Outlaw and First Born are all worth a *, Navy Cut is worth **.

Black Wall:
J.Lyall says that The Boardwalk Walls (SMCJ 2003) are the same as Black Wall (Hebrides guide p95). Colonel Huff (15m Severe *) is correctly graded and the same as Northern Soul (30m HVS **) - the first 15m are walking.
Diving Board (30m Severe *) is similar to Disco Fever (30m VS 4c **).

Around the Bend (30m V.Diff *) is correctly graded and the same as Funky Corner (VS 4c **), although it has a 3m direct start at Severe 4b.
Chapel Crack is correct at Hard Severe *.

Old Records   30m   VS 4b *. J.Lyall, S.Gillies. 12th June 2006.
Left of Colonel Huff/Northern Soul is another rock pool with a rock pedestal on its northern end. Start from this and climb up into a recess to gain a ledge, then follow a right-slanting crack to the top.

Aurora Geo, Cioch Wall:
The Pie Party   28m   E2. A Tibbs, H.Tibbs. 27th July 2006.
Start 4m left of President's Chimney.
1. 13m 5b Move left round the arête to an incut foot ledge which leads to a fine cracked wall. Climb the wall with a bouldery finish above good gear.
2. 15m Finish up the easy arête above.

MINGULAY, Creag Dhearg - The Red Cliff:
Firewall   58m   E6 6a ***. S.Crowe, K.Magog. June 2006.
Sustained climbing with good protection. Start off the ledge. Pull out right from the belay and make a rising traverse to a wide pink slot and continue to the narrow ledge. Make a hard move to good undercuts, thus far shared with The Scream. Follow the right-hand side of the flake, then pull leftwards, then move up to reach a prominent white quartz band. Climb directly through the bulges above to a ledge 6m below the top, possible belay but the hard climbing is not yet over! Climb the wall above stepping right to a testing last move.

Dun Mingulay:
Little K   35m   E5 6a ***. S.Crowe, K.Magog. June 2006.
A more often dry and splendidly bold variation on the first pitch of Big Kenneth. Follow Big Kenneth as far as the first roof to check whether it is dry. If not step down and traverse rightwards and continue slightly downwards until it is possible to pull round into a groove that leads back up to the roof of Big Kenneth (a few metres right of where you left it!) just in time to swing out strenuously right to a big jug, then trend up and slightly right to belay on a good ledge below the second roof.

Cobweb Wall:
Descent: Abseil as for The Undercut Wall and scramble round right (south-east) at barnacle level (mid-low tide and calm seas) to a good ledge system beneath a short V-slot above the initial roof.

Bikini Dreams   120m   E3 ***. A.Lole, G.Latter. 10th June 2006.
1. 40m 5c Climb easily up to good flakes and cross the initial roof on these. Continue directly, then up a fine right-trending pegmatite ramp to a recess.
2. 30m 5c Climb directly up the wall, then trend right on good flakes to an awkward step right round into a shallow groove. Step up right onto an exposed ledge, then pull directly through a roof to better holds above. Continue more easily up a right-slanting ramp to a large ledge above.
3. 50m 4a Continue easily up slightly right, then back left and direct to finish.

The North Wall:
Located on the west wall of Seal Song Geo (opposite Seal Song Wall). This wall consists of two steep walls. The right-hand steep wall has a black slab emanating from sea-washed slabs and has a sizable roof near its top. The left-hand steep wall is capped by smaller roofs and birdy ledges. At its left-hand end (around its nose/arête) is a chimney/cleft and a sea level niche/cave. On top of the walls is a large flat platform. At the left end of the platform is a block which is used to access the first three routes. Further to the right on the platform is a huge block which is used to access the remaining routes in this area. The following routes start from high-tide ledges, which also allow one to move around most of this area easily.

Dancing with Hens   30m   VS 4c ***. P.Hemmings, C.Pulley. 12th August 2006.
To the left of the chimney/cleft is a sea-level niche. Start to the left of this niche below an obvious orange band of rock and a corner. Climb the corner to the steep orange wall and pull up on powerful jugs to below a small roof and corner. Climb the corner and pull through the roof and step out right above the void. Space walk rightwards and pull through to a slab. Climb the slab to easy ground and the top.

Mistaken Identity   30m   VS 4c **. P.Hemmings, C.Pulley. 13th August 2006.
Start at the chimney/cleft near the left-hand end of this wall. Climb rightwards to the base of a steep crack at the left-hand end of the first steep wall. Climb this crack and a broken corner to reach the birdy ledges (possible belay). Break through the roof on the right and follow the steep and airy corner to the top.

Castlebay Hen Party   45m   E1 **. C.Pulley, P.Hemmings. 13th August 2006.
Start on the sea-washed ledges below the steep left-facing corner-line defining the right-hand end of the first steep wall. This can be reached by walking along the high tide ledge system running underneath the crag.
1. 30m 5b Climb up to the overhanging corner via blocks and a short chimney. Climb the overhanging corner until forced right onto a small ledge. Climb the continuation corner to a large ledge. Break through the awkward capping roof on the left (above a birdy ledge) to belay on the pink quartz ramp of Gneiss Helmet.
2. 15m 4c Traverse leftwards beneath the triangular roof and finish up the corner of Mistaken Identity. Alternatively, but a lot harder, traverse leftwards to finish up the bottomless groove of Gneiss Helmet.
Note: Gneiss Helmet is a bit of a non-route and is best described as an alternative finish to Castlebay Hen Party.

Guarsay Mor, The South Pillar:
The Gangplank   90m   E1 *. C.Pulley, M.Mortimer. 10th June 2006.
Start 20m above sea-level, on a ledge in a niche with a green corner (part of the way up the initial ramp line of Fisherman's Blues)
1. 20m 5b From the platform, follow flakes/grooves on the left wall of the green corner to a sloping ramp (the gangplank). Follow this boldly rightwards to step into the green corner above the belay. Move up to the roof and then swing rightwards to follow jugs to belay at the left-hand end of the big ledge one third of the way up the cliff.
2. 40m 4c Follow rounded cracks above the belay to the large roof. Swing/traverse leftwards onto the wall above. Follow the wall steeply to a large ledge below a prominent chimney.

3. 30m 5a Follow the exposed chimney steeply and then a small left-facing corner to the top.

PABBAY, Hoofer's Geo:
Rite of Passage 30m E4 6a *. S.Crowe, K.Magog. June 2005.
Follow the steep side of the arête just right of Squeeze Job. Powerful moves at the start lead to more technical climbing up the blunt arête above.

Fear an Bhata 30m E4 6a **. S.Crowe, K.Magog. June 2005.
Start up the black flakes of More Lads and Molasses, after the initial moves climb boldly up and rightwards to join As Sound as Mr J.A.

The Great Arch:
Northumbrian Rhapsody 100m E5. K.Magog, S.Crowe. June 2005.
1. 25m 6b Belay on a small ledge on the arête as for Child of the Sea. Move leftwards across the wall to cross an overlap to gain easier flakes above. Sweep right to belay on the right below a notch in the right side of the long roof.
2. 25m 6a Pull through the roof into a groove. Step left out of the top of this to gain the slabby headwall. Continue to a belay ledge.
3. 30m 5b Continue up solid but lichenous rock above.

Allanish Wall:
Youth of Today 40m Hard Severe 4b **. M.Airey, A.Dell. 16th August 2006.
This is the wall on the Allanish peninsula, at the rightmost end (looking in). The route takes the wall to the right of the big open VS "Unnamed" corner at the right end of the crag. Start from lowest of two ledges just above the sea on the left wall of the corner (abseil approach down the big corner, 35m). Traverse right from the ledge for 5m, then go up cracks past small left-facing corners and a band of black rock. Trend diagonally back left and finish up a fine thin crack just to the right of the big corner.

The Banded Wall:
Further south, beyond a more broken section, a prominent wide ledge at half-height divides a fine smooth lower wall, the left section dropping straight into the sea. There are tidal ledges (mid-low tide) at its southern end.
Descents: The first five routes are accessed by a 50m abseil from a large boulder on the edge of a grass terrace. Hanging belays. For the rightmost (southern) routes, abseil from good anchors 20m further south.

Wee Hottie 20m E1 5b *. G.Latter, A.Lole. 5th June 2006.
The prominent left-facing corner bounding the left end. Climbed from the start of the vertical section, the lower 10-12m left-slanting section would give a fine harder start when dry.
Note: Hyperballad E2 5c *** and Mollyhawk E1 5b ** (existing routes).

The Posture Jedi 25m E2 5c **. G.Latter, A.Lole. 5th June 2006.
Start from the same belay as Mollyhawk. Trend up rightwards and follow superb hidden holds to break through the roof where it dwindles at its right end. Continue easily up left to a large ledge.

A Horizontal Desire   40m   E2 5c *. A.Lole, G.Latter. 5th June 2006.
Start from a belay in the vertical crack at the base of a right-facing groove right of
the main roof system. Climb the groove to belay a roof, then break out left up a
crack. Easier ground leads to the top.

One Foot in the Grave   45m   VS 4c **. A.Lole, F.Murray, G.Latter. 6th June
2006.
Climb the initial corner of Warm Up, but continue to the roof and traverse right
underneath it. Finish up a fine easy groove and wall above.

Run Daftie Run   45m   E1 5b **. A.Lole, G.Latter. 5th June 2006.
The right arête of Warm Up. Climb easily up the wall on the left to protection in a
black plaque. Step right to good holds on the arête, then go up the right side and
continue more easily directly.

Squat Thrust, Right Finish   40m   HVS 5a **. G.Latter, A.Lole. 5th June 2006.
Climb the initial chimney corner of Squat Thrust, stepping up right to a shallow
groove in the arête and finish directly.

Wind Against Tide, Right Start   30m   E1 5b **. G.Latter, A.Lole. 6th June 2006.
Start from the belay at the base of Tide Race. Step left round the arête and follow
grooves to gain the wide horizontal fault at the base of the thin crack.

South Face:
The Curious Bulge   30m   HVS 5a *. C.Pulley, M.Mortimer. 5th June 2006.
Between Grey Cossack and Yob and Yag Go Climbing Part 2 is a left-facing corner
high on the face. Follow a rib to break through an overlap via a jug. Follow the
orange slab to gain the bulging wall. Swing right into the corner and follow it to
the top.

Shags and the City   30m   HVS 5b *. M.Mortimer, C.Pulley. 5th June 2006.
Climbs the right crack through the triple overhangs. After the second roof, follow
a crack to the right of the final off-width crack.

The Elephant of Surprise   30m   HVS 5a **. A.Lole, G.Latter. 6th June 2006.
The leftmost of the triple cracks, gained by traversing in from either of the adjacent
routes.

Off Wid Emily's Bikini   35m   E2 5b **. C.Pulley, M.Mortimer. 5th June 2006.
Right of The Shipping Views is a right-facing corner in the first recess. Follow
this into an off-width come chimney. Cut loose right and go up an overhanging
flaky corner to the roof. Swing left to join The Shipping Views.

The Bay Area:
B.A.R.T.   20m   E5 6a. I.Small, J.Clark. 5th June 2005.
Breaches the main roof where it narrows at the right end of the crag. Start a few
meters left of Jesus Wants Me... .Climb a wall and scoop passing the left of a roof
to gain a large flake-crack. This curves left and leads to a rest below large roof.

*Blair Fyffe climbs the second pitch on the First Winter Ascent of Knuckleduster (VIII,9), Ben Nevis.
Photo: Steve Ashworth.*

Follow a handrail out right to make a long reach over the roof for improving holds. Move up and right to a large flat triangular hold, then directly to top.

SANDRAY, Burrell Gallery:
Life Begins... 35m E5 ***. I.Small, T.Fryer. 26th July 2006.
A counter-diagonal to Pastiche, starting on the sea-level ledge below the leftmost black groove/corner and finishing up the main hanging corner on the right edge of Burrell. A magnificent line. Traverse in at high-tide level from La Louvre to the furthest (triangular) ledge. Calm seas only!
1. 15m 6a A series of hard and committing moves up a left diagonal crack and arête leads to a sloping overhung ledge (good rest). From its right end, a long move up gains a good quartz jug. Step right and climb a rib on small holds to a horizontal break. Traverse left to a foot ledge and step up a groove above to a horizontal break (junction with Pastiche).
2. 20m 6a. Traverse left on big holds to gain the corner and the right end of Burrell wall. Pull over a roof onto a slab, step left onto a wall and climb the wall and corner with interest until wild, steep finishing moves get through the hanging corner.

Physical Graffiti 20m E5 6b ***. G.Lennox (unsec). 26th July 2006.
Pull onto the Burrel wall as for Muscular Art. Move up left to a crack running into a flake then a niche. Climb up left to a horizontal break, then make a couple of huge reaches up left through the grey band of rock to better holds and the top.

Renaissance 20m E5 6b ***. G.Lennox (unsec). 27th July 2006.
Reached from the slab sloping into the sea right of Muscular Art, climb a crack to jugs and a rest in the corner to the right (Pastiche belay). Move back left and up on fingery holds to a thin left-facing edge and gain a jug on the left. Climb up to a break and then follow a line of holds leading out left to near the top of Muscular Art.

Note: Grade Comments
Mohr Air saw a couple of ascents this year and the grade confirmed as E4 6a, 6a, 5a ***.
C.Adam & A.Robertson made early ascents of *Finger Painting* and thought E4 6a *.
First Impressionist is a good stiff E4 6a *** with a very hard long reach at the top.

La Louvre:
The lines are close together, but all very good, and independent of existing routes.

Etch-a-sketch 25m E1 5b *. I.Small, T.Fryer. 24th July 2006.
On the right-hand side of the wall, following right-trending ramp system. Up black groove on slightly suspect rock, to gain and follow ramp/ledge, until possible to go straight up small but immaculate headwall near right edge.

Pointillist 25m E3 5c ***. A.Robertson, J.Clark. 25th July 2006.
A discontinuous crack-line to the left of First Impressionist. Start just left of First

Hamish Irvine cuts his way up Green Gully, Ben Nevis in traditional style on a Centenary Ascent, April 2006. Photo: Roger Webb.

Mount Shasta from Mount Lassen in The Cascade Range, US. Photo: Carl Schaschke.

Impressionist and climb direct up a bulging crack-line to a large niche. Traverse 1m left and follow a faint crack to the top via good breaks.

Art for Art's Sake 25m E4 6a ***. I.Small, T.Fryer. 25th July 2006.
Start at a thin crack 2m right of Dot to Dot. Follow the crack on good holds to a small triangular niche. Continue to a mini-overlap in orangey rock. Make a long move up to a good hold. Continue directly up the wall on hidden holds to the left of a hairline crack.

Crazy Horse 25m E5 6a ***. J.Clark, A.Robertson. 25th July 2006.
Low in the grade. Follows the left arête to climb the amazing Rockart face. Start in a groove just right of the arête (and left of Tormented Textures). Follow the groove and crack up the wall, trending slightly left until able to make committing moves onto "Indian face". Either pull into a huge guano niche, or better, hand-traverse at eye level and step onto a mouth. Pull round using good holds on the arête and up to a big break. Finish up the top wall on the left side of the arête, with continued interest.

Line of Beauty 25m E4 6a ***. T.Fryer, I.Small. 25th July 2006.
A rising traverse from right to left, following obvious breaks below the wavy quartz vein. Start just left of First Impressionist (at the base of Pointillist). Traverse up and left, crossing other lines, past a huge quartz splodge in the centre of the wall, and into corner of Tormented Textures. Move up wall left of TT to the right end of the overhung guano ledge below the roof (lie-down rest if required). Committing moves gain a camouflaged incut hold. Continue boldly to the top. Gorgeous.

MULL, Ardtun, The Blow Hole:
The Battle 12m HVS 5a *. C. Moody, A.Soloist. 24th August 2006.
The crack between Mud in your Eye and Juracell.

ERRAID, Beach Ball Wall:
(NM 289 194) Alt 8m South-East facing
This wall faces the left end of Mink Walls.

Orange Streak 10m HVS 5a *. C.Moody, C.Grindley. 2006.
Climb the crack just left of the orange streak at the left end of the wall.

Sun Trap 15m HVS 5a *. C.Moody, C.Grindley. 2006.
Start 6m right of the Orange Streak. Climb a steep corner-crack, then cracks up a right-slanting ramp.

Mink Walls:
(NM 289 193) Alt 8m South-West facing
Mink Walls run from a shallow gully on the left towards Asteroid Chasm on the right (to the south-east). The routes are often short but good quality. An abseil rope might be useful if climbing a few routes.

Pond Filler 13m VS 4c *. C.Moody, C.Grindley. 2006.
The obvious crack-line at the left end of the short crag where it gets higher. Start

at the left side of a pool either direct or on the left. The last few moves can be avoided at a ledge.

Pond Life   8m   E1 5a. C.Moody, C.Grindley. 2006.
Climb the off width crack in the left-facing corner at the right side of the pool.

Abby   8m   VS 5a *. J.Lines. 2002.
Just right of the off width, climb the shallow corner.

Emma   8m   E1 5a *. J.Lines. 2002.
Just to the right are some flakes, climb these and a shallow unprotected groove.

Orbit   7m   E2 5c *. C.Moody, C.Grindley. 2006.
Right of Emma is a thin crack which has wider section 2m from the top, climb the crack.

Toad Hole   7m   Severe. C.Moody, C.Grindley. 2006.
Right of Orbit is a black seam that runs up left. Climb a short right-facing corner to gain a ledge at the black seam, climb the crack above slightly leftwards.

Toad Crack   7m   HVS 5a *. C.Moody, C.Grindley. 2006.
The fine crack just right.

Just Spitting   7m   HVS 4c *. C.Moody, C.Grindley. 2006.
Gain a flake left of Jammer and continue up it, protection can be placed before the top.

Jammer   7m   HVS 5a. C.Moody, C.Grindley. 2006.
The corner crack.

Caroline   8m   VS 4c *. C.Moody, C.Grindley. 2006.
Just right of Jammer climb up to an undercut flake, continue up the flake.

Interrupted by Canoes   8m   E1 5b *. C.Moody, C.Grindley. 2006.
The cracks and flakes to the right, good climbing.

Wrecked   8m   HVS 5a *. C.Moody, C.Grindley. 2006.
The next line to the right finish up a right-facing flake.

Neanderthal   8m   E1 5b *. C.Moody, C.Grindley. 2006.
Climb a jam crack and continue up the thinner crack.

Need an Inch   8m   E2/3? 5c **. C.Moody, C.Grindley. 2006.
The hairline crack.

Red   8m   VS 4c *. C.Moody, C.Grindley. 2006.
Climb the cracks at the right end of the short wall.

Access Route   8m   Very Difficult.
The vegetated corner is useful.

The Mink 15m E2 5b **. J.Lines. 2002.
The wall is bigger at the right end with an arching overlap. Climb the right side of the slab, just right of a hairline crack, to gain the start of the overlap/arch on the right. Follow the overlap leftwards to finish up a corner-groove. A fine route.

Helga 15m VS 4c. C.Moody, C.Grindley. 2006.
Just to the right climb the left facing corner crack and finish up the continuation crack.

IONA, Raven's Crag:
Quartzyness 20m E1 5a *. C.Moody, C.Grindley. 22nd July 2006.
Between Skinhead and Mental Torment. Start at the edge of the crag. Move up the short corner and step left. Move up (junction with Skinhead), then right and climb the left side of the quartz seam. Strenuous but well protected.

SKYE

AN CAISTEAL, Coire Tairnealear:
West Buttress II. R.McGuire, N.Urquhart. 23rd February 2006.
The prominent buttress to the right of "Grey Gully" - see Skye Scrambles. The buttress is broad lower down with bands of rock and easy ground, becoming a narrow ridge towards the first pinnacle. The imposing tower at the top is bypassed on the right, easy ground leading to the main ridge near the summit.

Arrow Slot 140m III. N.Urquhart, R.McGuire. 21st March 2006.
This gully lies immediately right of West Buttress, and finishes at the northernmost deep gap on the ridge. Approach by snow slopes and a lower shallow gully. A direct finish to the gap was avoided by traversing left below a huge chockstone and loose looking blocks.

SGURR THUILM, North Face:
Truish Gil 350m II **. A.Fulton, B.Wear. 22nd March 2006.
The prominent gully bisecting the north face. Start in a snow bay above scree slopes. Trend left up easy angled snow until the gully steepens. Exit left up rock and turf, or directly if ice is present (100m). Move right on easy ground until the base of the obvious large gully. Climb up steep snow to a chockstone (possible belay). Climb steeply over the chockstone (crux, may bank out with build up) and continue on steep snow to the summit (220m). Likely to have been climbed before.

SGURR DEARG, North-West Buttress:
Aesculapius, Direct Finish, Hygeia Variation E2 5c **. C.Moody, W.Hood. 10th June 2006.
Previously A2. A worthwhile finish to a very good route.

SGURR SGUMAIN, North Buttress:
Notes from J.Preston: This is better approached direct from the loch in upper Coire Lagan up the left side of the scree slope. This is in fact the easiest descent back to sacks after climbing a route and does not include any Diff. climbing as mentioned in the guide. Once sacks have been collected, descend straight back

down the line of ascent to the loch. The description has been revised for the following route:

Purple Haze   110m   E1 5b **.
Low in the grade, maybe just top end HVS but run out at the top. Start where a small orange slab leads to a break in the overhangs.
1. 30m 4b Climb up through the break and continue diagonally rightward until cutting back left up a clean slab to a small square ledge (some suspect rock and poor protection).
Note: Climbing further left may be slightly easier but is extremely loose, plus there is a very obvious corner further right beyond "the cut back left above a clean slab", but this has nothing to do with the route.
2. 35m 5b Follow a right-trending ramp line and groove to a horizontal dyke (much better rock now all the way to the top). Make steep moves up an undercut wall to a good ledge. Climb a steep corner above (crux) to a large sloping ledge.
3. 45m 5a Climb a steep chimney at the back of the ledge and another corner above (possible belay). Follow a dyke line into a deep corner. Traverse left near the top along a small ledge and climb a bold arête to finish.
Note: The deep corner can be followed to the top, as in the original Mackenzie guidebook.
Walk off right, cross a gully and traverse a ramp line rightwards to the top of the West Face of the Final Tower.

SGURR SGUMAIN, West Buttress:
Nuggets   15m   HVS 5a **. G. and K.Latter. 8th May 2006.
About 10m left of the belay at the top of pitch 1 of Sunset Slab and Yellow Groove is a striking diagonal crack. Climb it, pulling out right at the top on good holds. Traverse down right to regain the parent route.

SRON NA CICHE, The Cioch:
Diuru   65m   E3 ****. J.Lines (on-sight solo). July 2005.
A combination of Dilemma and Uhuru gives probably the best climb on the wall.
1. 40m 5c Climb the crack of Dilemma and when it fades, continue up to a small overlap, then take a diagonal line out left to a further thin crack which leads past the protruding block to a ledge. Step left.
2. 25m 5b Climb Uhuru crack to the top.

MARSCO, South West Buttress:
The Yellow Jersey   50m   E1 5b **. R.Hamilton, S.Kennedy. 2nd July 2006.
A fine, well protected route following a prominent crack-line on the small buttress a few metres right of the wet gully near the far right end of the lowest band of rock. The buttress is located about 100m right of and at a slightly higher level than the waterfall just right of the start of Snark.

MARSCO, North Face:
Wooly Gully   150m   III,4 *. M.Lates, M.Beeston. 7th February 2007.
Follows the obvious central groove-line. This lies right of the conspicuous black overhanging wall. Five short hard pitches are linked by the easy angled gully bed.

Continue easily in the same line to the summit. Frozen turf and rock under thin snow.

BLA BHEINN, South Buttress:
Note: *Il Dort dans les Choufleur* (SMCJ 2006) is largely the same as as Rosie's Stash.

ELGOL, Schoolhouse Buttress:
This line can be found round to the north of the overhanging face on the left-hand end of the cliff. Better than it looks - but only just.

I'm Glad you Think it's Funny 18m Difficult. D.McAulay and party. April 2006.
Start up the wall on the far left of the cliff, and climb a short clean wall on horizontal breaks to a V-groove. Move then up past two vegetated ledges, the second with a small tree, before finishing up and right via a corner.

Suidhe Biorach:
Right of Tree Route is a 10m stretch of wall before the big corner of Fertility Left is reached. At half-height, just below a big overlap, three short hanging cracks can be seen in parallel. The next two lines make their way up the wall taking in the left and right of these cracks.

Busted Flush 30m E2 5b *. A.Holden, S.Marriott. 30th September 2006.
This takes in the left-hand of the three vertical cracks. Start below the crack. Climb the lower wall (sometimes wet but on big holds). Continue past a right-facing flake up to the short crack. Climb this and move up to a break (crux). Go up the fine headwall to the top.

Analogue Wall 30m E1 5b *. A.Holden, M.Hudson. 31st May 2005.
A line 2m left of the corner of Fertility Left, via a slim hanging crack, the rightmost of the three. Move easily up the lower wall to a large sloping ledge. Continue up the steeper wall on good pockets to another ledge. Climb to the base of the hanging crack and pass this (crux) to continue pleasantly to the top.

DIY Arête 30m E1 5a **. M.Hudson, A.Holden. 31st May 2005.
The bottomless arête right of the corner gives straightforward climbing in a spectacular position.
1. 15m 4c Follow the initial wet wall of Fertility Left to the first sloping ledge. Step out right onto the pocketed wall and climb diagonally to a belay beneath the upper arête. A direct pitch up the initial hanging arête still awaits.
2. 15m 5a Climb the higher arête past a break on the right wall at 4m (good cams) with a crucial mono hold above. The upper section is much easier.

The next lines are found 40m right of the main cliffs on a vertical wall of flakes and wafers.

The Madcap 20m VS 4c *. R.Brown, N.Bassnett. 25th July 2006.
This atmospheric outing takes the left end of the wall finishing on the jutting beak, and gently overhangs for most of its length. Climb easily to the left-hand side of a tufty ledge. Continue leftwards on good holds with ankle-biting exposure, before finishing right at a made-to-measure jug.

Big Ben   20m   VS 4b. M.Hudson, J.Sutton. 15th July 2005.
Start centrally, 10m right of Madcap, and head upwards towards a vague groove.
Not much fun, as the rock becomes steeper and looser with height. Belay on the
huge beak of Madcap that tops the arête 10m to the left.

One hundred metres east of Big Ben is a cave with a hidden raised entrance,
Prince Charles' Cave.

Why Why Why   22m   VS 4c. M.Hudson, R.Brown, A.Holden. 30th May 2006.
Start 10m right of Prince Charles' Cave below a seeping brown corner. Zigzag up
easy wafers and ramps to the brown corner. Avoid the corner by moves up the
steep wall just to its right (crux) to gain the easier-angled headwalls. Finish direct
or up a right-facing flake-corner 2m left of the upper corner of Green Green Green.

Right again the cliffs gradually decrease in height and in places form huge square
stack-like features riven by narrow alleyways. Access to this section is best made
by walking east from the main clifftop for 400m. Follow good paths along the
clifftop before a short scramble down to the shore, then double back towards the
sea down a curious tilting alley filed with tidal debris. This corridor, though moist
and claustrophobic, offers interesting traverses on both sides and a couple of esoteric
lines.

Otter Alley   8m   HVS 5a. A.Holden, M.Hudson. 7th July 2006.
A short technical route on the gentler northern wall of the alley, taking the extreme
left-hand end of the long smooth stretch of wall, next to a smaller cleft. Good thin
moves lead up the wall immediately right of the arête. Plenty of slot and pocket
placements for the creative leader, none totally reassuring.

Canale   27m   Very Difficult *. N.Bassnett, R.Brown. 26th June 2006.
Start on the south wall of the alleyway, 20m in from the mouth, just to the right of
a subsidiary alley, and almost opposite the start of Otter Alley. Climb the obvious
shallow diagonal line rightwards until it lands on a massive ledge above the
shoreline. Belay on the right-hand end before climbing easy flaky steps to the
final steep corner shared with Scholat.

Scholat   15m   E1 5a. R.Brown, A.Holden, M.Hudson. 30th May 2006.
This climb takes the grossly overhanging wafers left of the big corner of *Legover*
(SMCJ 1998). Start 3m left of the big corner. Gain a ledge before stepping gingerly
right into the short flakey scoop immediately left of the more obvious Legover.
Climb jutting flakes urgently to a good ledge. Take the steep hedgehoggy wall
above then finish up the big corner.

SUISNISH:
Lelou   35m   VS 5a *. D.McAulay, M.Bishop. 25th August 2005.
This route takes the concave slab to the right of Afternoon Tea (SMCJ 2001), via
a choice of two finishes. Scramble up to the right past big blocks to a grassy bay
below a damp gully and black streaked wall. The route climbs the wall to the left
of the black streak to gain good holds in a horizontal break (small wires). An

interesting move up to the right gains a rounded jug and before a layback up the improving rounded flakes to a large ear below the concave slab. The slab can be climbed by the right arête (bold) or by the centre (good small friend protection). Belay round a large boulder below the clifftop. The rounded flakes can also be gained from the right.

DUIRINISH, Harlosh Point, Stob nan Uamha (NG 282 401):

This remarkably slim stick-stack seems to defy nature in that it is barely two feet thick throughout, yet it stands perched like a devotional obelisk in the teeth of all south-westerly onslaughts. It offers a short but sharp route to its slender top, accessible at all but the highest tides, though big seas should be avoided.

Stob nan Uamha 10m VS 4b. M.Hudson, A.Holden. 8th July 2006.
Scramble round onto the seaward side and up to a spacious raised platform. Climb the vertical face above over a slight bulge. Descent by simultaneous abseil.

NEIST, LOWER WALLS, Destitution Point:

Leftovers 10m HVS 4c *. M.Hudson, J.Sutton, L.Jones. 6th June 2005.
Follow the initial corner of Haggis and place protection in a small brown niche at 4m. Step out left and gain the arête by a long reach, then follow it to the top.

Twisted 10m E1 5b/c. J.Sutton, L.Jones, M.Hudson. 6th June 2005.
The blank corner just right of Tatties (SMCJ 2005), climbed by contorted palming and bridging. The exact grade depends on the amount of gear and holds borrowed from adjoining lines. Small cams useful on the shelves on the right.

Sissy 10m E1 5a **. J.Sutton, L.Jones, M.Hudson. 6th June 2005.
A bold, well-positioned line up the front of the blunt rib that forms the southern side of the bay. Move up to a spike runner, then use pockets above to move right to a scary mantel on good knobbles. Easier than it looks.

Euro Zone:

Notes from C.Moody: Spindrift (SMCJ 2005) is undergraded. Rope Gripper (SMCJ 2005) is Very Difficult. There are now two belay stakes about 5m above the top of Optimum Snore Time.

Shoals o' Herrin' Area (NG 128 483):

A difficult area to locate from above, Shoals o' Herrin' is best located by first finding the seaward end of the wall that runs down from the southern end of the Financial Sector (Wish You Were Here). Going seaward for 30m in line with the wall brings you to the top of the Fallen Arch area (Bavaria and One Way Bottle - SMCJ 1999 - are probably just to the north but yet to be located). Fifty metres south from here is a slightly lower grassy headland, just after a small right-angled inlet. Shoals o' Herrin' walls are immediately below. Stakes for abseil descents are in situ (Sept 2006). There is a good ledge system below the routes, although not linked at high tide. Descriptions go from left to right (north to south) looking in. There are a stake and a crack in a boulder for Friends at the corner; abseil rope required. The cliff is a fairly uniform 25 to 30m in height.

Abseiling from the northerly stake and boulder gains the base of Yo Sea Whales.
Route descriptions now start from the left corner of the wall. Around the corner
on the north facing wall is a prominent white scar. A fierce little crack springs
from the right side of the scar leading to fine yellow then grey corners. There's an
even fiercer crack on the left side of the scar leading all the way up the black wall
in a stunning position – both unled. A metre or so in from the left edge on the
seaward face is a fine black crack which is the logical start to the following route,
but is not led as yet.

Mix and Match   VS 4c. M. & K.Tighe. 5th June 2005.
Climb the fine black cracked groove about 5m from the left edge; this is the left
side of a gently sloping pillar that runs the full height of the crag. Avoid a fierce
looking crack in the headwall by traversing left into the upper corner to finish. A
bit rattly at the top.

Yo Sea Whales   E2 5b *. M.Tighe, I.Sykes. 6th June 2005.
The prominent groove on the right side of the pillar runs through a small overlap
at one-third height and continues up through the cracks in the headwall to finish.

Right of here is a chimney-corner line as yet unclimbed. This is followed by a
yellow rib, with a prominent crack covered in green lichen on the upper half - not
led. Ledges are at their highest here, well above high tide. Right of here a small
waterfall runs over the cliff. There are two excellent crack-lines just right again.

Gannet Track   VS 4c *. M. and K.Tighe. 5th June 2005.
The gently right-sloping crack going up into the yellow zone. The direct start via
a small chockstone at 3m is much harder than the rest of the climb; more in keeping
is to go up ledges on the right and traverse in at 6m.

Shoals o' Herrin'   HVS 5b **. M. and K.Tighe, S.Fraser, J.Hart. 14th August
2005.
Just right again is an excellent crack-line that runs up a shallow depression in the
middle of the yellow wall. Fabulous climbing on excellent rock with an abundance
of protection.

The Squeeze   VS 4c. M. and K.Tighe, S.Fraser. 23rd September 2006.
The deep chimney-line in the corner. Start in the chimney proper, or gain it via
giant steps from the left. Get inside at about one-third height, then get out if you
can. Avoid in the nesting season.

A big rib now limits progress south to low tide. Access to the following routes is
perhaps best via stakes into the next bay south. Stakes were placed for the following
two routes. The first route is in the middle of this rib.

Billy Basko   HVS 5b ***. M. and K.Tighe. 5th June 2005.
The fabulous cracked groove is hard to start but eases higher up

Fishermen Friends   Mild VS **. M. and K.Tighe, S.Fraser, J.Hart. 14th August
2005.

A wide recess lies right (south) of Billy Basko. This climbs the excellent left-hand chimney-corner of the recess.

A big green pillar forms the right-hand (southerly) side of this recess. A deep chimney recess forms its left-hand side. A small, impassable sea-inlet lies around the corner to the south.

The Green Chimney   VS 4c. M. and K.Tighe, S.Fraser, P.Coates, J.Hart. 14th August 2005.
The route avoids the initial Green Chimney by climbing a fine and quite tricky layback crack in the middle of the wall before traversing diagonally right to finish up the corner, which is a little fragile.

Dogs Head Wall:
This is just north of Citronella Wall (see below), running north to Dogs Head Buttress. Below Wish You Were Here are belay stakes. Walk south from here till the ground rises slightly at a small outcrop. Forty metres north of the edge of the outcrop is a ditch. Twelve metres north of the ditch are two belay stakes, one stake where the ground slopes down to the cliff and one 5m inland from it. Twelve metres north of the belay stakes is a block (the back of it has been dug out a bit), there is a large block belay below it that can be threaded.

Stop Start   28m   VS 4c *. C.Moody, C.Grindley. 18th August 2006.
The crack-line left of Yellow Flake with a shallow chimney about 6m up. Thread a large block belay just below the top.

Yellow Flake   30m   Severe **. C.Moody, C.Grindley. 18th August 2006.
Climb the crack that goes past the right side of the big yellow flake at two-thirds height. Same belay as the last route.

Barnacle Soles   30m   Hard Severe **. C.Moody, C.Grindley. 18th August 2006.
Right of Yellow Flake is a shallow corner. Climb the crack-line to the right of the corner to a slabby ledge then the final 5m of easy grassy ground to the first belay stake.

Rope Retiral   30m   VS 4b *. C.Moody, C.Grindley. 18th August 2006.
Climb the crack-line just right through a slight bulge with some blocks to the slabby ledge and finish of the previous route.

Nest Crack   30m   VS 4c *. C.Moody, C.Grindley. 18th August 2006.
To the right is a left-facing chimney-corner. Climb the crack to the left of the chimney past a nest. A detour left, then back right at two-thirds height was made. Finish up the corner to reach a ledge.

Dry Escape   20m   Very Difficult *. C.Moody, C.Grindley 18th August 2006.
Round left of Dogs Head Buttress is a crack. This is close to (and may be part of) Very New Seafront Area (SMCJ 2001).

Citronella Wall:

Below Wish You Were Here are belay stakes. Walk south from here till the ground rises slightly at a small outcrop. Citronella Wall is below, at the north end of the wall where a rib runs north-west into the sea. North of the rib is Dogs Head Wall (see below).

Another Green World 20m VS 4c. C.Moody, C.Grindley. 30th September 2006.
The green crack at the left end of the north face of the rib. Green but positive with good protection. Move right on a large ledge below the top and climb the easy rib to flat ledges.

Waterworld 20m VS 4c *. C.Moody, M.Tighe. 14th October 2006.
A thin crack in the corner left of One World to reach flat ledges.

One World 20m Severe *. C.Moody, C.Grindley. 17th August 2006.
The shallow chimney at the west end of the north side of the rib to reach flat ledges.

Short and Sweet 8m VS 4c *. M. and K.Tighe, C.Moody, P.Rosher. 14th October 2006.
A fine little crack off a large platform between One World and Citronella. Might be another wee crack below when the tide is out.

Citronella 20m Severe *. C.Moody, C.Grindley. 17th August 2006.
The corner-crack at the south side of the rib.

Rocas Dubh 30m Hard Severe **. M. and K.Tighe, C.Moody, P.Rosher. 14th October 2006.
Eight metres right of Citronella a corner-crack runs the full height of the cliff. Good climbing, better than it looks from above.

Silurian 20m VS 4b *. M. and K.Tighe, D.Cameron. 1st October 2006.
A slim unclimbed crack lies in the buttress just right of Rocas Dubh. Right of this is a fine chimney-cleft.

Rib Tickler 20m VS 4b *. M. and K.Tighe. 24th September 2006.
A rib now bars southerly progress, except at very low tide. This route takes a fine recessed crack in the lower half of the rib before breaking out right and finishing up Huge Jugs.

Huge Jugs 20m VS 4c *. C.Moody, C.Grindley. 30th September 2006.
Start at the left side of the next bay to the south below twin cracks. The cliff drops into the sea just north of this route. Start up the right-hand crack, pull left and continue up the other crack on big holds. Climb a crack in a shallow yellow corner to a large ledge.

Moodyloo 20m VS 4c** M. & K.Tighe. 24th September 2006.
The next crack come slot to the right gives a fine tussle.

Had to be Done   25m   VS 4c. C.Moody, C.Grindley. 30th September 2006.
Right of Huge Jugs is a corner-crack. Start just right, make a steep layback move then follow a ramp line up right to where a short corner leads to a belay.

Right of Had to be Done progress southwards is once again difficult, except at low tide. The next bay south is best accessed by an abseil from the large boulders at the top of the grassy knoll which takes you past a large ledge with a wee pool halfway down and lands you below fine twin cracks above a prominent white scar.

The Wedge   30m   E1 5b. M. and K.Tighe. 15th October 2006.
The first crack-line right of the twin cracks and scar runs the full height of the cliff and has a prominent wedged block at half-height which provides the crux.

The Seafront:
The smooth upper wall right of Sofa (SMCJ 2001) is climbed by a striking line. It can be reached by abseil or by climbing the first pitch of Sofa. The first route is 40m south of The Wedge.

If I Don't Do It, Somebody Else Will   20m   E3 6a **. J.Sutton, L.Jones. May 2006.
The blank yellow wall, 10m high and 10m wide starts from the broad ledge 12m above the sea. The route follows a series of technical laybacks up the thin crack just right of centre. Scramble to the top or traverse off.

Pink n' Mix   18m   E1/2 5c. B.Wear, J.Sutton, M.Hudson. 30th Oct 2005.
The line of steps across the wall to the left of Kickabout (SMCJ 2001). Start at the cracks below the beak as for Kickabout and make hard fingery moves up and left to reach a big square shelf at 4m. The grade depends on the amount of protection placed to the right in the Kickabout cracks. Move up and then traverse left to finish up a crack at the left end of the upper face.

Kickabout, Direct Finish   E1 5c *. J.Sutton, M.Hudson, B.Wear. 30th October 2005.
A good logical finish following the lower crack straight through the bulges above with the hardest moves at the top.

Little California:
This name has been adopted locally for the routes in the sunny bay just south of the descent containing the routes Smeg, Senora etc.

Gloominous   20m   HVS 5b. J.Sutton, B.Wear. July 2005.
About 10m south of the descent, and just left of a sharp arête, is a crack starting from a higher ledge. Gain the crack and wriggle up over a small roof (crux), before easier climbing follows an obvious corner to the top.

South of Bay 4:
End of the Era   14m   VS 4b *. C.Moody, C.Grindley. 1st October 2006.
North of Headless Chicking (SMCJ 2006) are twin cracks. Abseil down the

northerly of the cracks to a small platform. Climb the wide crack and then the twin cracks.

Foghorn Cove:
This is the cove south of the lighthouse, containing the route Horny Corner and various DWS's on the other side. West of Horny Corner a 15m-high wall of compact rock has two faces that drop straight into the sea. These lines are just left of Gary Latter's existing DWS's.

Hypertension   15m   E1 5c ***. J.Sutton, L.Jones (both solo). August 2004.
The first line of thin cracks on the steep north-west facing wall. Traverse in from the left to below a small roof. Pull over the roof and follow the steep crack on improving holds.

Diaper Mention   5m   E1 5c **. B.Wear, J.Sutton. August 2005
The next line 4m to the right of Hypertension needs very low water to traverse in to and gives a superb deep water solo. Gain the bottom of the crack – a lot harder at high tide – and climb it to a brilliant cross-through to gain a flat ledge. Take a deep breath, mantel, and blast on up for the top.

Narrow Buttress:
Patsy Says   18m   VS 4c *. M.Hudson, M.Francis. 4th June 2005.
A steep right-facing corner in the middle of the west face, the leftmost of the three obvious cracks. Abseil to a ledge below the corner, or scramble in from the grassy gully to the left.

The next three routes all start from the same ledge, a block jammed 15m down the wide chimney at the seaward end of Narrow Buttress. Approach by abseil down the chimney.

Thunderland   15m   Hard Severe 4b. M.Hudson, M.Francis. 4th June 2005.
From the ledge, step up left and follow a ramp blindly onto the left-hand face. A short crack above, 3m right of Patsy Says, leads back to the top of the buttress on gritty jams.

KILMALUAG AREA:
A large inlet defines the northern end of Sgeir nan Eathar Bana. Two routes lie 20m north of here, clustered around a much narrower sea-slot at NG 446 747, sharing the same abseil access. The clifftop fence turns a sharp corner 30m north of these routes, and a slumped terrace of huge boulders above the routes makes a good sheltered base. The first line is a north-facing corner-crack, visible from terraces just below the clifftop a little to the north. Abseil to good sloping ledges next to the dark sea-slot.

Goodbye Arthur   20m   VS 4c *. M.Hudson, R.Brown. 5th August 2006.
Bridge and layback up the excellent corner past a steepening near the top.

Golf Girl   15m   Severe. R.Brown, M.Hudson. 5th August 2006.
Using the same abseil, the next route can be reached a few metres north across the
sea-slot. Start below a stepped crack opposite the previous line, which gives
straightforward climbing over bulges to a good ledge and block belays.

The next routes lie 100m north again on the short cliffs at the south end of the bay
at Balmacquien. The first route is a crack-line leading to a final overhanging brown
corner found just past the easy-angled slabs, and opposite a small golden-topped
islet. Abseil in or traverse in across the slabs, with mid to low tide helpful.

Secret Weapon   18m   Severe 4b. M.Hudson, R.Brown. 5th August 2006.
Climb easy flakes and bulges to the well-protected crux up the final corner. Belay
on huge blocks 6m back.

Nomoreagain   25m   Hard Easy. M.Hudson, R.Brown. 5th August 2006.
Twenty metres right again a diagonal route takes the slabs to the same belay. Start
at the bottom right of the slabs by an overlap and take a diagonal stroll towards a
small overlap, finishing up the well-positioned left edge of the higher slab.

TROTTERNISH, Storr Area:
One hundred metres south of the Old Man is a cluster of three pinnacles. The
southernmost of these is the tallest, clearly seen on the approach from Portree as a
conical mound to the left of the Old Man, and providing a reasonably solid route
to the summit. Scramble up to a sloping shelf on the southern side of the feature,
and belay at two large blocks on the shoulder.

The Big Sister   20m   Severe. M.Hudson, R.Brown. July 2006.
Climb the arête above the blocks to a sling runner, step right to an airy footledge
making use of crystal portholes and so reach the other arête. Brief but airy moves
up the arête above lead to the turfy top.

Carn Liath, The Macleods:
Parallel and 100m west of the Thief Buttress walls, this row of five huge pinnacles
towers over a highly complex and impenetrable area of mammoth blocks and
crevasses. The following clean and elegant jamming route is worth seeking out,
on the west side of the fourth MacLeod, heading downhill from the Main Cliff.

Frajar   12m   HVS 5b. M.Hudson, J.Sutton. 3rd August 2006.
Start steeply to reach a jammed block. The fist-sized crack eases above.

The Blade Variation, Left-Hand Start   HVS 5a. J.Sutton, M.Hudson. 3rd August
2006.
Follow a well protected zigzag jam crack low down on the left side of The Blade
to a big ledge. Make a grovel traverse rightwards along this under the nose to join
the original route.

NORTHERN HIGHLANDS NORTH

BEINN DEARG:
Finlay's Buttress   250m   V,8. O.Metherell, J.Edwards. 8th February 2007.
The arête between Fenian Gully and No Surrender.
1. 60m Start at the lowest point of the arête. Climb a ramp going leftwards towards the edge of the arête. Go up and back right at around 45m up a line of weakness. An airy move leads to a good stance below a slab.
2. 20m Go up the slab and traverse leftwards along a moustache of turf (in-situ high hex for a back rope) to a comfortable ledge below an overhang. Climb the overhang on the flying prow on excellent hooks and gear (crux) to easier ground.
3. 30m Move right on easy ground around the buttress and go up an icy wall to easier ground.
4. 30m Go up the easier ground the base of a triangular capped chimney in the middle of the wall.
5. 25m Climb the chimney and move out right and continue up and right on excellent turf to easier ground.
6. and 7. 85m Easier ground leads to the top.

RHUE SEA-CLIFFS, Main Cliff:
Rhue-Mania   25m   E4 6a **. I.Taylor, T.Fryer. 7th June 2006.
Round to the left of Cat's Whisker is a steep wall. Start at the right end of this wall. Climb straight up on sculpted rock to a big break, then go up and slightly rightwards to gain a hanging groove. Follow the groove to a roof, then traverse left to a big corner and finish up this. A rattling flake at the top of the corner appears to be well keyed in!

Kanga-Rhue   25m   E6 6b **. I.Taylor, T.Fryer. 4th September 2006.
Starting left of Rhue-Mania, climb a thin crack-line until it fades, then move left to good holds in a break. Continue up and rightwards via difficult moves, then move left and up to gain the big corner (junction with Rhue-Mania). Finish up the corner. Headpointed.

Trawler Walls:
Paddling With Pollock   8m   HVS 5a. M.Robson, S.M.Richardson
24th September 2006.
The hanging corner between Swimming with Sharks and The Jester is gained from the left by a steep pull onto the ledge at its base. Follow the corner to finish as for Swimming With Sharks.

Rhued Kid   12m   E1 5c. M.Robson, S.M.Richardson. 24th September 2006.
Start between Midget Gems and Buoys in Blue and climb up to a small rattly thread beneath the roof. The thin crack splitting the roof takes good wires and is followed to the top.

CAMAS MOR AREA, Creag an Airgid (NC 092 012):
The crag previously named Camas Beag, see Blitzkrieg (SMCJ 2006). Approach as for Camas Mor but continue for further 1km, crossing a small gorge. Soon

after, the crag comes into profile on the left. Descend to a large boulder beach at its base via a gully at the landward end of the crag. This steep crag faces west overlooking a pleasant bay. Routes on the main face are non-tidal. At low tide it is possible to boulder hop around to the far end of the south face and gain a small tidal geo (Broken Barrel Geo).

Main Face:

Walking the Rock   60m   E4. I.Small, J.Clark, N.McNair. 25th June 2005.
Takes the striking crack-line up the overhanging right face of the prominent central prow to the right of Blitzkrieg. A fantastic, sustained pitch.
1. 30m 5b Previously climbed by C.Cartwright, I.Small, 24th September 2000. Start directly below the prow at a ledge with two rowan trees at the base of an arête. Climb the right side of the arête to a crack, then traverse hard right to gain another crack. Follow this past a large flake to a comfortable ledge below the prow.
2. 30m 6a The continuously overhanging crack above. Make a hard entry into the crack and climb past a wedged block and an easing. Follow the wider crack above into a corner and over a roof. Finally, pull out left from a large undercut to finish.

Broken Barrel Geo:

Stave   20m   E1 5b. I.Small, C.Cartwright. 24th September 2000.
Start up a large flake in the centre of the west face, then gain a hanging corner above.

ARDMAIR, Beast Buttress:

Note: Timorous Beastie (SMCJ 2006) was headpointed.

Monster Buttress:

Soor Plums   20m   E5 6a**. I.Taylor, T.Fryer. 7th September 2006
The arête right of Summer Isles City. Using a thin crack, climb the wall directly below the arête to gain a ledge. Continue up the technical arête, then finish by the final crack of Summer Isles City.

All-Day-Buckfast   20m   E4 6b *. I.Taylor, A.Cunningham. 20th February 2007.
The arête right of Breakfast Corner. Climb Breakfast Corner to a large flake, then traverse right to good holds on the arête. Make a long move to a pocket and continue to a ledge. Finish up the pleasant cracked wall above.

Roof Buttress:

How Soon Is Now?   18m   E7 6c **. T.Rankin, C.Adam. 13th May 2006.
A fine fading diagonal crack-line up the wall left of Siesta. Start up the left-facing groove of 99 to gain the crack. Follow it easily at first to a good break, then move up using a hollow flake and side pulls to gain a thin break and crucial protection (Friend 00 hard to place and two RP1s). From here, hard sustained climbing leads slightly right up the immaculate orange wall to the top. Best to belay up left from the large boulder. Red pointed with the crucial protection in place.

KEANCHULISH INLAND CRAGS, Evening Wall:

Plan B   10m   E3 6a *. I.Taylor, T.Fryer. 14th October 2006.

A short action-packed route starting right of Tick Collector. Climb steeply to gain a left-slanting crack in the slab above. Pull onto the slab and finish more easily.

CUL MOR, Coire Gorm:
Four Eagles 150m IV,5. J.Edwards, R.Webb. 5th March 2006.
Start at the foot of Easy Gully about 10m down from the start of Three Chimneys, at the very right-hand base of the gully. Climb the buttress above by the easiest line to below the upper wall. This is split by two prominent chimneys, with Three Chimneys finishing up the left one. Climb the right one, with the crux at the top.

CUL MOR, Creag nan Calman:
Inverpolly Pillar 65m E2 5c. I.Small, S.Jensen. Summer 2005.
Takes the obvious steep pillar in the centre of the crag to the left of a large overhanging bay. Start from a grass ledge on the right side of the pillar.
1. 20m 5c Gain and climb a black corner to its top (crux). Exit left onto a slab and go up a further corner to a large ledge on the left.
2. 45m 5b Step delicately back right across wall into a corner and follow a continuation groove to jam cracks and large perched boulder on ledge. Climb a slab above and a crack through a bulge to easier ground.
Scramble up easy ground to finish.

BEN MOR COIGACH, North Face:
To the left of Consolation Gully is a deep easy cleft and left of this are two right-slanting fault lines that lie on the right side of the extensive north face. The following route climbs the right-hand fault line. Optimum conditions would be hard frost and little snow as it is a watercourse.
Nobody's Fault 300m II. J.R.Mackenzie, N.Wilson. 10th February 2007.
Climb the thinner right-hand fault over ice pitches to easier ground to near the top where a narrow icefall leads up to the left-hand fault and the top. Optional, but more interesting than continuing up the right-hand fault.

BEN MOR COIGACH, Cona' Mheall, Crucifix Buttress:
Da Vinci 25m E2 5c **. A.Nisbet, J.R.Mackenzie. 23rd September 2006.
The right-hand companion crack to Crucifixion Crack, giving good technical climbing, well protected and low in the grade. Climb the little corner that leads into the main crack and climb this past the first crux, a constriction, then more easily to the roof which gives the second crux and so to the top.

Class War 40m HVS 5b *. J.R.Mackenzie, A.Nisbet. 23rd September 2006.
This is the left-facing corner crack immediately left of Anarchist Crack. Well protected with a strenuous but entertaining crux. Either start at the base and climb the lower dirty groove (4c) into the main corner or step left into the corner from the ledge that runs below Crucifixion Crack. Climb the corner, up an overhanging crack and then more reasonably to the top. A perfect thread belay can be found up and right.

REIFF:
Stone Pig Cliff:
Bond to See You, M 15m E5 6a. I.Small, T.Fryer. 8th September 2006.

Starts just left of One for Q. Takes the left side of the cave recess by a small hanging corner with a tricky entry. A thin crack leads to a break. Arrange gear, then tackle the overhang directly and strenuously move left to finish up the arête.

The following routes are not in the new guide, but were thought worthwhile although they may have been climbed before.

Pinnacle Walls:
Little Old Wino   10m   Severe 4a *. R.Hamilton, T.Hamilton, S.Kennedy. 2nd September 2006.
Right of the slabby corner at the foot of Sip from Wine are twin breaks running horizontally right. From the corner step right then pull up onto the first break under a small roof. Pull right into a corner then directly up via a large rounded hold to finish up the edge.

Barrier Reiff, Left-Hand Finish   8m   HVS 5b *. S.Kennedy, R.Hamilton. 2nd September 2006.
Surmount the small roof, then move left and finish up the hanging corner.

Pooh Cliff
Tigger Happy   Difficult. J.R.Mackenzie. 21st February 2007.
Climb the generous wall left of Rose Root.

Heffalump Trap   VS 5b *. J.R.Mackenzie. 21st February 2007.
Two metres right of Rose Root and left of the short corner leading to the raised platform is a pink alcove bottomed by an overhanging wall; this gives a good problem if climbed straight up.

Note from I.Small: Spaced Out Rocker's Cliff:
A better description for the start of Headlong would be, "Climb the wall to below the thin diagonal crack then traverse horizontally left along a break to gain the arête at the right end of the big roofed area."

Rubha Ploytach:
Aquarium Arête   8m   Severe **. M Barnard. June 2006.
Climb beside the left edge of the black seaward wall, to the left of Marie Celeste.

ACHMELVICH, Clean Cut:
Calypso   14m   E3 6a **. D.McGimpsey. 2nd September 2006.
The fine bottomless corner left of Flawless. Bold moves in the upper half, protected adequately with RPs (two RP2s useful). Pre-practiced.

Stereo Sushi   7m   Severe. E.Christison, D.McGimpsey. 2nd September 2006.
The short but very pleasant corner right of Hed Kandi.

Note: FA date of Hed Kandi should be 22nd August 2004. Also, the guidebook approach to the crag doesn't go past the Hermit's Castle, which is on the north side of the campsite inlet.

Ardroe Slab (Guide p199): Note from D.McGimpsey. Both Loch Dubh Arête and Tease and Seize are good, relatively clean and avoid the worst of the seepage. The crux on Tease and Seize is hard and a long way above gear, E2 5b.

OLD MAN OF STOER:

Original Route, Variation to Pitch 4 25m HVS 5a. P.Allen, W.Moir. 9th September 2006.
On pitch 4, traverse and trend up right until you reach the point in the description "avoiding the first upward break". Climb the chimney and right edge above, poorly protected. Belay at the big ledge common to final pitch of Original Route.
Note: The current description for pitch 4 says to "avoid the first upward break". Maybe it should say "avoid the first chimney and go right to below another chimney-groove.

INCHNADAMPH CRAGS:

Straven Route 50m VS. R.Manby, J.McKinley. 13th May 2006.
Some way left of the right end of the left sector, directly above a gate on the road and an easy way through the lower tier, the base of the crag rises somewhat for a short way. There is an obvious double facing corner and just to the right a small cave with a level grass floor. The cave is reached by steep grass.
1. 35m 4c From a belay in the cave step down right under a small roof and go up a broad rib with mainly vertical cracks. Continue past a small grass ledge stepping right past a large block. Go up slightly left to gain a steep ledge and traverse delicately right and then up. Gain a good belay on a steep sloping grass ledge.
2. 15m Go up with care to the left and then up over poor rock to reach a good belay.
Note: There was as much good rock as bad and the runners were good making the climb worthwhile. Basically the party couldn't find any of the routes described and settled for this line.

SCOURIE CRAGS, Rubh' Aird An t-Sionnaich:

J.Preston thought the crag was in a stunning setting. The approach takes 20mins. All the other starred routes on the crag were good, well worth a visit. Pugwash Ahoy was probably Severe, needs low tide and was a bit awkward traversing into it.

Blistering Barnacles 20m HVS 5a *. J. and D.Preston. 24th September 2006.
An obvious line to the right of Chokestone Corner. Start as for Chokestone Corner, at the first large jammed stone in the gully. Climb up and right (Chokestone Corner goes up and left). Continue right under the leaning headwall following an obvious crack. The final steep well protected moves to the top are the crux, in a fine position.

Notes: TARBET CRAGS AND SEA-CLIFFS:

Creag an Dubh Loch: Very vegetated, nice setting. Updraught not a 2* route.
Warm Up Buttress: Black Wall Special, Severe (poss. Hard Severe), not VS.
Scottish Layabout, bit loose and vegetated, possibly VS. Barmy, VS worth a *.

Tarbet Sea-Cliffs, Balmy Slabs, Western Sector:

Violator 30m E1 5b **. S.Kennedy, R.Hamilton. 25th June 2006.

A sustained route climbing the steep wall left of Cornucopia. Best at low tide. Abseil descent to start on small ledges just right of a chimney-groove about 4m left of Cornucopia. Steep initial moves lead to small ledges. Continue up a thin crack-line (crux) then pull onto a slab (Rooftop Finish, see SMCJ 2006). Make thin, exposed moves out left on the lowest lip of the slab to finish up a crack near the edge.

Captain Hook   30m   HVS 4c *. R.Hamilton, S.Kennedy. 25th June 2006.
The slab forming the left wall of the deep chimney of Black Tidings. Keep to the centre of the slab all the way before pulling onto the left arête at a point just above the level of the chockstone in the chimney.

Dolphin Crag:
Inshallah 30m E1 5b *. S.Kennedy, R.Hamilton, D.McGimpsey. 9th September 2006.
The current guide mentions (p244) the existence of "a suicidal downward pointing flake" near the top of the slab right of Central Crack. This route takes a line up the slab starting directly beneath the flake. On an earlier visit the flake resisted a spirited attempt to liberate same by the heaviest member of the party who gained the flake by abseil. Climb the initial slab moving rightwards into right-facing grooves which lead up and left. Continue directly up the thin slab above which leads to the dreaded flake. Step gingerly onto the flake from the right then finish directly up a rust coloured slab.

Last Train to Satansville 30m E1 5b **. S.Kennedy, R.Hamilton, A.MacDonald. 22nd July 2006.
Climbs the slab midway between Meal for a Seal and Central Crack. Start directly below a right-facing corner situated just above mid-height. Climb the slab to a small overlap. Surmount the overlap using a finger crack then climb the corner to the upper overlap. Step up left, then traverse horizontally left under the overlap to reach a sharp edge. Climb a cracked slab right of a groove to finish.

Sneak Preview   30m   E1 5b *. D.McGimpsey, R.Hamilton, S.Kennedy. 9th September 2006.
A jagged overlap runs diagonally leftwards across the lower section of slab left of the groove of Meal for a Seal. Belay in a small corner just above the high tide mark. Climb the slab on the left for 3m, then surmount the overlap between two downward pointing sections. Negotiate a small overlap above and pull into a short left-facing corner. Continue fairly directly up the thin slab above to finish.

Solitary Man 30m E1 5b *. R.Hamilton, S.Kennedy, A.MacDonald. 22nd July 2006.
Takes a line up the slab left of Sneak Preview. Traverse to the left end of the jagged overlap, then climb directly up through a bulge by a thin crack (crux) onto the slab. Climb the slab moving slightly left then back right to finish.

The Fin 10m Hard Severe 4a ** R.Hamilton, D.McGimpsey, S.Kennedy. 9th September 2006.
On the leaning black wall on the south side of the geo are two obvious breaks near

the centre. This route follows the steeper right-hand break. Abseil down the left-hand break to a huge boulder. Traverse rightwards to the base of a crack which leads into a pod. From the pod pull out left onto a narrow fin of rock which is climbed to the top in a fine position.

Rock Garden Crags:
Philosophers Stone 10m VS 4c. J.R. and J.C.Mackenzie. 29th July 2006.
Takes a direct line via a crack on the left of the downward pointing flake of Gold Rush.

SHEIGRA, First Geo, South Side Inner Wall:
Maybe Later E7 6c ***. D.MacLeod. 4th May 2006 .
The thin seam between Ape Escape and Here and Now gives hard and technical climbing. Start up the diagonal crack as for Here and Now, but move left and up the wall to good undercuts. Climb the right side of the seam and place crucial runners with difficulty (BD stopper 3, microstopper 2). Step left and make a hard move to gain the undercut break and good runners. Traverse slightly left and make another hard move to gain good holds leading up the overhang to finish. FA: Abseil inspected, a few moves practised.

South Wall:
Note from I.Taylor: *Tell Tale Signs:* Climbing the crack direct is E3 6a.

CREAG RIABHACH:
Note: The Map Ref should be NC 280 639 (Guide p317).

WHITEN HEAD, Stac Thormaid (NC 5485 6780 Tidal):
This is a fine looking 35m stack that deserves more ascents based on its easy access, situation and climbing. The stack has remained unreported. Mick Tighe made an ascent with a party on 20th May 1993 by the landward arête (Original Route). This was assumed to be a second ascent as halfway up, a wooden wedge with a small hemp rope tie was found.
Approach: Park at Achininver and follow a track west through a farm yard and up the hill until it ends. Continue across moor to where the burn cascades into the sea at Rubha Thormaid (1hr). The stack can be seen to the east. Access is gained up an easy scramble to the bay and wading across ledges 1.5hrs either side of low tide.

Original Route 40m Hard Severe 4b **.
A fine route that takes the landward arête. From the base climb to a ledge and then up to a steep wall. Step left around the arête and climb a wall for 2m, then the arête to the top.

Rùn-dìòmhair 40m HVS 4c. R.I.Jones, R.Reglinski. 22nd April 2006.
Start at the chimney to the left of the seaward face. Climb the wall above for 3m before making bold moves right and upwards to sidestep an overhanging wall. Pull through blocks to a large ledge and an easy scramble to the summit.

NORTH CAITHNESS, Brims Ness:
The following routes are located in a rocky bay immediately before the recorded

routes of Pure Caithness Crack and X Club. Bring turf spikes for anchors to abseil onto a non-tidal ledge that runs the width of the bay. Three metres above the starting ledge, a terrace ledge runs along most of the width of the bay.

Brim Pin   16m   Severe 4b. R.Wallace, R.Christie. 15th August 2006.
The left end of the ledge is bounded by a pillar. Climb a crack and groove in the middle of the pillar to a blocky overhang, then go directly up the wall above on horizontal breaks taking care on friable edges at the top.

The Outer Brim   16m   Severe 4b. R.Wallace, R.Christie. 6th August 2006.
Climb a crack up to the left end of the terrace. Surmount a couple of large blocks and climb the sharp corner above and left.

Point Break   16m   VS 4c. R.Christie, R.Wallace. 6th August 2006
Climb a curving crack 2m right of the previous route, then an open corner to the terrace. Climb an open groove, directly over a jutting nose at mid-height.

Brimstone and Treacle   16m   VS 4c. R.Wallace, R.Christie. 19th July 2006.
Starting in the middle of the cliff, climb a short tapering groove and crack up to the terrace. Continue up an undercut groove and exit out an easy wide chimney.

Answer the Inky Calling   16m   VS 4c. R.Christie, R.Wallace. 19th July 2006.
Climb a flake 2m right of the previous route to a small roof that is turned to the left, move into a groove and onto the terrace. Climb a corner onto a large black block, then continue up onto a sandy coloured ledge. Layback a cracked corner.

CAITHNESS, AUCKENGILL, North Auckengill:
Ziguratt   10m   HVS 5a. R.Christie, R.Wallace. 5th June 2006.
Around the right wall from Bonsai Baby is a roofed corner. Bridge up the corner, then traverse under the roof on the overhanging right wall to break free on the overhanging front wall.

Snappy When Wet   8m   VS 4c. R.Wallace, R.Christie. 5th June 2006.
Starting 5m right of Ziguratt, bridge this corner on occasionally friable rock.

SARCLET, First Bay:
Seek'n'Seal   10m   VS 4c. R.Wallace, S.Ross, D.Pain. 29th April 2006.
Climb an open book groove 2m left of In the Pinks, with brief excursions onto its left-hand arête.

Split Rock (ND 352 430):
This small square-cut buttress sits on the sea 100m north of First Bay and provides some varied mini routes. Access is by scrambling down its north side and along non-tidal ledges on the seaward side. Routes are described from right to left.

Remembrance of Fast Things   9m   Severe 4b. R.Christie, R.Wallace. 21st May 2006.
Climb an open groove at the right side of the wall finishing with a layback at the top.

Terns of Endearment 9m E1 5b *. R.Wallace, R.Christie. 21st May 2006.
Climb the centre of a smooth looking wall on small pockets and edges keeping off
the left arête.

Madeleine 9m VS 4b. R.Christie, R.Wallace. 21st May 2006.
The overhanging left wall has a black crack running up its right side. Climb the
steep crack on large jugs.

Tern It Up 9m E1 5a. R.Wallace, R.Christie. 21st May 2006.
Climb the left side of the overhanging wall with barely adequate protection.

Achtern 9m Severe 4a. R.Wallace, R.Christie. 21st May 2006.
Back and foot up a narrow groove on the left.

Cave Bay:
Thrumster Regatta 25m E1 5b. I Small, S Jensen.13th May 2006.
Climbs the left side of the prow of Occum's Razor. Abseil to a ledge at sea-level
below Occum's Razor's pedestal. Climb the corner to a steep crack and follow it,
passing two ledges. From the second, climb the blank-looking wall out right to
finish.

Big Buttress:
The Orchid Hunter 35m E3 5c. I.Small, J.Walker. 1st July 2006.
Follows the groove and flake line on the left side of the rounded pillar to the left of
The Adventures of Baron von Midgehousen. Abseil to small ledges at the base of
the route. Tricky moves gain the groove which is followed with interest until it
becomes a flake, forming the large top of the rounded pillar. Step off this to finish
up the short wall.

MID CLYTH, North Geo:
A Wing and a Prayer 30m E2 *. R.I.Jones, J.Sanders. 30th April 2006.
Start 2m right of Cormorant Crumble.
1. 18m 5a Climb the wall below an overhang and traverse rightwards to a corner.
Step up and right onto the hanging corner and climb the wall above to a large
ledge (belay here on micro cams placed 2m up the wall above or use the abseil
rope).
2. 12m 5b Bold and technical climbing up the middle of the vertical wall and
hanging right-facing corner at mid-height (small micro wires and cams essential).

Over the Water:
Scooter's Last Scoot 15m HVS 5a. R.Wallace, R.Christie. 2nd July 2006.
Between Velvet Scooter and Mac-attacked is an overhanging capped groove. Climb
the groove until forced right onto an undercut ledge. Scramble up onto the next
ledge and make a few moves up the short steep headwall to the top.

Born to Bloom Unseen 15m HVS 5a. R.Christie, R.Wallace 2nd July 2006.
Start up the corner left of Mac-attacked and squirm up the top of the off-width.
Exit right into a capped chimney and climb this to its roof, then move right around
the pillar into Mac-attacked and bridge directly through the roof.

OCCUMSTER, The Gully:
Perseus   15m   HVS 5a *. R.Wallace, R.Christie. 3rd June 2006.
Directly opposite Andromeda, climb a steep sustained layback crack to a good
ledge, then diagonally up the slab to the left and some big ledges to the top.

LATHERONWHEEL, Pinnacle Area:
The following route climbs the other side of the arête of More Noise. Access is
gained through the arch on the right as you first enter the Pinnacle Area before the
stacks. The bottom of the route is accessible 1hr either side of low tide.

Mystic   15m   Hard Severe 4b. R.I.Jones, R.Reglinski. 23rd April 2006.
The route climbs the left wall of the narrow inlet as you come through the arch.
Climb the wall for 2m, traverse right to a right-facing corner and climb this to the
top.

Immediately north of the Pinnacle Area is a north facing wall with a distinctive
2m diving plinth at its left end and a small roof running along its left side at mid-
height. Access is by abseil onto non-tidal platforms at the base. The first two
routes start from platforms below the central open groove.

Accapulco Lathero   12m   Severe 4b. R.Wallace, S.Ross, D.Pain. 20th May 2006.
Traverse right onto the hanging arête on sharp jugs and continue up the front of
the arête avoiding loose blocks on the left.

Stick Up   12m   VS 4c. R.Wallace, R.Christie. 19th May 2006.
Move onto the left wall aiming for a tiny block below the small roof. Pull over the
roof and follow twin cracks to a ledge then step right and climb the narrowing
groove.

Sysygy   12m   VS 4c. R.Christie, R.Wallace. 19th May 2006.
From a platform at the left side of the wall, move left onto the arête. Climb towards
the left arm of a V-crack and follow this through the roof, passing the left side of
the diving plinth.

Stack Area:
Salt and Sauce   10m   Severe 4a. R.Christie, J.Nicol. May 2006.
Start on the flat ledge 3m right of Personalised Dwarf. Climb directly to the grassy
ledge, finishing left of a small corner.

SOUTH CAITHNESS SEA-STACKS:
Cleit Mhor   40m   HVS. R.I.Jones, J.Sanders. 29th April 2006.
Cleit Mhor is the largest of the three stacks. Access was gained by abseil from the
solid fence (no stake required) and the stack can be accessed by traversing around
the south side at low tide. The return is a swim or a long wait.
1. 20m 4c From ledges on the right side of the seaward face pull through a hanging
crack and climb the wall above to a wide ledge traverse 5m left and ascend 2m to
belay on the wall.
2. 15m 4c Climb up 5m to a ledge of loose blocks on the left arête. Pull up on to
the arête with care and climb the groove on the left to the top.

Note: No previous evidence of ascent was found. The local farmer has seen repeat ascents of Cleit Bheag and Cleit Ruadh, but not Cleit Mhor.

SHETLAND, ST NINIAN'S ISLE, Loose Head Stack (HU 3605 2194):
The 40m stack at the northern tip is separated by a deep 5m channel. Access is gained by a 40m free hanging abseil from the cliff face opposite to a niche in the centre of the south side of the stack. A 50m rope attached to the trig point provides an anchor.

The Cheesegrater   70m   VS 4b. S.Calvin, R.I.Jones. 27th May 2006.
1. 40m Pull out of the niche (crux) and climb up leftwards on a rising cracked ramp.
2. 30m Scramble up easy ground to the summit.

NESS OF HAMAR, Dragon Geo:
(HU 2972 7432)   Partly Tidal   South-West facing
Only affected at high tide.

Smaug   20m   E2 5b **. R.I.Jones, P.Sawford. 30th May 2006.
Right of the corner of Taming the Dragon is a buttress with a chimney on the left. Start in a small corner to the right. Climb the short corner to a roof and pull round onto the face. Climb a crack before pulling right onto a sloping ramp. Finish direct up a hanging wall.

Lamp Geo:
(HU 3010 7424)   Tidal   North-West facing
Accessible near low tide.

Lamp Crack   20m   HVS 5a. P.Sawford, R.I.Jones. 30th May 2006.
The crack-line up the prominent left-facing corner. Poorer rock on the final headwall.

ESHANESS:
The Silmaril   40m   HVS 5a ***. R.I.Jones, P.Sawford. 9th June 2006.
Start from a small ledge just above the sea at the bottom of a small left-facing groove to the right of Scooty Alan. Climb the crack-line to a ledge at half-height. Climb the wall just left of the arête for 5m and then the arête direct in a fine position.

The next two routes take the grooves to the half-way ledge and the wall above just left of the chimney-groove below the fence.

Anglachel   40m   E1 5a. R.I.Jones, J.Sanders. 8th June 2006.
From a ledge above the sea, climb the prominent groove/corner to the half-way ledge and climb the wall just left of the arête.

Anguirel   40m   E1 5b *. R.I.Jones, J.Sanders. 8th June 2006.
A fine route let down by the rather intrepid nature of the second pitch.

1. 18m 5b From the ledge climb the small groove/corner to the half-way ledge. A fine pitch.
2. 22m 5a Climb the centre of the wall above to finish up a broken groove at the top.

Foy Corner 40m VS 4c ***. P.Sawford, P.Whitworth. 5th June 2006.
The large right-facing corner. Start from ledges and pull out of the chimney into the corner.

Ringil 30m HVS 5a **. R.I.Jones, N.Carline. 3rd June 2006.
Climbs a small left-facing corner to the right of Foy Corner. Start from a narrow ledge 6m above the undercut wall. In calm seas it is possible to climb the left-facing corner below the ledge.

Guthwine 35m E1 5b *. R.I.Jones, N.Carline. 3rd June 2006.
Start from a hanging belay just above the centre of the overhang. Climb to a narrow ledge at 5m and the direct up the centre of the wall right of Ringil.

Glamdring 35m E1 5b *. R.I.Jones, J.Sanders. 6th June 2006.
Start from a hanging belay on the right arête of the overhang. Climb the right side of the wall.

The next lines are right of the wall of Aisha.

Herugrim 35m E1 5b. R.I.Jones, S.Calvin. 27th May 2006.
Climbs the wall starting just left of Mhairi and right of a right-facing corner. Climb the middle of the wall direct to the overhang. Pull up onto the right-hanging arête and traverse left on to the wall above. Climb up the wall and then the small right-facing groove to the top.

Corrected wording for the existing route:
Mhairi 35m Hard Severe (1989)
About 15m right of Atlantic City is a fine grooved rib which climbs through the second right-facing corner before a cave. Start from a ledge just above the sea. Climb the grooved rib for 15m, then the right wall to an overhang. Climb the wall on its left and finish up the right-facing corner.

Aranruth 35m VS 4c *. R.I.Jones, S.Calvin. 27th May 2006.
Right of the cave is a fine large rib that divides two narrow caves. From ledges above the sea climb the centre of the wall and shallow groove near the top to a ledge just short of the top and then the final wall direct.

Behind the wall that is breeched by Team Specsavers (2005) is a smaller zawn. The following climbs are on the south-west and south facing walls.

Swell's Up 25m Severe. R.I.Jones, N.Carline, P.Whitworth. 3rd June 2006.
Climbs the right-slanting crack up the wall furthest left. Belay in a small alcove and pull up onto the wall at the bottom of the crack (crux) and climb to the top.

Watching Whales   25m   HVS 5b. R.I.Jones, P.Whitworth.11th June 2006.
Right of Swell's Up is a chimney. Just right of this is a wall with a roofed groove/
cave at its base. From the cave, make hard moves on damp rock to pull up and out
leftwards on to the wall above. Climb this and the arête above to finish the final
moves on the left of the arête.

Right of this wall is an arch through to a zawn to the north. The corner and crack-
line above this has been climbed and called Overhole (20m VS 4c 2005) by
P.Sawford & P.Whitworth. Right of the arch is a wall that caps the arch and has a
crack-line that runs up and rightwards to a large right-facing corner/flake. The
following line climbs this.

Fated Seal   20m   HVS 5a. R.I.Jones, P.Whitworth.11th June 2006.
From a hanging belay on the abseil rope, climb the right-slanting crack and right-
facing corner/flake. Not as good as it looks and damp lower down.

Stuvva Cave Area:
A small shallow cave lies 150m south of Stuvva Cave. The first route climbs the
rib to the right. From the cliff-top the route finishes 10m north of a cairn of large
blocks.

The Charles Jones   25m   E2 5b *. R.I.Jones, N.Carline. 3rd June 2006.
From a ledge above the sea climb the wall to a large V-groove. Pull up onto a
ledge on the right and then climb the wall on the left of the groove to beneath the
capping overhang and pull through on the left up a small hanging groove.
The Charles Jones was a ship that was wrecked with all souls lost a couple of
decades ago in Stuvva Cave.

Fifty metres south of the route is large left-slanting ramp and corner with two
routes.

One Way Ticket   25m   VS 4c *. R.I.Jones, P.Sawford, J.Sanders. 9th June 2006.
Climb the middle of the slab and the wall above.

Lost Hopes   25m   Mild Severe. J.Sanders, R.I.Jones, P.Sawford. 9th June 2006.
The corner-groove which can be damp.

THE FAITHER, Arched Wall:
You Need Look No Faither   40m   Hard Severe 4b *. J.Sanders, R.I.Jones. 5th
June 2006.
Belay in a niche next to Sea of Change. Climb the left-facing corner for 6m and
pull on the ledge on the right below a capping bulge. Traverse right 2m and then
up and traverse back left 2m above. Pull up on to another ledge below a roof and
traverse out left onto a hanging rib. Climb this and the pocketed wall above. Large
slings are useful as protection is limited.

Prophecy Wall:
Partly tidal   South-West facing

This is the next wall easily seen to the north of the Arched Wall. The routes can be climbed at mid to high tide from a hanging belay.

The Oracle   50m   E2 5c **. R.I.Jones, J.Sanders. 6th June 2006.
This climbs the left arête. Climb the smooth black rounded and poorly protected wall of the arête (crux) to a break at 7m and then climb the wall above trending right and then leftwards to a large ledge at 15m (possible belay). Climb the corner-grooves of the arête to a larger ledge at 30m and an easy scramble up the pocketed wall to the top.
Variation: Traversing into the route by climbing the first 8-10m of The Faither Prophecy reduces the grade to HVS 5a, but not the quality.

The Faither Prophecy   55m   E1 5b ***. R.I.Jones, J.Sanders. 5th June 2006.
An outstanding route which follows a slanting line of weakness through hanging roofs up the wall. Start at the bottom left of the wall.
1. 35m 5b Traverse right for 3m and pull up through a bulge onto the wall. Climb up and rightwards to a roof and pull up on the wall on the right. Pull through a roof into a niche below a roof and pull out of this on the right into a right-slanting crack-line and belay on a small ledge 5m higher on the right.
2. 20m 5a Traverse left 4m and pull up on to the wall on the left of the crack-line. Climb up and leftwards to finish on the arête.

Hidden Wall:
Tidal   North-West facing
The wall cannot be viewed from the land and is accessed by abseil just left of the arête of Prophecy Wall.

The Seer   50m   E1 5b. R.I.Jones, J.Sanders. 6th June 2006.
1. 10m 5b From green ledges climb up to a large hanging crack-line. Climb this and pull out onto the wall on the right. Pull up on a ledge on the right and then pull back left into a niche above the crack-line and belay on the abseil rope.
2. 40m 5b Climb the slab wall above to an overhang with a left-facing corner-niche. Pull up in the niche and climb the crack-line above followed by easy climbing up the pocketed wall to the top.

LUNNASTIN:
The cliffs north of Lunning and around Lunning Head provide a range of short 10 to 20m climbs on gneiss rock. Most of the climbs are found a few hundred metres to the west of the bay of Orra Wick and a few more lines have been climbed on the crags on the hillside above Lunning.

Lunning Crags, East Wall:
(HU 5030 6735)   Tidal   North-East facing
Approaching from the east this is the first wall that has been climbed and is accessible at mid to low tide. It has a triangular sloping slab with a right-facing V-groove on the left.

Into the Groove   15m   Mild Severe. P.Sawford, P.Whitworth. 22nd May 2006.
Difficult moves up to the V-groove and then easier climbing to the top.

New Computer 15m E1 5b. P.Sawford, P.Whitworth. 22nd May 2006.
Pull up on to the hanging wall right of the V-groove. Pull through this and climb the wall above.

West Wall:
(HU 50406 86738) Partially Tidal North-West and North-East facing
The climbing is around a small geo. The first two routes are approached by abseil.

Hidden Corner 15m Very Difficult *. P.Sawford, P.Whitworth. 22nd May 2006.
The left-facing corner on the left of the left-hand wall.

Rising Crack 25m Severe. P.Sawford, P.Whitworth. 22nd May 2006.
Just right of the corner, climb a rising crack-line up the wall to the top.

The following routes are accessed by an easy scramble to the right of the climbs.

Lunning Corner 20m VS 4b. R.I.Jones, P.Sawford. 29th May 2006.
The black corner that splits the two walls.

To the right of the corner is a wall with an overlapping rock wall above.

Dallicam Wall 12m Hard Severe 4b. R.I.Jones, P.Sawford. 29th May 2006.
The shallow groove to a ledge at 8m and a pull through the overlap on the crack-line above.

Orra Crack 12m Very Difficult. P.Sawford, R.I.Jones. 29th May 2006.
The central crack-line up the wall and groove above the ledge.

The Vidlin 12m Severe. P.Sawford, R.I.Jones. 29th May 2006.
Climbs the wall right of the central crack and the overlap above.

Lunning Head:
There are a number of small crags but only a few lines worth climbing. The first route is non-tidal and can be found in a small geo at HU 5090 6740.

Split Personality 15m E2 5b. R.I.Jones, P.Sawford. 29th May 2006.
A climb in two parts. Climb a thin crack-line up the centre of the wall on crimps and smears to a small niche. Pull up and rightwards onto the overhang and pull through in an exposed and poorly protected position.

The next route is non-tidal and can be found by scrambling down to the cliffs from the east at HU 5150 6745.

Single Minded 15m E1 5b. P.Sawford, R.I.Jones. 29th May 2006.
The fine looking crack-line up the large groove.

RONAS VOE:
The crags are easily accessible by boat from Heylor, or by a 1.5 to 2hr walk from the east. Most of the routes are on granite outcrops set back from the sea.

Hollanders' Crag is the name given to it by local climbers. It is referred to as Low Crag in the SMCJ2006. Hollanders' refers to an incident in 1674 when a crippled Dutch East Indiaman, the Wapen Van Rotterdam, sheltered in the voe and was captured after a fight with an English frigate, having stayed and traded with the locals for 4 months due to strong winds and storms. Five routes in SMCJ 2006 are also included.

Hollanders' Crag:
South-West facing (HU 2968 8137)
The clean crag 50m above the beach. The following routes climb the wall to the left of the bulging nose.

Unnamed   8m   Very Difficult. P.Whitworth. July 2004.
The crack-line furthest left of Hollanders' Corner.

Hollanders' Corner   10m   Mild Severe. A.Whitworth, T.Robertson. July 2004.
The left-facing corner.

Ronas' Herring   10m   E2 5b *. P.Sawford, R.I.Jones. 31st May 2006.
Climbs the wall just right of the arête. Low in the grade.

Houllan   10m   VS 5a. P.Sawford, R.I.Jones. 31st May 2006.
From the niche 2m right of the arête, pull up onto the wall and climb the wall and small crack to finish with a pull through onto the left of the hanging slab.

Abram's Crack   10m   E1 5b *. R.I.Jones, P.Sawford. 31st May 2006.
Climbs the small central crack-line and then direct up the final hanging slab.

Grunafirth Watch   10m   HVS 5a. R.I.Jones, P.Sawford. 31st May 2006.
Pull up onto the wall from the niche to the left of the bulge and then the shallow niche/cracks to finish right of the hanging slab.

Mussel Beach   10m   E3 6a *. W.Moir, P.Whitworth. 23rd July 2005.
The central crack-line through a bulging nose. Go up right of the crack, then pull back left and up via twin cracks.

Hollanders' Slab   12m   Very Difficult. P.Whitworth, R.I.Jones, J.Sanders. 7th June 2006.
The rising slab right of the bulge to finish up a break in the wall.

Wapen van Rotterdam   10m   HVS 4c   R.I.Jones, P.Whitworth, J.Sanders. 7th June 2006.
Climb a short rib that crosses Hollanders' Slab and pull up through the overhang onto the wall above.

The East Indiaman   12m   Hard Severe 4b. J.Sanders, P.Whitworth, R.I.Jones. 7th June 2006.
Climb the large detached flake to the left of the overhang and the wall above.

1674 Route   10m   HVS 5a *. R.I.Jones, P.Whitworth, J.Sanders. 7th June 2006.
On the next wall right of a narrow steep band of grass. Pull up on to the wall and climb cracks and the wall to the top.

Trade Winds   10m   Hard Severe 4b *. J.Sanders, P.Whitworth, R.I.Jones. 7th June 2006.
Climb the right-slanting crack-line and then the wall to finish up the bulge to its left.

Gulliver's Wall:
This is the small triangle-shaped wall 50m to the left of Hollanders' Wall.

Gulliver's Crack   10m   VS 4c **. P.Whitworth, J.Posnett. July 2004.
The right-trending crack-line and bulge above on its right. The bulge direct makes this HVS 5a.

Gulliver's Toe   10m   VS 4b *. P.Whitworth, J.Posnett. July 2004.
Climb horizontal crack-lines left of the arête.

Unnamed   8m   Very Difficult. J.Posnett, P.Whitworth. July 2004.
The crack-line to the left.

Sea Walls:
These are the walls 100m to the left of the abandoned fishing station which separate the beach from the beach below The Trip. There are three walls. Ripple Wall is the farthest to the left and is capped by a hanging roof and bounded by a left-facing corner on its right.

Ripple Effect   25m   VS 4c. R.I.Jones, P.Whitworth. 7th June 2006.
Climb the rising left-slanting corner to a V-groove. Pull into this and traverse up and rightwards through the hanging wall above to finish.

To the right of this is Beach Wall provides three lines.

Old Puffer   18m   VS 4c *. R.I.Jones, P.Whitworth. 7th June 2006.
Climb the left side of the wall with a tricky mantel onto the higher section and the left-facing shallow corner to finish.

Kermit   18m   Severe 4a. J.Sanders, R.I.Jones. 7th June 2006.
The central crack-line.

It's Not Easy Being Green   18m   Very Difficult. J.Sanders, P.Whitworth, R.I.Jones. 7th June 2006.
The right crack and wall to its right.

Upper Teog's Crag (Called High Crag in SMCJ 2006):
The slabby upper tier.

Up on the Hill   10m   Severe *. W.Moir, A.Whitworth. 23rd July 2005.
The obvious right-facing corner.

Up the Hill Backwards 10m VS 4c *. W.Moir, A.Whitworth. 23rd July 2005.
Takes the thin crack through the bulge left of previous route.

Breech 35m Severe *. P.Whitworth, A.Whitworth. 23rd July 2005.
Climb the crack-lines on the lower and upper tier to the right of Up on the Hill.

Lower Teog's Crag:
Self Sufficiency 30m VS 4c **. P.Whitworth, J.Posnett. July 2005.
1. 15m 4c Climb the obvious crack-line from the lowest point of the crag.
2. 15m 4b The wall above.

Unnamed Crag (Right-Hand Crag):
The crag below and right of the Teog's Crags

The Blade 14m E2 5c **. W.Moir, P.Whitworth. 23rd July 2005.
A fine route up the left-slanting crack-line.

Heylor High Water 10m E1 5b *. W.Moir, P.Whitworth. 23rd July 2005.
A crack left of The Blade, joining it at the top.

RONAS HILL CRAGS:
There are a number of good short granite crags which are being developed around
the area of Hevdadale Water (HU 29 89) a few miles north of Ronas Hill. They
provide a good range of graded routes up to 10m from Very Difficult to E2. There
are around 40 routes, mainly by P.Whitworth, A.Whitworth and P.Sawford. The
following is not a complete set.
Approach: Take a gravel track from North Roe, which leaves the public road at
HU 366 897 drive along this for 3km and park at the side of the track at HU 336
897. The 1:25000 map shows a track that heads south west between the Beorgs of
Uyea before heading west. The path is ill defined, but follow the course of this to
the north of the lochs Brettoo Loch before heading south west to Heevdadale
Water. The crags are spread across the area to the east and south east of the loch.

Hevda Wall (HU 294 896):
A 6–10m high wall on the edge of the loch. Routes are from left to right.

There She Goes 7m Hard Severe. R.I.Jones (solo). 10th June 2006.
The crack-line up the left-facing shallow corner.

By The Water 8m Hard Severe 4b. R.I.Jones (solo). 10th June 2006.
Three metres right. Pull through onto the hanging wall and climb this direct.

Sunshine 10m Severe. J.Sanders, P.Sawford, T.Robertson. 10th June 2006.
Four metres right. Climb the shallow V-groove. Trend leftward 2m and then the
wall above. A direct start is possible at 4c.

Singing in the Rain 8m Hard Severe 4a. J.Sanders, P.Sawford, T.Robertson.
10th June 2006.

Two metres right. Climb the wall direct just left of the stepped ramp. A direct start is possible at 5b.

Bumble 9m Very Difficult. J.Posnett, P.Whitworth. 2004.
The stepped left–trending ramp.

A Pale Blue Colour 8m HVS 5a *. P.Sawford, J.Sanders, T.Robertson. 10th June 2006.
From the bottom of the ramp climb the wall direct and up the left side of the hanging groove/wall.

Is That an Angel? 8m E1 5b *. R.I.Jones, P.Whitworth, P.Sawford. 10th June 2006.
Two metres right. Climb the wall to a hanging flake. Pull through to its right.

No It's Pete 8m HVS 5a *. P.Whitworth, R.I.Jones. 10th June 2006.
Two metres right. Climb the wall and hanging wall above.

Eazzy 7m Very Difficult. P.Sawford, J.Sanders, T.Robertson. 10th June 2006.
Two metres right. The left–facing broken scoop.

Right of the Scoop 7m HVS 5a. P.Sawford, J.Sanders, R.I.Jones. 10th June 2006.
The wall right of the scoop.

Beat the Bulge 6m HVS 5a. P.Whitworth, R.I.Jones. 10th June 2006.
Two metres right. The wall and mantelshelf onto the wall above.

Notes from R.I.Jones:
The Trollcatcher (SMCJ 2006), at Picts Ness, Muckle Roe should be **.

PAPA STOUR, Breigeo Head Area (HU 154 603):
The following routes were climbed by S.Calvin in May and August 2005.

Perched Block Crag:
The most northerly of these geos with a huge block hanging above its back. There is a big cave at the back of the geo. Approach by abseil to good ledges.

Push me, Pull me 10m Severe.
A big corner come groove at the seaward end of the crag. Good climbing, good pro.

A Bonxie Stole my Piece 10m Hard Severe.
An obvious flake-line 12m right of The Trundler.

Foula Doon 10m VS 4b.

A wall and flakes left of the previous route. Bold.

A Kingdom for my Crowbar   10m   VS 4b.
A vague groove/wall just left of Foula Doon; go right at roofs at top.

The Trundler   10m   HVS 5b **.
An obvious fine crack at the left end of the wall. Good route.

Old Man Watching   10m   HVS 5b *.
A steep groove to the right of The Trundler. Start from the same ledge. Crux at top, seepage.

The Prow   13m   HVS 5b **.
A fantastic line up a prow between two sea caves to the right of the perched block. Follow quartz cracks above a good ledge and a steep, reachy crux at the top.

Stack Crag:
The next big geo to the south containing a fine unclimbed stack. Routes are left of a stepped rake in the centre of the crag. Abseil down into a "crevasse" close to an impressive unclimbed prow.

The Jaffa   10m   Severe 4a. S.Calvin, J.Eves.
Climb a line of flakes just left of the rake.

Papa Mike   10m   VS 4c. J.Eves, S.Calvin.
Thin flakes just left of The Jaffa. Bold.

Shutting up Shop   10m   VS 4b. S.Calvin, J.Eves.
Climb the crozzly prow from the left end of the belay ledge. Reach a ledge and climb a wall to the right of a corner above. Bold start.

Breigeo Crag:
The most southerly of the three geos. Climb down the landward side of the north facing wall. There is a double barrel sea cave at the back of the geo.

Knife Edge Groove   10m   Very Difficult.
An obvious groove at the seaward end of the wall.

Irish R'n'R   10m   Severe.
Flakes to the left of the previous route.

Mamas and the Papas   10m   Severe.
A fine crack at the left side of the wall.

Papa Smurf   10m   VS 4c.
Start up Papa Smurf and branch out right up the wall.

NORTHERN HIGHLANDS CENTRAL

BEINN LAIR:
Monster Munch 280m VI,6. S.M.Richardson, I.Small. 10th February 2007.
A natural winter mixed line taking the groove system on the right flank of Molar Buttress. Good sustained climbing with some good positions overlooking Y Gully.
1. 40m Climb the first pitch of Y Gully and move left to the foot of the chimney-groove.
2. 50m Climb the chimney-groove past several steep sections to an easing below a steep hanging chimney.
3. 40m Move up into the chimney and back and foot on a jammed flake to a rest. Continue past a large perched chokestone (crux) and move up and right to easier ground to belay below twin short grooves. A sustained and serious pitch.
4. 50m Climb the right-hand twin groove and continue up and left to where the buttress steepens.
5. 50m Move up and climb a short steep wall, then move right to gain a narrow slanting shelf overlooking Y Gully Left Branch. Climb this and make steep exit to a good stance.
6. 50m Move up and left up easier ground and finish along a shallow neck to reach the summit slopes.

Marathon Ridge III,4 ***. M.Edwards, D.McGimpsey, A.Nisbet, D.Bell. 9th February 2007.
ME/AN started up a groove at the very toe of the buttress, left of the summer route, but this was Grade IV,3. DM/DB started higher up on the left and traversed in, then descended to the top of the groove. Thereafter the summer route was followed via its tricky chimney (crux). The thin fissure on the crest was the highlight.

MULLACH COIRE MHIC FEARCHAIR:
No Place for Hubris 120m IV,4. S.M.Richardson, R.G.Webb. 21st January 2007.
The prominent gully line right of centre that climbs into a deep V-slot in the skyline.
1. 50m Climb the lower gully over a couple of steep sections to an easing.
2. 40m Move up deceptively awkward mixed ground to enter the V-slot. Climb this to a square-cut amphitheatre.
3. 30m Exit right up a steep chimney-groove to easier ground and the top.

GRUINARD CRAGS, Pink Streak Slab:
(NG 960 889) Alt 120m South-West facing
This is an area of scrappy looking rock on the hillside above left of the waterfall. A prominent pink streak runs centrally and a short steep lower tier lies below an area of glacis. Descend to the left (facing).

Scrooge 35m HVS 5a. A.Cunningham, A.Fyffe. 10th December 2002.

A more or less direct line left of the pink streak. Start at the top left of the glacis and climb the initial short wall to a heather ledge. Step right and climb by a vague groove to a left-curving overlap. Move left and up to below a small Rowan, traverse right by a horizontal crack and climb up to finish at the top of the diagonal crack of Pink Streak.

Humbug Rib 40m VS 4c *. A.Cunningham, A.Fyffe. 10th December 2002.
A direct line right of Pink Streak finishing up the pale blunt rib. Start at the glacis of Pink Streak and climb direct by the right side of the pink rock into a vague scoop. Work up and left into the top of a flake-crack and finish up the rib directly above.

The Artful Dodger 45m Mild VS 4b. A.Fyffe, A.Cunningham. 10th December 2002.
Climbs the cleanest rock diagonally right from the start of Pink Streak and Humbug Rib. Start by a big block and climb up into a large vague scoop past a flake-block. Continue trending up and right on pink rock to a move right again and up a left-facing slab corner to below a steeper wall. Climb the cracks in this to a heather ledge and finish by the cracks in the wall above.

The Sidewalls:
Up and right of Pink Streak Slab and directly above the waterfall is a short sidewall narrowing into a small gully. Just below the narrows is a buttress with an overhung recess at its base. Descend to the right (facing).

Dusty Rib 20m VS 4c. A.Cunningham, A.Fyffe. 17th December 2002.
From the base of the recess move left into a short hanging corner and climb this to a ledge. Move right and climb cracks in the crest to the top.

Little By Little 20m Very Difficult. A.Fyffe, A.Cunningham. 17th December 2002.
Climb bubbly rock right of the recess and a steeper section between roofs to gain a ledge. Climb the crack in the brown rock to the top.

In the narrows is a short compact wall leading to a terrace

Nut Cracker 25m VS 4c *. A.Fyffe, A.Cunningham. 17th December 2002.
Climb cracks in the left edge of the short wall to the terrace. Pull over directly above and follow cracks to the top passing a prominent black pegmatite inclusion.

Choughed to Bits 25m Very Difficult. A.Cunningham, A.Fyffe. 17th December 2002.
Climb the wide crack in the middle of the short wall to the terrace, move right and climb centrally via an open stepped groove line.

Riverside Slabs:

Fade To Grey 20m E1 5b *. A.Fyffe, A.Cunningham. 17 December 2002.
A worthwhile route crossing Sunlight Slab. Start just right of Sunlight Slab and climb diagonally right towards the edge. Pull over the bulge and trend left up to the highest point of rock and junction with Sunlight Slab. Step left and climb the slab direct through a left-trending crack and horizontal break.

GRUINARD CRAGS, Jetty Buttress:

Hopes and Expectations 30m HVS 5a *. A.Wallace, R.Wallace. 13th August 2006.
Starting 3m right of Route 11, follow a slightly vegetated crack. At the top pull out right, onto the ramp of Route 11. Make an exciting bridge left into a hanging corner and climb this onto a ledge below a slightly scooped area of yellowish rock. Interesting moves over this lead to an easy slabby finish.

Hands, Knees and Bumpsy-daisies, Rib Finish 25m E3 6a. I.Small. 15th October 2006.
A better finish giving a more sustained climb. Follow the original line over the roof, then step right and follow the rounded rib over two bulges and a final wall.

BEINN DEARG MHOR:

Finny's Cave 400m V,6. J.Edwards, R.Webb. February 2007.
The wall on the east side of the corrie, near the rocks climbed by Sang and Morrison in 1899. An obvious cave feature lies high in the middle of the wall with an ice gully below it. On the first ascent the true direct start was not formed so a traverse was made to the line along a ledge on the left. Climb the gully on ice into the cave. From the cave an iced wall on the right allows escape (crux). Continue up and rightwards till easier ground is reached. Continue diagonally leftwards on easier ground to overlook a gully coming up from below. Climb across to gain the gully and up to the top.

AN TEALLACH, Glas Tholl:

Crashed Out 80m VII,7. G.Hughes, V.Scott. 7th February 2007.
Climbs the upper section of the left wall of Hayfork Gully. Start just below the fork in Hayfork Gully.
1. 25m Climb a slabby ramp leftwards to gain a ledge. Traverse an airy foot ledge leftwards to just left of an overhanging band above a slabby wall.
2. 25m Climb straight up on spaced turf to gain a small left-facing corner beneath a vertical wall just above and left of overhangs. Swing rightwards above the overhangs and traverse right for a few moves until the corner of an upper slabby ramp can be gained. Go up this then rightwards across slabs to the base of an upper chimney. A serious pitch.
3. 30m Climb the chimney above direct through a blocking roof and continue to the top of the wall. Well protected with good hooks and turf.

Toll an Lochain, Sail Liath:

The Upper House 200m VI,6 **. M.Edwards, A.Nisbet. 11th February 2007.
Climbs the face of the left buttress, left of Opposition Couloir. Some bold

climbing leads to a well protected technical crux. Start below a grooved ramp which is parallel and left of Opposition Couloir.
1. 30m Climb easily up the initial groove.
2. 35m Continue up the groove over two steep sections.
3. 45m A steeper and thin section of groove leads to an easier continuation up right.
4. 50m Gain a ledge above and traverse it right for 25m. Climb turf to a bulge and up sods in a smooth slab to below an overhung niche.
5. 40m Climb through the roof of the niche, overhanging but very helpful, to an easier line of turf which leads to easy ground.

SGURR NAN CLACH GEALA:
Skyscraper Direct   240m   VI,7 ***. P.Benson, G.Robertson. 21st January 2007.
This version follows the true crest all the way, with some strenuous and exposed climbing. Start by either of the variations described, then belay directly beneath the overhanging nose of the upper buttress, about 15m right of Gamma Gully.
1. 30m Climb the obvious open groove up left to a perch on the very edge, then pull wildly out right before stepping back left into a flying groove. Follow this to a step right and a commodious perch on the crest.
2. 30m Move directly up, then go back right onto the crest of the buttress. Follow this more easily for 10m or so, then climb parallel cracks to an excellent stance where the buttress rears up again.
3. 30m Continue directly up cracks through improbable ground to where the angle eases.
4. 30m Continue less steeply but still with interest in the same line to where the angle eases.
5. 50m Follow the horizontal ridge to the top as for the normal route.

SGURR NA MUICE, North-East Face:
There is a serious error in the diagram in the new Northern Highlands Central guide (page 338), due to the late addition of a route. The key is correct but each number on the picture needs to be increased by one, except 14 which is correct.

STRATHFARRAR, Sgurr na Fearstaig, South Top, East Face:
Rising Damp, Direct Start and Finish III. S.Nadin, N.Wilson, J.R.Mackenzie, A.Nisbet, D.McGimpsey. 3rd March 2007.
To the right of the gully start of Rising Damp is a broken buttress. Either climb up the rib to the right of the gully, joining the parent route where it bends back right, or take the buttress edge left of Sea Pink Gully, joining Rising Damp at the saddle stance. Follow the normal route to near the final pitch but belay at a big block, and finish directly up a fine narrow groove, crux.

BEN WYVIS, Coire na Feola:
Proletariat   215m   V,5. M.Edwards, D.McGimpsey, A.Nisbet. 7th February 2007.

Climbs a mixed line based on the central icefall left of Laird of the Rings (and which very rarely forms). Start 5m up right from the toe of the buttress.

1. 35m Gain a ledge at 2m on the left, then climb a short vertical wall. Trend right up turfy ground and a short icy ramp, then traverse back left along a ledge into the centre of the wall.

2. 30m Continue to the left end of the ledge and move left round an arête. Go up trending right to easier ground.

3. 50m Move left into the icefall and either climb this or turfy ground on the right to a ledge below overhangs.

4. 30m The ice line goes right up a ramp but Laird follows this. Instead, move left round an arête and climb near the arête to an airy platform and the steep wall above to easy ground.

5. and 6. 80m Climb to a final tier and finish through this by a turfy groove (common to Discovery Buttress).

BEN WYVIS, Coire Mor:
Swine before Earls 180m III,4. R.G.Webb, S.M.Richardson. 2nd January 2007.

The right edge of No.1 Spur (overlooking the Grade I gully to the right), gives a pleasant mountaineering route. Start below the steep lower tier that is characterised by a right-facing corner-chimney in its top half.

1. 30m From directly below the corner-chimney, move right along a shelf and climb a corner-crack on the right edge for 5m before moving back left to a bay just right of the corner-chimney.

2. 40m Climb the corner-chimney and pull over the capping bulge to easy ground. Move up the right edge of the spur and belay in a small col.

3. and 4. 100m Continue up an easy ramp on the right, then break out left on blocky mixed ground to reach the flat top of the spur. The climb ends here and 100m of easy ground leads to the An Socach spur.

NORTHERN HIGHLANDS SOUTH

The following routes just missed the new guide.

GLEOURAICH:
Flatiron 60m II. R.Hamilton, S.Kennedy. 11th February 2007.

Situated on the sprawling, slabby buttress in the northern corrie between Gleouraich and its east top, Creag Coire na Fiar Bhealaich. The buttress is crossed by two diagonal terraces. Start at the toe of the buttress and climb a right-trending ramp (just right of a slabby rib) leading to open ground. Climb a short wall on the left then mixed ground to finish.

BEINN EIGHE, COIRE MHIC FHEARCHAIR, Eastern Ramparts:
Olympus VII,8 ***. B.Fyffe, M.Moran. 20th March 2007.

By the summer line. Continuously steep but highly amenable climbing in good cracks but a thin scary crux reaching the big flake near the top.

CAIRNGORMS

LOCHNAGAR, The Sentinel:
Left Spiral 60m II. S.M.Richardson. 10th December 2006.
Start below the left edge of the crag and climb a line up turf flanking the steep left edge to an easing. Continue up and right over steep steps to reach the neck.

Starlight and Storm 70m V,5. S.M.Richardson, J.Edwards. 18th November 2006.
A good mixed climb based on the well defined right edge of the buttress.
1. 20m Start below the right edge and climb up to a small right-facing corner-flake leading to a crack through a bulge. Continue up the easier crack above to a stance on the arête.
2. 50m Step left onto the front face, climb a short crack and make a long reach to turf. Move diagonally left, then up and right to regain the right crest after 15m. Continue up the easier right edge to reach the neck and finish along the easy ridge.

Sentinel Couloir 70m II. J.Edwards, S.M.Richardson. 18th November 2006.
Climb the attractive gully tucked into the right edge of the buttress to the neck and finish along the easy ridge to the top.

Red Lightning 60m II. S.M.Richardson. 10th December 2006.
The short buttress just left of The Sentinel. Start at the lowest rocks and climb the crest via a line of short stepped corners to reach the plateau.

The Cathedral:
Ghost Dance 90m V,6 *. S.M.Richardson, J.Edwards. 18th November 2006.
The groove and pillar defining the left edge of the crag. Good climbing but escapable at half-height.
1. 45m Start as for Transept Groove and climb the left-hand of twin fault lines. Move on to the left bounding rib just below a prominent chokestone and move up to a stance below the imposing final tower.
2. 35m Move up and right below the stepped roof and pull over it at its right end. Climb the steep wall above on good hooks and step left into easier ground. Continue up the flake-chimney and stand on the pinnacle to gain the steep wall above to finish just below the plateau. An enjoyable pitch.

Eagle Buttress:
State of Independence 65m VII,8. E.Tresidder, V.Scott. 18th December 2006.
An excellent mixed climb taking the superb right arête of the Where Eagles Dare wall.
1. 30m Start at the top of the easier ground of Eagle Buttress, directly below the soaring arête. Climb icy and turfy grooves leading up and slightly right, before a short horizontal traverse leads to a large flake at the foot of the arête.
2. 35m Step left then up on to the top of the flake, then traverse easily rightwards on a ledge to underneath an overhang. Arrange some protection beneath the overhang, then step out and right onto a steep wall (involves some guile and cunning). Climb the wall to turf on the right hand end of the ledge above. Walk

back along the ledge to the foot of the superb crack in the arête. Climb this, strenuous and in a superb position, to more broken ground. Continue in the same line over several steep walls to gain the top

The Stuic:
Serendipity Pillar 90m IV,5. S.M.Richardson, I.Small. 14th January 2007.
The corner and pillar left of Morning Has Broken. Good climbing, but interchangeable with adjacent routes.
1. 40m Start just right of New Boot Groove and climb the open right-facing corner to a stance below the upper pillar.
2. 25m Climb the pillar to a good stance at its top. Junction with Morning Has Broken.
3. 15m Step left and climb the left-hand crack in the headwall to reach the left arête. Finish easily up this to the top.

Coire Lochan na Feadaige:
Cleft Chimney 70m V,5. S.M.Richardson, I.Small. 14th January 2007.
A counter-diagonal to Feadaige Buttress.
1. 30m Start 5m left of Feadaige Buttress and climb a short steep wall to enter a wide chimney. Climb this to where it splits into two and climb the right branch to a large turfy ledge.
2. 40m Move right across the ledge and climb a short steep crack to easier ground that leads up right of the crest to the top.

GLEN MUICK, Creag na Slabhraidh, Darrarie Slabs (NO 315 843):
The Chain 40m VS 4b. R.Archbold, G.Strange. 18th June 2006.
On the most continuous rock above a solitary rowan. Start just left of black mossy streak. Climb to a prominent horizontal undercut crack. Move right below this, go up left, then right and up to reach heather at the top of the lower slab. Belay up right on an upper slab (30m). Climb the upper slab by cracks going left to a flake, then up right to finish.

BEINN A' BHUIRD, Coire an Dubh Lochain:
The Scent IX,8. R.Cross, G.Robertson. 2nd March 2007.
Follow the summer line throughout, except on pitch two, quit the corner above the belay and go up an obvious short flared crack. On the first ascent there was useful snow on the ledges, perhaps crucial, particularly to gain and climb the "awkward ramp" on pitch two. The step right to the first belay is hard, and pitches two and three are sustained in difficulty throughout, pitch 2 being serious, but pitch 3 being relatively well protected. Hooks or warthogs are essential for protection.

COIRE SPUTAN DEARG, The Red Slabs:
Fifty metres left of Sundance is a wet recessed area of pink rock. Left again is a clean east-facing slab of green rock. The following three routes climb this slab and all are worthwhile solos.

Rooibos 20m E5 6a. J.Lines. 30th August 2006.
Link the blind runnels up the left edge of the slab. Absorbing and bold (on-sight solo).

Echinacea   30m   E4 6a/b. J.Lines. 24th August 2006.
Climbs the centre of the slab, steping off the right end of the higher ledge, make thin moves up and right to gain the flake, easier but bold climbing remains.

Ginseng   30m   E4 6c. J.Lines. 30th August 2006.
The right-hand line. Start from the lower ledge just right of a small corner. Heinous scratching up the centre of the slab leads to the centre of a diagonal crease. Move right to the end of the crease and climb the slab to the top.
Variation: Alternative Start (June 1996): Climb on tiny edges just to the right of the true start (6a/b) to gain the crease.

Rain Shadow   100m   VS 4b. A.Nisbet. 29th July 2006.
A quicker drying line up a rib right of Umbrella. Start at the same place as Umbrella, just right of any overlaps at the cliff base. Climb the vague rib formed right of various corners to reach the right end of the main overlap, where it turns into a corner. Descend a small hanging slab through the overlap and finish slightly rightwards up friction slabs.

Grey Man's Crag:
Little Gem   100m   V,6 *. R.G.Webb, S.M.Richardson. 7th January 2007.
The well defined V-shaped buttress between the two branches of Slab Gully. Excellent varied climbing in a superb position.
1. 35m From the junction in Slab Gully move up the main (right) branch for 5m, then move left onto a wide hidden ramp. Follow this up to a stance on flakes on the buttress crest.
2. 25m The headwall above is cut by a narrow right-facing corner. Climb the corner for 5m to where it becomes blank. Hand traverse right along a flake; move up 3m, then foot traverse left along a parallel ledge back into the corner. Surmount a small roof and continue up the corner to easier ground.
3. 40m Continue up the buttress crest to the top.

Rough Diamond   100m   V,7. R.G.Webb, S.M.Richardson. 17th December 2006.
The steep crack system cutting the vertical left wall of Grey Man's Crag (hidden behind the arête taken by Sapphire) overlooking the right branch of Slab Gully. Thuggy climbing up steep, well protected cracks.
1. 15m Start from the junction in Slab Gully, make an awkward move up a steep wall and continue up turf to a good stance below the steep cracks.
2. 35m Climb the cracks to the buttress crest. Junction with Plumbline etc.
3. 50m Continue up the crest overlooking Slab Gully to the top.

Anchor Buttress:
Lanyard   130m   III. D.McGimpsey, A.Nisbet, J.Preston. 9th December 2006.
Climbs the right face of the buttress containing Anchor Route. Start just right of its toe. Climb a snow groove, then slabby ground as directly as conditions allow to reach the upper tier. Climb a central groove in two pitches to the top.

Snake Ridge Area:
Mousehole Gully   120m   II. A.Nisbet. 19th December 2006.

The next gully to the right of The Ladders starts easily, then steepens to a big corner. Above this is a huge chokestone which blocks the gully. Climb a groove slanting up left almost into The Ladders, then return right and cross a ridge to enter the upper gully above the chokestone. Follow this to the top.

Narrow Buttress 100m II. A.Nisbet. 19th December 2006.
A ridge formed on the left wall of Narrow Gully. The upper part has a well defined crest. The lower part would merge with the gully given a big build-up. Start about 50m up Narrow Gully (depends on the definition of the start). Climb the slabby lower crest to where a shallow gully cuts across. Continue up the steeper upper section, which has many flakes, to the top.

Spider Buttress, Lower Tier:
In the centre of the lower tier is an impressive arête bounded on the right by a prominent chimney-groove.

Ataraxia 25m E6 6b **. J.Lines. 30th August 2006.
A fine varied route, which might be slow to dry at the bottom. Start 10m right of the chimney-groove at a fine layback corner. Climb the corner to below a roof and jam left under the overlap to reach the base of a slabby rib (escape left here gives a good E2 5c). Step onto the rib from the right and climb it cautiously before mantelling into a scoop. Trend left and up to the top. Bold but technically straightforward. The crux rib was pre-rehearsed after two previously failed on-sight solo attempts.

Terminal Buttress:
Remontado 30m E6 6a *. J.Lines (on-sight solo). 30th July 2006.
A stunning line taking the challenge of the blind crack up the blank wall to the left of The Chute, is ultra-serious and only for those with a death wish. Wander up a slab to the base of the crack. Climb the crack, which is sequential for 8m after which it eases dramatically and joins Contra Flow.
Note: A hollow flake at the base of the wall may just prevent a leader falling 20m into the gully. Then again it may snap!

ANGEL'S PEAK, Corrie of the Chokestone Gully:
Big Foot 100m V,5. D.McGimpsey, A.Nisbet. 7th March 2007.
The rib right of The White Hotel is pleasant but escapable. Start in the centre of the rib where a groove leads up and slightly left. Follow the steep groove, moving left and back right high up, to reach easier ground. Follow this to a steepening (Sasquatch is close on the right) – 40m. Move left on to a middle section of rib, then climb a groove on the left side of an upper section. The easy upper corner of The White Hotel is close on the left.

Slovenian Death Water 90m V,6. S.M.Richardson, S.Isaac. 26th February 2007.
The rib between The Waster and The Wanderer defined by a prominent overhanging slot at half-height.
1. 45m Start just right of The Waster and climb easy ground for 20m to a small breche. Move up and right on to deceptively steep mixed ground and climb this to a small platform on the left below good cracks.

2. 30m Move up into the slot and exit through its roof on the left. Continue for a further 15m up mixed ground to a stance.

3. 15m Finish up more mixed ground to the cornice.

BRAERIACH, Garbh Choire Dhaidh:

Wombat 130m VS *. A.Nisbet, J.Preston. 30th September 2006.
The rib right of the corner of Koala. Start at the same place as Koala.

1. 30m 4b Climb cracks immediately right of the rib to gain its crest. Step right and follow wider cracks.

2. 40m 4b Continue up steps with wide cracks and some hollow blocks to an easier section gaining the top of the rib.

3. 50m 4c Go up to the final slabby wall and move right to below a wide crack left of a left-facing corner (which is Kangaroo). Gain and climb the crack. Finish through a bulge and the wall above.

Winter: V,6. G.Ettle, J.Lyall. February 2007.
By the summer route for the first two pitches but finishing up Koala.

Coire Bhrochain, Braeriach Pinnacle:

East of Eden 140m VI,5 *. M.Edwards, A.Nisbet. 17th February 2007.
A groove line mid-way between West Wall Route and a more obvious chimney line taken by The Lampie. Start from Slab Terrace below the groove.

1. 30m Climb easily to below the groove.

2. 30m Climb the groove to a ledge on the left.

3. 30m Continue up the groove, thin and poorly protected unless icy.

4. 50m Follow the airy ridge to the top of the pinnacle.

BEINN MHEADHOIN, Summit Tor:

Silk Worm 10m E3 5c *. J.Lines. 30th August 2006.
Takes the obvious quartz vein in the west face.

Classic Crack 10m HVS 5a *. J.Lines. 30th August 2006.
Climbs the superb central crack up the west face.

SHELTER STONE CRAG:

The Pin True Start 85m VS. A.Kassyk, A.Tibbs. 28th July 1994.
Start 15m left of a wet mossy patch at the base of the crag below a grass ledge 5m up.

1. 50m 4c Climb up directly passing two grass ledges to a blocky bulge. Climb this and continue up the corner above to a belay. A good pitch.

2. 35m Easier climbing leads to the lower ledge.

The Camel 255m E5. I.Small, T.Fryer. 5th August 2006.
(Pitches 1, 2, 6 climbed previously; I.Small, C.Cartwright, July 2005)
Sustained, independent climbing threading around the line of The Needle; leads to a final crux pitch tackling the exposed headwall right of The Needle Crack. A double set of small cams is useful. Start right of Stone Bastion at grassy ledges.

1. 50m 5c Climb easily up right to an overlap and gain a grassy fault above. Step

left onto the slab and follow a seam leftwards to its end (bold). Move up to a steep wall, take the left-facing inset corner in the arête, continue up the rib then step right onto a slab and traverse rightwards to a good ledge.

2. 35m 5b Move up left-trending ramps heading for a steep alcove right of the Needle Rib. Climb the steep wall (stubby spike runner), to the terrace.

3. 45m 5c From the left end of a long narrow ledge above, make tricky moves up thin flakes then swing right to a grassy ledge. Step back left into a groove leading to a steep wall and take a crack on perfect spaced slots to a footledge. Move out left onto a rib, finishing up its left side to a square-cut ledge.

4. 20m 4c Move right and up to a bigger ledge and follow the flake-crack, then a dirty groove onto a big ledge below a leaning wall.

5. 30m 5c Start up the Crack for Thin Fingers and make a long reach left for a handrail flake leading to a ledge. Take the corner at its right end and climb easier ground up left to the foot of the Steeple corner.

6. 25m 5c Follow a diagonal crack in the fine right wall (awkward start) to gain a small corner leading to a narrow ledge below the Needle Crack.

7. 45m 6a Sustained and intricate face climbing aiming for the niche at the source of the pink weep. Step down right off the ledge making steep moves past a rounded spike and up to a disappointing crack-line and break. Move left to follow a thin flake, then back right to gain the pink streak. Move up to a thin break and traverse right to a footledge. Arrange RPs and make committing moves up the wall, then step right to a haven in the niche. Move out right to finish up the headwall on excellent breaks with a blocky exit.

Lectern 80m V,8. J.Edwards, P.Warnock. 25th January 2007.

1. 40m Start high on the side of Pinnacle Gully and climb up and onto a pyramid of blocks below a smooth steep corner. Belay on the Lectern block.

2. 20m Climb the corner and left wall using very small footholds and a hidden hook at the top of the wall behind a block. Move left onto a sod of turf and go up to belay when easier ground is reached.

3. 20m Climb blocky easier ground above with the occasional step to the top.

HELL'S LUM CRAG:

Cruella De Vil 50m E1 5b. A.Fyffe, I.Peter, S.Peter. 2nd July 2006.

Takes a line of discontinuous cracks up the lower slab just right of The Bats, The Bats. Descend by traversing left or right down the diagonal fault. Start at a short, mossy left-facing corner just up from the lowest point of the slabs and about 3m left of The Bats, The Bats. Climb a short crack just left of the corner and gain the crack above its mossy start. Follow this crack up and right to gain another hair-line crack in a pink slab. Climb the slab up and right to an overlap and follow this left to gain a short but obvious left facing corner. Climb this and the continuation crack to the next overlap, go right below it till possible to move left on to the upper slab and up to the terrace.

Note: I.Small and J.Clark climbed a similar line to Unleashing Hell (SMCJ 2001) but felt it deserved hard E4 6a. Follow the right-facing corner to pull out right at the roof to join Evil Spirits.

The Lower Slab:
Noddy 35m Severe. A.Nisbet. August 2006.
An easier mossy crack-line which leads into the upper corner of Hell's Gate. Finish up the easier slab 2m right of the corner.

SADDLE SLABS (NJ 015 037):
The slab consists of two sections separated by a wide flat rib between two right-slanting parallel faults. The left section is a wide open area of smooth slab. The right section is steeper low down and with a central pink streak. There are two routes on the right section in SMCJ 2001. Much of the slab is low angled and can be walked up by those used to padding on granite, although this is still fun. The routes may have been climbed before.

Side Saddle 120m Difficult. A.Nisbet. 5th July 2006.
Start just left of the left parallel fault. Climb a slight rib left of the fault to a crack in a bright pink streak. Climb this into a layback groove which leads to an easing. Go diagonally left across low angled smooth slabs and use a dyke to finish up a slightly steeper section. Probably slow to dry.

Saddleback 100m Difficult. A.Nisbet. 5th July 2006.
Climbs the flat rib between the two parallel faults. Easy angled slab gains a prominent central crack shaped as a slight S. Climb this (crux) and finish by easy padding.

COIRE AN T-SNEACHDA, Mess of Pottage:
Crack Pot Severe *. A.Nisbet, K.Haldane. 22nd July 2006.
A version of the winter route on clean rock. Start up Opening Break and climb its crack-line direct to the base of the corner to join the winter route. Follow this to the final buttress climbed by a slightly different line. A start up the middle led to the same delicate left traverse, but then the arête and back right gained the top.

Melting Pot Hard Severe. A.Nisbet. 24th July 2006.
As for the winter line except that the middle pitch followed pleasant but scrappy blocky ground left of the diagonal fault to reach the top groove which was the crux (4b).

Note: On an ascent of Pot of Gold by A.Nisbet on 24th July 2006, instead of climbing the easy final chimney, moves left gained a fine crack in a slabby buttress. The route overall was thought possibly to be worth three stars on immaculate crampon cleaned rock.

Aladdin's Buttress:
Witchcraft 40m E2 5b. A.Nisbet, J.Preston. 2nd July 2006.
The slab between the Magic Crack and Damnation corner. Start from the base of Damnation corner either by a 40m abseil from the top of Magic Crack or by climbing the start of Damnation or Genie. Go out leftwards on low angled slab to reach and climb a shallow left-facing corner in the centre of the slab. Where this merges with a left-rising overlap, follow it to near Magic Crack. Reach over the

overlap to a crampon scratched hold, then move back right into the centre again before climbing boldly to the overlap of the White Magic traverse into Damnation. Step left to a big ledge on Magic Crack (25m). Follow Magic Crack to its abseil point.

Fiacaill Buttress:
Cap in Hand 75m IV,4. J.Lyall, A.Nisbet. 19th January 2007.
A counter diagonal to Trampled Underfoot. Start as for Rampant where a short step out of Fiacaill Couloir leads to the big ledge (5m). Go left up the lower of two ramps (Rampant is the higher) to gain and climb the short corner of Trampled Underfoot. Move left to another ramp which leads left (40m). Follow this left until a short wall leads right to easier ground and the top (30m).

Physical Graffiti 70m V,6 *. A.Fyffe, J.Lyall. February 2007.
A fairly direct line up the vague buttress below the big top groove of Rampant. Start on the big ledge 75m up the gully as for Rampant.
1. 35m Climb a short way up the start of Rampant, then go straight up into a V shaped niche. From the top right-facing corner of the niche, make awkard moves to exit left, then follow the fault passing the left side of a block roof to gain a ledge.
2. 35m Climb up to the foot of the main groove of Rampant and take a short chimney cutting the left wall to gain a big pinnacle. Altenatively, gain the pinnacle by the fault on its left side. From its top move up a wall to a niche below an overhang, then climb the slanting groove on its right to gain blocky ground which is followed to the ridge.

Swan Song 70m V,6 *. G.Ettle, J.Lyall. 17th February 2007.
Takes a parallel line to Physical Graffiti to finish up the obvious crack in the left wall of the sharp rib on the right of Rampant. Start on the big ledge.
1. 35m Climb steeply up the fault just left of the big block as for Burning and Looting but continue straight up into a curving corner. Climb a thin crack in a slab to climb a tricky fault through a short slot to a big ledge. This is right of the block roof of the previous route.
2. 35m Take the ramp on the right, below the main groove of Rampant, then pull out right and climb the prominent crack on the left of the sharp rib.

The Seam Difficult. A.Nisbet. 27th July 2006.
By the winter line via Fiacaill Couloir and Invernookie. An unpleasant start but the chimney was on good clean rock.
COIRE AN LOCHAIN, No 1 Buttress:
Cardiac Arête 85m HVS **. J.R.Mackenzie, A.Nisbet. 13th July 2006.
The arête left of Ventricle is impressive but has good holds and protection. Start as for Ventricle.
1. 20m 5a Climb the overhanging crack of Ventricle, then move left to below the groove of Open Heart (SMCJ 2006). Continue easily left to a smaller groove (Ventriloquist).
2. 20m 5a Climb this groove for 5m, then make an impressive but easy traverse right to the upper section of Open Heart's groove. Climb this to the big sloping rock ledge. Move right to the arête.
3. 35m 5a Step round the arête into the left-hand of two shallow grooves (Ventricle

climbs the right one). Climb this to near its top, then step back on to the arête. Climb immediately right of the arête, then the arête itself to a ledge. Make a move up the wall 3m left of the arête and traverse back to the arête. Go up to a bulge again passed 3m on the left followed by an immediate return to the arête. The bulge direct is 5b. Climb the arête to a ledge at the top of Ventricle's wide crack.
4. 10m 4a Finish up the wall above as for Ventricle.

LURCHERS CRAG:
Drystane Ridge   100m   II. A.Nisbet. 14th January 2007.
The ridge forming the left side of the amphitheatre at the south end of the crag is pleasant but slightly artificial. The crux is at mid-height, a steep blocky section with some good flakes.

Collie's Ridge   120m   II. A.Nisbet. 8th January 2007.
A ridge which forms the right side of the amphitheatre. The gully of Quinn joins it high up.

SRON NA LAIRIGE:
High on the left is a short but prominent ridge with a steep front (50m III,4), starting at the first break up on its right side. Climbed by D.Crawford, J.Lyall, D.McGimpsey, A.Nisbet on 10th January 2007.

Neon Ridge   120m   II *. J.Lyall, A.Nisbet, J.Preston. 20th December 2006.
A ridge left of Lairig Ridge and starting higher up. It has a steep but very helpful lower wall composed of flakes and blocks. This is right of a well defined groove which would be an alternative start. After this lower wall, follow the crest as closely as possible on flakes and blocks.

Lairig Gully   120m   I/II. J.Lyall, A.Nisbet, J.Preston. 20th December 2006.
A narrow gully between Neon and Lairig Ridges. Grade II when lean but banks out.

Lairig Rib   200m   II *. D.Crawford, J.Lyall, D.McGimpsey, A.Nisbet. 10th January 2007.
Follow the rib which overlooks Lairig Gully throughout. Steep but helpful and quite exposed in places. The start is a bit scrappy but excellent higher up when Lairig Ridge joins.
Sinclair's Last Stand, Cerro Norrie Finish   40m   V,5. D.McGimpsey, D.Crawford. 9th March 2007.
Climbs the thin groove avoided by the normal route to reach the ridge. This was a thinly iced and poorly protected groove containing a bizarre snow mushroom.

Braer Rabbit   130m   IV,4. J.Lyall, A.Nisbet, J.Preston. 20th December 2006.
The ridge right of Gormless. Start up and right from the base of the ridge and climb a steep groove for 25m before moving left to the crest (45m). Continue more easily up the crest to the plateau (50m, 35m).

GLEANN EINICH, Fan Corrie:
Nig   III. J.Lyall, D.McGimpsey, A.Nisbet. 15th November 2006.
By the summer route.

Cholatse (6440m.) and Taboche (6367m.), two spectacular peaks just a few miles west of Everest. Photo: Geoff Cohen.

Indicator Wall, Ben Nevis, during the International Meet. Photo: Des Reubens.

Nog   II. J.Lyall, D.McGimpsey, A.Nisbet. 15th November 2006.
An easier route just left of the summer line. From near the pinnacle, an easier descent to the south was made rather than the probable summer descent to the north.

Fan Rib   III. J.Lyall, D.McGimpsey, A.Nisbet. 15th November 2006.
The route, which starts much lower than Nig and Nog, had some thin moves near the start, then easier.

No. 4 Buttress:
Gooey Rib   150m   III. J.Lyall, D.McGimpsey, A.Nisbet. 19th November 2006.
The right rib (Einich Rib being the central). Start on its right side and climb a shallow groove. Continue under steep walls which form the crest and gain the crest beyond them (50m). Finish up the small but well defined crest.

A' Phocaid:
Eureka Ridge   160m   III,4. S.Allan, K.Grindrod, J.Lyall. 23rd January 2007.
Start at the foot of the rocks just left of the deep gully and climb easily to a block below a steep wall (60m). Slant right up a groove, then move left onto a ledge. Cross the ledge before going back up to belay on the ridge (35m). Continue directly up the crest and its easier top section.

Mixed Spice   150m   III *. J.Lyall. 5th February 2007.
Start 20m up Deep Pockets and climb a thinly iced open corner on the right wall to reach a ledge. Climb an icy vegetated groove on to a faint rib and follow this on thin turf to the top.

Deep Pockets   150m   I/III. J.Lyall. 24th December 2006.
The deep gully contains two chokestones which can be tricky to pass, or banked out to straightforward snow.

Tangy Edge   150m   III,4 *. H.Burns, J.Lyall. 7th March 2007.
The rib to the left of The Sporran. Head up rightwards into an easy amphitheatre right of Deep Pockets and go up the crest of the rocky rib in one good pitch. Follow easier ground up and left to the top.
Pursed Lips   150m   II. J.Lyall. 5th February 2007.
Start 10m right of Pick Pocket and follow a right-slanting fault which runs out at a rock wall after 90m. Traverse left around a rib 5m below the rock wall to gain easy slopes.

Pouch Gully   150m   II. J.Lyall. 24th December 2006.
Start just right of Spyglass Gully. Go up a slanting chimney, then continue up the easier gully to a possibly large cornice, which had a helpful fissure on the first ascent.

Chili Seasoning   150m   III. J.Lyall. 5th February 2007.
Start 10m right of Spyglass/Pouch Gullies. Slant up right to gain the crest of the rib overlooking Spyglass Gully. Climb up, keeping left of the edge, until the final tower which is climbed direct.

Easter Meet 2007, at the Inchnadamph Hotel. Photo: Dick Allen.

NORTH EAST OUTCROPS

FINDON NESS, Findon Ness South:
The Peacekeeper 12m E1 5a *. R.Birkett, M.Reed. 8th August 2005.
Follow the steep juggy line up the right-trending crack right of Warzone to an interesting finish.

Pow Kebbuck:
Rest in Peace 12m E3/4 5c **. R.Birkett, M.Reed. 8th August 2005.
The line left of Pow-Wow gives good sustained climbing. Climb a small left-facing corner to move right at a break. Go direct up a black wall (crux) to gain a big flat hold above. Finish direct.

SPORTLETHEN:
Power Hound Variation 10m 8a+ *. T.Rankin. September 2006.
A super direct variation to The Portlethen Terrier missing out all the big holds! Eliminate but superb sustained climbing. Climb the boulder problem start to The Terrier, then use only holds on the hanging ramp to the left to gain a break. Take the wall above direct on small crimps to join The Terrier at the 5th bolt; finish up this.

BOLTSHEUGH, Upper Right:
The Grand Masters Traverse F8a/8a+, Font 7c. W.Moir. Spring 2003.
A very sustained left to right super low traverse. Start sitting below the crack of The Enemy Within. Traverse right on the lowest holds around the arete to a low flake where hard moves gain a rest at a ledge. Continue right and use a crimpy block to cross a corner (no feet on low blocks in the corner) and gain a good long flat edge in another small corner. Drop very low around the next arete to good low flakes above the pool. A big move gains a flange on the lip of the roof and slopers on the lip lead to a good low triangular hold. Use the sloping lip again to cross the next corner. Super low heel hooking now leads slightly up to an obvious little slot on a faint arete and a finish up the wall and crack above.

Lower South:
Cheeky Madam 15m 6b *. T.Rankin. July 2006.
The line of bolts climbing out of the left side of the big cave to join Trouble Monkey at the lip. Finish up this.

Hunchback Direct E2 5c. N.Morrison, W.Moir. 7th July 2006.
Climb over the capping roof where the original escapes left along the slab, then take the next roof direct.

Three Roofs 10m E3 5c *. T.Rankin (solo). 30th December 2006.
An exciting little solo or reasonably safe boulder problem with a mat and spotters. Climb the three roofs direct just right of the start of Trouble Monkey. Finish up the easy ramp above.

JOHNS HEUGH:
Rhythm of the Heart 25m E4 6a **. T.Rankin, A.Coull. August 2006.

The crack and groove-line right of Vein Spotting gives another excellent well protected route. Start below a short right-facing corner at 6m. Climb to the corner, surmount the roof above using a crack on the right and move up to the large break. Move slightly left and up to excellent holds below the groove. Make an awkward move up to get stood in the groove (Wallnut 2 in the break above), then reach up right to good holds that lead onto a slab above. Step left and continue direct to the top left of the easy upper groove.

Asystole   25m   E5 6a *. T.Rankin, A.Coull. August 2006.
A wild route based on the roof and shield feature right of Rhythm of the Heart. Start below a left-trending thin crack-line right of Rhythm of the Heart. Follow the crack to a guano ledge below a roof. Cross the roof rightwards (hard) to an excellent quartz pocket and move up and slightly left to the large break. Use an undercut at the back of the roof to reach good holds over the lip (Tri-cam 1 in a quartz pocket on the lip and Quadcam 00 above). Move up slightly left, then back right to a good hidden hold above the shield (crux). Rock up right onto a slab, step left and climb a shallow groove leading to the easy upper groove. Well protected but strenuous to place at the crux.

Spanked Roof Monkey   25m   E5 6a **. T.Rankin, R.Birkett. August 2006.
A sensational line over the roof and up the wall between the two crack-lines. Climb the overhanging right arete of the cave to ledges. Follow thin cracks up the wall to a break below the roof. Use a flake in the roof to gain a good hold on the lip and pull over leftwards. Step up right to a break and junction with Jaded Ledge Lizard after it moves left. Follow Jaded up the wall to a good break where it returns right to the crack, but continue straight up the wall above to a roof. Pass the roof on the left to finish in a fine position. Very well protected steep and sustained climbing, which is low in the grade.

DOONIE POINT (NEO p196):
Magical Mystery Tour   12m   E2 5b *. P.Mather. 27th May 2006.
This takes an unusual line, providing a daft exercise in bridging. There are two arches at Doonie point. Start underneath the arch furthest inland. Climb the slabby north side of the arch to a roof, then pull up into a bridging position. Traverse the roof of the arch in an easterly direction, until forced onto the steep southern wall. Continue a rising traverse on jugs above the second arch. Well protected.

I am the Walrus   10m   HVS 5a *. P.Mather, R.Mather. 27th May 2006.
This is the arete to the left of Hang Fire. Start just left of Hang Fire and take a diagonal line of jugs up and left to the break on the arete. Continue directly up the arete on good holds. A good climb, similar to routes on the Back Door Wall of Newtonhill.

COLLIESTON, The Graip:
The Seedless Graip Variation   15m   HVS 5a *. R.Birkett, B.Jermieson. 29th September 2006.
Start as for Graip Vine to below its main crack. Move left along a horizontal break to gain a small roofed left-facing corner. Go up this and left to an arete through a steep grey bulge on good holds to regain and follow the original up the left arete.

Never mix Graip and Grain   15m   Hard Severe *. B. Jermieson, R.Birkett. 29th September 2006.
Climb the start of Bogus Corner till just past the roof on the right. Use an obvious big foothold to swing right onto the hanging arete which is followed to the top.
Variation: Graip and Pillage   15m   VS 4b *. R.Birkett, B.Jamieson. 29th September 2006.
Pull through the roof on the right direct using a good hold above the lip on the right. Step left to follow the arete to the top.

GREY MARE SLABS, Southern Rocks:
An easily accessible wall of superb pink granite essentially a continuation round the arete from the Pocket Wall. All climbed on-sight.

Jargon   25m   VS 4c *. T.Rankin, M.Reed. 6th August 2006.
At the right of the wall is a fine little corner. Climb this and slabs to the fault line of Ledgeway. Pull left into a hanging groove. Follow this to a ledge on the right, then step left onto a slab. Climb this trending left to a pedestal on the left edge of the wall.

To Far for Grampa   20m   E5 6b. T.Rankin, M.Reed. 6th August 2006.
A line based on the hanging flake-crack in the wall right of Gobbledygook. Good climbing but it involves a short committing crux. Start just left of Ledgeway and climb the wall to a junction with Gobbledygook below the bulging crack. Arrange protection (good thread on the arete above), then swing right around the nose to gain the crack. Hard moves up this lead to better holds and welcome protection. Move right then back left on to the slab above. Climb this to the belay pedestal on the edge.

Not Bad for Grandad   15m   E3 6b *. T.Rankin, M.Reed. 6th August 2006.
Left of Gobbledygook is an innocuous hanging crack in the arete. Climb the lower wall direct to the crack. Powerful laybacking leads to an easier finish.

LONG HAVEN QUARRIES, Scimitar Ridge, Seaward Walls:
High Hopes   25m   E4 6a **. T.Rankin, C.Adams. 29th October 2006.
An excellent exposed pitch up the right side of the impressive arete. Abseil to the Sea-Scoop belay perch. Climb the left-hand groove as for Sea-Scoop but continue up the large flake corner to below a bulge. Undercut the bulge left to reach a good break above. Gain a standing position above the bulge (crux) and step left to a thin crack. Follow this with sustained interest to an easy finish up the upper wall.

Comfortably Numb   20m   E8 6c ****. T.Rankin. 23rd April 2006.
The challenge of the overhanging south wall. Red Pointed with all gear in place. Abseil in to the spacious platform below the wall. Climb the left-hand crack directly above the platform until you can make hard moves right into the right-hand crack. Further hard and very committing moves gain the break and the more positive upper crack. A stunning line with equally stunning climbing. Generally well protected. Escape is difficult so it is probably best to abseil in from the old quarry building and leave the rope in place.

ROSEHEARTY, Quarry Head:
Egg On Face 10m E4 5c *. T.Rankin, C.Adam. May 2006.
Climb Free Range until it moves left. Step right and climb the shallow crack-line to the top. Sustained and well protected.

CUMMINGSTON, Doubt Wall:
No Doubt about It 10m Hard Severe. J.Preston, J.Lyall. 24th April 2006.
Climbs the wall left of the "chossy ramp". Start at the base of the chossy ramp and without setting foot on this, climb the steep wall left of the ramp, finishing on the arete in a fine position.

Sunshine Stack:
A small stack in between The Stack and Sentinel Stack. It is situated 25m north of Easy Arete on Sunshine Wall. The route has almost certainly been climbed before.
Sea Lichen 10m Severe. S.Lynch, J.Roberts. 28th August 2006.
A seam of hard rock on the south-east face of the stack.

COVESEA:
Note: M.Reed climbed Paul Tax on 22nd September 2006, the first ascent after its rockfall, at E5 6b. M.Reed thinks Sandanista (E2 5c) is not as sustained as the (excellent) Domino Effect but might warrant E3 also as the gear is mostly dubious cams, and hard fought at the start. The Domino Effect – finish straight up, not as for Sandanista. There are no belays above the Family Affair routes, and really nasty gorse to wade through in the vain search. Banana Republic, bordering 3 stars.

REDHYTHE POINT, West Head Area (NJ 573 671):
This area is located west of Redhythe Point just beyond a line of rocks jutting out to sea (West Head). The first routes are in an inlet with a 15m high east facing wall, the Black Wall. This has two corner-lines, the right of which is Black Wall Corner. The left section of the wall beyond the left corner is of poor rock and seeps continuously. The seaward end of the wall leads round to a short steep wall dropping direct into the brine. The routes require low tide.

The Black Wall:
The first route starts just right of the left-hand corner. Care is required with the rock at the top.

Paint it Black 15m E1 5b. P.Greene, B.Duthie. 16th May 2004.
Good sustained climbing. Climb twin cracks to a break, then move slightly left along the slanting break. Pull directly over a bulge to easier ground.

Black Wall Corner 15m Hard Severe. B.Duthie, P.Greene. 16th May 2004.
Step off a boulder and climb the corner direct.

News Story 15m VS 4c. B.Duthie, P.Greene. 16th May 2004.
Step off the boulder and climb the first obvious scoop direct. Follow the crack-line to the next scoop, climbed direct again, finishing straight up.

The Darkness   15m   VS 4c. P.Greene, B.Duthie. 16th May 2004.
Start up News Story but traverse right out of the first scoop below a small overlap.
Climb up round to the right of this.

Rolling Stones Buttress:
This is the steep blocky buttress facing the Black Wall.

The Rolling Stones   20m   E1 5b. B.Duthie, P.Greene. 30th May 2004.
This climbs the wall via hanging flakes at mid-height. Starting at the left side of
the wall, climb the crack-line moving right at the sloping ledge to gain the lower
flake. Layback up the flakes to good ledges leading to a big shelf at two-thirds
height. Finish up an obvious corner crack.

Wee West Wall:
Forty metres west of the top of Black Wall is the Logie-esque Wee West Wall, cut
by the left to right slanting crack of Doon the Watter. Routes are semi-tidal.

Ferry Cross the Mearnsy   10m   HVS 5a. P.Greene, B.Duthie. 30th May 2004.
Start at the left side of the wall beneath a right-trending crack. Climb the crack
and pull over the bulge. Avoid stepping left to the arete and pull over the next
bulge to finish directly.

Doon the Watter   10m   Hard Severe. P.Greene, B.Duthie. 16th May 2004.
The central crack-line is harder than it looks.

Abstemious   8m   E1 5b. B.Duthie, P.Greene. 30th May 2004.
Quite a bold start but difficulties ease with height. Start just left of twin cracks.
Move up trending right over the bulge to a rest. Pull up moving slightly left and
finish towards the highest point.

Wide Crack   6m   Very Difficult. B.Duthie, P.Greene. 16th May 2004.
The right-hand crack-line.

The Warm up:
This area lies around the left arete of Wee West Wall and is accessed by
downclimbing a short north-west facing corner. The right wall has three short
lines from left to right; the crack (Very Difficult), the corner (Difficult) and a line
2m right of the corner (Severe). The left wall has four routes from left to right; the
slabby scoops (Very Difficult), the crack (Difficult), a line through a niche to a
ledge and up a tiny right-facing corner (Hard Severe) and the deceptive wide
crack (Severe). All routes by P.Greene and B. Duthie on 30th May 2004. Several
hundred metres further west is a grassy gully with an obvious open-book corner
on the right wall. There is an ancient rusty peg in-situ. An ascent on 11th May
2005 by B.Duthie and P.Greene gave a grade of HVS 5a.

GLEN CLOVA, The Red Craigs, Central Crag:
Sunset Song   30m   E5 6b. I.Small, J.Clark. 18th September 2005.
A forceful route climbing the wall right of Empire of the Sun. Start below and

right of the orange patch of rock. Climb the slab to an overlap, pull over and move left over shattered rock to gain a slabby ledge. Step right onto the impending wall and gain a flake. From its top make committing moves up and left to a small overlap. Pull out right to a short slot/crack. Final steep moves lead to a good hold from which balancy moves right allow a hanging corner to

HIGHLAND OUTCROPS

Note from M.Gear: Edge of Perfection on Carn Mhic a'Ghille-Chaim is very dirty but E1 grade is probably about right. No belay at the end of pitch 2 as described, so had to carry on an extra 15m (of very mossy and poorly protected VS climbing) to excavate an anchor. Pitch lengths become 20m, 35m, 25m and 15m. It's a great line, but given the awful state of the rock, hard to justify even one star.

STRATHNAIRN, Ashie Fort:
Note: Website (Highland Outcrops, p159) was first climbed by R.B.Frere around 1937. He named the crag Dun Riach. Kenny's Revenge (SMCJ 1999) was climbed by R.B.Frere on 27th July 1938, named The Big Crack and Pickpocket climbed and named as The Wall. Three other routes, now dirty, were also climbed, including a line past a block some 10m from the left end of the crag, with K.A.Robertson.

INVERFARIGAIG:
A suggested name of Dun Dearduil Crag after the hilltop forts. The other routes on the crag were repeated and confirmed as worthwhile.

Echo Beach 15m E1 5c. A.Tibbs, D.Moy. 30th August 2006.
Start from the belay at the top of pitch 1 of Wild Roses. Climb a wall and the short steep groove above to a tree. Finish direct.

DUNTELCHAIG, Dracula Buttress:
Mummy 20m E1 5b **. R.Mackenzie, D.Moy. Summer 2006.
Start 15m left of Balrog. Climb a slabby arête to a small overlap. Go over this to a hollow flake (gear). Step right and up 1m to a crack. Finish directly to the top .

BFG 10m VS 5a. D.Moy, D.Allan. 27th July 2006.
Just right of Balrog is a left-facing corner. Climb it and into a right-facing corner.

Puff 9m Severe. D.Moy, D.Allan. 27th July 2006.
An arête 3m right of BFG.

Scrag End 9m Very Difficult. D.Moy. 20th July 2006.
Just right of Puff is a right-facing corner. Ascend this and break out left at the top.

The Main Crag:
Between Top Corner and Edir there is a 40m slab which is overhanging at the

right side. At the top right of the slab Mica Slab slants up right. Hours of cleaning produced the following routes.

Mica Direct   35m   Mild Severe. D.Williamson, H.Wyllie. June 2005.
Go up the left side of a blank slab to a steeping. Pull through on cracks and flakes and continue direct up the cracked slab to the top. Pleasant well protected climbing.

Mica Crack   35m   Hard Severe. H.Wyllie, D.Williamson. 8th May 2006.
Start at the middle of the slab, 4m right of Mica Direct. Climb the right edge of the lower slab to the ledge below the overhang. Step left into a niche, and then follow an obvious crack-line straight up. When the angle eases, continue up right to the highest point of the upper slab.

Dennis the Menace   30m   E2 5c **. P.Macpherson (unsec). 30th April 2006.
Start at the right end of the slab below blocks under an overhang. Go easily up the slab to the blocks. Pull strenuously through the overhang to a crack which splits. Climb up to an obvious hand jam and pull over a bulge on to the upper slab. Continue more easily up the cracked slab.

DIRC MHOR:
Bogart Corner   55m   E2 5b **. H.Burrows-Smith, J.Lyall. 15th June 2006.
Start down right of Bournville below a striking grey corner which lies on the right wall. Scramble up into a rock bay.
1. 40m 5b Climb black rock at a break right of a quartz dyke and go boldly up into the corner. Follow the corner and go round a roof on the left to a ledge.
2. 15m Finish up a short wet wall and easy heather.

West Flank:
White Tower   45m   Very Difficult. J.Lyall. 5th November 1983.
Climbs an obvious white tower beyond Schist Hot and opposite Carry on up the Khyber. Climb a crack up the front and continue to the top of a tower. Descend into a gap and climb the next tower to finish.
Note: This route is a good landmark for finding the top of the descent gully beside Carry on up the Khyber, as it is directly opposite this gully and easily seen.

ARDVERIKIE, White Slab:
(NN 505 852) Alt 500m   North-North-West facing
The climbs located on Creag a' Chuir. To approach, cycle in past Adverikie House and strike straight uphill at two prominent clumps of rhododendrons. White Slab is close to the crest of the ridge, left of a prominent rocky ridge with a small pine tree growing at the top.

M.O.G.   55m   Severe. N Crookston, C Prowse. 21st September 2002.
On the left-hand side of the slab, climb shallow cracks to an easier finish above.

Hector   55m   Hard Severe 4a *. C Prowse, S Grove. 28th September 2002.
Start 3m right of M.O.G. Climb the slab on small quartzite holds to a runner at 10m, then the easy slab above.

Hextor 50m Difficult. S.Grove, C.Prowse. 28th September 2002.
At the right side of the slab, climb a shallow cracked groove to a steepening at a niche and an easy slab to finish.

Behind the white slab is a shorter reddish slab, Red Slab. The four crack-lines have been climbed at around Difficult by N.Crookston, S.Grove and C.Prowse. Fifty metres to the left of Red Slab is a narrow whaleback slab.

She Likes Eels 20m VS 4b *. S.Grove, C.Prowse. 28th September 2002.
Climb the whaleback slab to a bulge. Pull over this boldly and continue to the top.

At the east end of the hill two prominent crags sit not far above tree level. The right-hand crag has a slabby left-hand side and an arête with a prominent groove on the right-hand side.

Lexie 25m Hard Severe 4a **. C.Prowse, S.Grove. 29th September 2002.
Climb up the left-hand side of the slab to runners at 10m. Traverse hard right across a hanging slab to gain the groove in the arête. Finish up the groove.

The left-hand crag has a slabby front face and a pile of boulders on its right-hand side.

Gardeners Question Time 25m Severe. S.Grove, C.Prowse. 29th September 2002.
Start at the left-hand side of the crag. Climb up the slab and traverse left along heathery ledges until below a prominent flake. Gain the top of the flake by good moves. Traverse right and up the slab to finish. Better than it sounds, should improve with more cleaning.

CRAIG A' BARNS, Upper Cave Crag:
Ching F8a **. G.Lennox (Second ascent by T.Rankin). 3rd April 2006.
A new sport route between Silk Purse and Marlena. Follow Silk Purse to the second bolt, then move out left to new bolts and take a direct route cutting through the horizontal break of Marlena to rejoin Silk Purse half-way up the left-slanting diagonal crack (points will be deducted for traversing to the resting jugs on Silk Purse).

GLEN LEDNOCK, Low Wall:
Brokeback Mounting 12m E1 6a *. A.Fulton, A.Inglis. 30th April 2006.
Start on top of a small boulder, below a groove with twin cracks, midway between the original and direct start to Sultans of Swing. Make a bouldery start on a left-hand sidepull and reach for a high left-hand layaway. Follow the groove directly to the top, crossing over Sultans of Swing. RPs can be placed from the ground to avoid spinal injury on the boulder below.

BEN NEVIS, AONACHS, CREAG MEAGHAIDH

BEN NEVIS, Little Brenva Face:
Wall of the Winds   320m   VI,5. S.M.Richardson, I.Small. 27th January 2007.
A major line up the previously unclimbed headwall right of Super G. Climbed on ice.
1. to 4. 180m Start as for Slalom and climb straight up the vague rib on moderate mixed ground to the foot of the headwall.
5. 20m The foot of the wall is undercut, but 25m right of the Super G icefall, a short blocky ramp leads onto the wall. Climb the ramp, traverse right for 10m and climb a steep groove to reach a snow bay.
6. 40m Traverse up and right for 20m to reach the left-facing corner system that cuts through the wall. Move right to belay in a large niche.
7. 30m Continue up the corner to reach a large vertical square-cut corner.
8. 50m Climb the left wall of the corner and continue up the corner-line to reach the plateau at the same point as Super G.

Indicator Wall:
Ship of Fools   150m   VIII,7. S.M.Richardson, I.Small. 1st April 2007.
An outstanding icy mixed climb taking the steep pillar between Riders on the Storm and Albatross. The route uses the narrow sinuous groove just right of Riders on the Storm to bypass the huge overhang defending the lower pillar, and then continues up the crest.
1. 30m Start directly below the pillar and climb a discontinuous icy groove up the crest of a broad rib to belay below the steep lower section of the pillar.
2. 30m Move up the hanging slab right of Riders on the Storm. Climb this on thin ice and pull over an overlap (crux) and climb a second slab to a foothold ledge. Continue up the narrow groove right of Riders on the Storm to its top. Move right for 3m above the overhang along an exposed break and belay at the foot of the upper pillar. A demanding and serious pitch climbed on very thin ice.
3. 60m Climb a steep break in the centre of the wall above and move up then right to the edge of the pillar overlooking the depression of Albatross on the right. Move left along a horizontal crack for 2m then pull onto a thinly iced slab above topped by a roof. Pull through the roof onto a second thinly iced slab and climb this to easier ground. Continue up the crest of the buttress via a short steep gully section and belay at the foot of the final icefall of Le Nid d' Aigle. Another difficult pitch.
4. 30m Climb an icy fault diverging left from the icefall for 10m, then step left onto the sharp front arête of the buttress. Climb this on ice in a sensational position to reach the upper ice slopes. Follow these easily to the top.

Arctic Tern   140m   VII,5. S.M.Richardson, I.Small. 25th March 2007.
A good thin face route based on the icy grooves cutting into the left side of the pillar between Riders on the Storm and Albatross.
1. 30m   Start as for the Left-Hand Start to Albatross and climb straight up icy slabs to belay in the steep V-corner 5m left of the twinned groove of Albatross.
2. 45m Step left and climb a steep ice runnel to exit at the top of the slab of Fascist Groove, and continue up an easier groove for 10m. The left wall is cut by a thinly

iced, stepped groove-line. Delicately climb this for 20m then continue up the crest of the rib to reach the traverse line of Flight of the Condor.

3. 45m Step right and climb a 5m icy chimney to reach an open left-facing groove. Follow this for 20m and step right onto the blunt rib between the exit gullies of Nid d'Aigle and Riders on the Storm. Climb the rib until below a final steepening.

4. 20m Climb ice on the right edge of the steepening and finish up a short snow slope to the top.

Rhyme of the Ancient Mariner Direct Start 90m VII,7. I.Parnell, V.Scott. 24th March 2007.
A more direct start to Rhyme of the Ancient Mariner. Start just left of Stormy Petrel (the original attempt on Rhyme also started up here).

1. 50m Climb icy slabs just left of Stormy Petrel for 30m to a steep rock prow. Arrange gear in a crack on a right-facing wall, then descend slightly and climb an obvious steep corner-groove. From the top of this, step left onto a hanging icy slab and traverse this leftwards to gain ice leading to an obvious hanging icicle. Belay below and right of the hanging icicle.

2. 40m Steep mixed moves up an overhanging groove gain the icicle (good small to medium cams in a crack at the back of the groove). Pull over on ice to join Rhyme and follow icy grooves above to the base of the headwall.

3. Break through the headwall as for Rhyme.

Gardyloo Buttress:
Close to the Edge 100m IV,4 *. R.Hamilton, S.Kennedy. 3rd February 2007.
Takes a line close to the true north-west edge/arête of the buttress. Right Edge follows a line further to the right. Requires a good build-up of ice. Start almost directly below the edge at the lowest rocks. Follow a narrow left-trending groove just right of the edge. From the top of the groove move right then back leftwards onto a slab. Climb the slab to a small bulge close to the edge which leads to another icy slab trending rightwards to below a cracked wall. Move left under the wall then up to a small overlap with an icicle fringe. The overlap leads leftwards to a snow shelf which leads left to an exposed belay on the edge below a rock wall (50m). Step right onto the icy upper slab below a right-trending overlap. Climb the slab over a bulge, then trend right to easier ground (30m). Easy snow slopes lead to the cornice (20m).

Note from R.Webb: The guide should say that Murphy's Variation to Kellett's Route starts midway between Kellett's and Smith's beneath a groove and climbs direct to the icicle fringe, then pulls through the fringe to join Smith's at the end of its second pitch.

Raeburn's Wall:
Life on Mars 100m VI,6. D.McGimpsey, A.Nisbet. 2nd April 2007.
A large iced hanging slab right of The Upper Cascade. Climb steep ice to an alcove underneath the the roof (two spike runners). Step right on to a bottomless ice pillar which leads on to the hanging slab. Climb this (50m). Continue up the groove above to the cornice; on this occasion the first break was about 30m left.

Chiquita 100m VI,5. D.McGimpsey, A.Nisbet. 31st March 2007.
A thinner icefall left of Adieu and Farewell (shown as an unclimbed white stripe

on the diagram on p126-127, Ben Nevis guide). The icefall started up an inset slab under a left curving overlap. The overlap was crossed by moving left and back right to gain the thicker upper section which flowed out of a banana shaped groove curving right. A direct line led to a fortunate weakness in the cornice.

The Comb:
Isami   130m   VIII,8. D.McLeod, H.Manome, K.Yokoyama. March 2006.
Climb the first pitch of The Good Groove. Instead of heading up the right-slanting ramp, step left and up (onto Comb Left Flank for a move) and then back right to gain a higher right-slanting ramp. Climb a steep corner above (good gear) and take a belay above this at the foot of the next right-slanting ramp (40m). Move along this into the right-hand of two short but blank looking overhanging corners. Climb the corner with good gear initially to a strenuous and bold finish (good belay on the slabby arête above, 30m). Step right into a deep groove and climb it to the knife edge finishing ridge of the buttress (30m).

Number Three Gully Buttress:
Unleashed   170m   VII,6 ***. M."Ed" Edwards, A.Nisbet. 23rd March 2007.
A line up the left side of the large ice sheet which is climbed less directly by Vulture.
1. 50m Start as for Vulture (Aphrodite) to a rock outcrop below the left side of the overhangs which block access to the ice sheet.
2. 40m Climb a right-slanting weakness through steep ice left of the outcrop. This is as for Vulture, but then continue straight up to a point 6m from the left end of the overhangs.
3. 35m Pull through the left end of the overhangs (crucial there is enough ice here) and climb the left side of the ice sheet to where a ramp leads off left.
4. 25m Go left up the ramp and leave it by steep thin ice above, then snow to a rock outcrop.
5. 20m The finish was direct but very steep to a small cornice.

Knuckleduster   120m   VIII,9 *** B.Fyffe, S.Ashworth. 12th Febuary 2007.
A winter ascent of the summer route. The summer route was followed except on pitch three where instead of traversing back into the main grove, smaller grooves in the arête were climbed (this may be part of Last Stand). The route was sustained with the second pitch being the crux.

Curly's Arête   175m   VIII,8. S.Isaac, I.Parnell. 8th March 2007.
A committing and sustained line based on Last Stand.
1. 15m From the foot of the big Knuckleduster groove, head diagonally up right to below deep cracks in a slab in the arête.
2. 35m Follow the deep cracks to a ledge beneath the steepest section of the arête. A thin traverse right gains a ledge on the right side of the arête. Boldly traverse diagonally up right to a junction with Sioux Wall. Make one move up Sioux Wall and then traverse back left to a short crack just before the arête. Very committing climbing leads up and left to a belay on the arête itself.
3. 40m The groove above leads to a steepening below which a serious pull right gains another right-angled groove. Follow this until below the capping bulges where a traverse line leads 6m right to a belay on Sioux Wall.

4. 30m Follow the direct finish to Sioux Wall to the platform of Number Three
Gully Buttress.
5. 55m Follow Number Three Gully Buttress to the summit plateau.

Note: An ascent of Sioux Wall including the upper pitches by F.Wilkinson and
R.Zalokar on 1st March 2007.

Creag Coire na Ciste:
Salva Mea   90m   VIII,8. V.Scott, D.Bojko. 1st March 2007.
Gains, climbs and leaves the obvious left-slanting hanging chimney just left of
the icicle on South Sea Bubble. A serious route on blind and brittle rock.
1. 30m Start just right of directly below the hanging chimney. Climb up and
leftwards to gain a broad easy groove. This leads to the base of a steep right-
facing corner/ramp with a steep smooth left wall. Climb this corner on good turf
into the chimney. Much of this ground is shared with South Sea Bubble.
2. 60m Climb the wildly leaning chimney to its top. Move up to beneath an
obvious slot and pull steeply through this to gain a steep groove above. From the
groove climb up and leftwards to gain steep blocky ground (possible belay) which
leads (moving rightwards) to the snowslope and cornice. A serious pitch with
very little and poor gear on blind shattered rock.

Creag Coire na Ciste:
Wall Street   120m   VII,7. R.G.Webb, S.M.Richardson. 23rd March 2007.
The ramp and groove right of South Sea Bubble. The second pitch is steep and not
well protected, but overall the route is low in the grade.
1. 30m Climb South Gully as for South Sea Bubble.
2. 20m Climb mixed ground just right of the entry gully of South Sea Bubble to
gain the ramp. Follow this up and right to the foot of the steep corner.
3. 30m Climb the corner (1 rest) to reach a tongue of ice that leads to a stance by
a large block overlooking South Gully.
4. 40m Continue up the crest of the buttress above on thinly iced slabs and finish
up snow to the cornice.

Fore "n" Daft   120m   IV,4. J.Lyall, S.Frazer, M.Twomey. 10th March 2003.
The shallow icy chimney right of Fore Play leads to a ledge, then a left-slanting
fault is followed to belay on Four Play. Go back right onto the edge and up by a
short wall and crack to the easier upper slopes.
Note: This would seem to be the same as a line climbed by S.M.Richardson,
R.G.Webb, 23rd March 2007.

The Girdle Traverse   4000m   V,4. S.M.Richardson, B.Davison. 21st April 2006.
A right to left girdle traverse from Castle Ridge to North-East Buttress. Loosely
based on Bell's summer Girdle Traverse, but climbed in the opposite direction to
minimise the amount of direct sun on the route. Climb North Castle Gully to gain
the top of Castle Ridge, head over The Castle, then move down across mixed
ground into Castle Corrie. Climb the upper section of Ledge Route, cross the
Trident Buttresses, descend Number Four Gully, climb North Gully, and traverse
across Creag Coire na Ciste into Number Three Gully. Climb Thompson's Route,

descend Number Three Gully Buttress, climb Green Gully and descend Hesperides Ledge. Traverse across Comb Gully Buttress, move along the first part of Raeburn's Easy Route and continue left into Glover's Chimney. Drop down from the Gap into Observatory Gully and head off under Indicator Wall and across Observatory Buttress and enter Point Five Gully above the Rogue Pitch. Exit Point Five via the Left-Hand Finish, continue across Hadrian's Wall, Observatory Ridge and Zero Gully to finish up Slav Route and reach the crest of North-East Buttress.

AONACH MOR, Coire an Lochain, North-East Face:
South Pole   60m   IV,5. D.McGimpsey, A.Nisbet. 16th January 2007.
An icefall in the centre of the leftmost buttress, left of Sprint Gully. Start below the right side of an inverted-V recess capped by a very steep groove. Climb up into the recess, then pull over its right wall on ice. Continue up the icefall (40m). A short step gains the easier upper crest (20m). Either continue to the plateau (often no cornice here) or descend to the south for another route.

Sixty Metre Dash   60m   III,4. A.Nisbet. 18th February 2007.
A parallel line, more of a right-facing corner, 10m left of Sprint Gully. Climb to a barrier overhang, pass it on the right on ice overlooking Sprint Gully, then continue up and left on increasingly easy ground to open slopes. Finish as for South Pole (not included in length).

Ribbing Corner   100m   IV,4. D.McGimpsey, A.Nisbet. 16th January 2007.
Right of Ribbon on Edge is a steep gully curving right. Next right is a steep ice-filled corner which leads direct to the top of the gully. Climb the corner and continue to below a chimney (40m). Move right and climb steep snow to the top.

Two Queens   70m   IV,5 *. D.McGimpsey, A.Nisbet. 16th January 2007.
Start 5m left of Three Kings. Climb a steep groove, then an easier corner leading into a shallow gully. Climb the gully (50m). Climb a short wall and the upper slope (20m).

Whitecap Gully   80m   IV,5. M."Ed" Edwards, A.Nisbet, C.Plant. 18th February 2007.
The gully left of Back Street Boogie, often topped by huge cornice. Start at the short gully below Back Street Boogie but climb leftwards on ice close under the buttress to join an easier line which comes up from the left (this may have been climbed by R.Payne and partner who then finished as for Sideline). Continue up the combined gully line to the cornice, which on this occasion was climbed by chimneying an overhanging fracture line which separated the snow arête on the left from the main cornice.

Ribbed Walls:
Man Friday   90m   III,4. A.Nisbet. 23rd February 2007.
The gully right of Pernille is mostly easy but has a short steep ice pitch. There were footsteps already in it (and finishing!), so this was not the first ascent.

Castaway   90m   II. A.Nisbet. 23rd February 2007.
Start 10m right of Pernille. Climb an iced groove into a bay on the right. Continue

on ice above the bay, then move left to finish through the cornice as for the above gully (actually as for Pernille).

Muppet Show 90m III. M.Green, A.Nisbet, E.Wardle. 3rd February 2007.
A line up the centre of the often heavily corniced area right of Pernille. Start about 20m right of Pernille and climb to below a wide rectangular ice-filled gully. This led to a big cornice so go diagonally right into a smaller runnel of ice which led to the upper slopes and a rock outcrop. The finish on the right was 10m of 80 degree snow (a noteworthy crux) topped by a short overhanging ice wall.

Hidden Pinnacle Gully 70m III. S.M.Richardson, R.G.Webb. 4th February 2007.
The right half of the Ribbed Walls is defined by four large towers. This route takes the gully defining the left edge of this section. Climb the gully to where it narrows and climb ice past the hidden pinnacle to where the angle eases. Continue up the wide upper gully and pass the cornice on the right.

Unnamed 70m IV,5. S.M.Richardson, R.G.Webb. 4th February 2007.
The right edge of Hidden Pinnacle Gully finishing up the hanging chimney on the left side of the fourth tower.
1. 40m Climb the edge and move up to a snow-field. Continue up this to a wide overhanging slot. Climb this (crux) to belay below the headwall of the fourth tower.
2. 30m Move up and right to enter the chimney. Climb it and surmount the cornice on the left.

Twins Area:
On an ascent of Lost Boys, A.Nisbet climbed straight up a line of shallow icy grooves about 8m right of Right Twin. This may have been more direct than the previous complex description. The following route was then climbed up a central line of ice.

White Noise 100m IV,5. A.Nisbet. 23rd February 2007.
Start just right of Lost Boys. Climb to the barrier wall where the ice was too steep and thin in the thawing conditions. Move steeply out left on mixed ground and traverse back right to the ice immediately above the steep section. Continue on easier ice to a steeper mixed section which led to the upper slopes. An arête on the left finished with no cornice (same finish as used for Lost Boys).

White Bait 100m IV,5. M."Ed" Edwards, D.McGimpsey. 5th February 2007.
Climbs the right-hand side of the icy wall containing The Lost Boys. Start just left of the lowest rocks, approx. 20m right of Right Twin.
1. 40m Climb a short ice groove, then up and right into an icy bay. Follow this up and left to its top, then gain a narrow ledge on the right and break out through steep walls to a ledge.
2. 30m Continue up then move right into a large snowy bay. Climb up the left side to the top of the bay.
3. 30m Exit the bay and continue out left, then straight up to the cornice.

AONACH BEAG, West Face:
Stalking Horse VI,7. D.Hollinger, A.Turner. 18th January 2007.

Follow the summer line. A very good main pitch was split under the overhang. The wide crack was the crux, involving successive can opener moves. The moves around the overhang were exciting but a helpful crack on the left wall provided good hooks.

An Aghaidh Garbh, Summit Buttress:
Close Encounters 65m IV,5 **. R.Hamilton, S.Kennedy. 18th February 2007. The steep open slopes to the right (north) of the "Goblet" buttress lead to a small steep buttress which is two tiered and usually crowned by large summit cornices. The buttress is bounded on the left by a small amphitheatre overhung by huge cornices and a further buttress to the left again. To the right, straightforward snow slopes lead to the top section of the North-East Ridge. This route takes a line of icy grooves left of centre. Start left of the toe of the buttress and climb an icy slab to a snow slope and a slabby wall. Climb the wall on the left to a snow bay then the steep groove above to a snow terrace. From the terrace an icy ramp leads up leftwards to the base of a V-shaped groove. Follow the groove to the top of the buttress (50m). Steep snow leads to a problematic cornice finish not far from the summit cairn (15m). The ascent was noteable due to the leader taking a 20m peel from the cornice (unscathed).

STOB COIRE AN LAOIGH:
Some Like it Hot 70m VII,7 ***. M."Ed" Edwards, D.McGimpsey, A.Nisbet. 13th February 2007. Climbs a right-facing corner in the steep wall between Jammy Dodger and Serve Chilled. A fine line, steep and sustained. Start about halfway along the wall, below and just right of the corner, which starts 20m up.
1. 25m Climb over a short wall into a roofed V-groove. Pull out left from the groove and step back right on to a "diving board" above its roof. Climb a steep wall above to turf. An earlier attempt climbed direct to the base of the corner, but this ascent stepped right, moved up and returned left to below the corner.
2. 45m Climb the corner!

White Heat 65m VI,7 *. M."Ed" Edwards, J.Edwards-Lihocka, A.Nisbet. 20th March 2007.
Based on the opposing left-facing corner right of Some Like it Hot but forced out on to its sensational right arête. Start as for Some Like it Hot.
1. 15m Climb into its roofed groove but pull out right on to blocks. Climb a shallow groove on the right to below the corner.
2. 30m Climb the corner to a block pinnacle below overhangs. Stand on the pinnacle and step out right, then move up to a small platform on the arête. Climb blocks and cracks mostly just left of the arête to a ledge below a roof.
3. 20m Move right into the finishing groove of Serve Chilled. Go up this for 10m but move left and finish up the rib on the left.

CENTRAL HIGHLANDS, Carn Liath, Coire Dubh:
Stormrunner 100m II. S.M.Richardson. 3rd December 2006. The corrie is ringed by a frieze of schist crags. The most prominent line is the central buttress that descends furthest into the corrie. Start below the left edge of the buttress and climb a short ramp that leads up to the right edge. Follow this to a short easing at half-height, then continue up mixed ground to the top.

Mount Remote, Canadian Coast Mountains. Simon Richardson and Don Serl climbed the obvious couloir splitting the face. Photo: Simon Richardson.

GLEN COE

BUACHAILLE ETIVE MOR, Eagle Buttress:
Note: Raptor was climbed by D.McGimpsey and A.Nisbet, grade HVS 4c, 5a **.
A star less than Pontoon, climbed that day and an excellent route.

Curved Ridge Area:
Cracked Rib 150m II/III. D.Bell, R.McGibbon. 18th March 2006.
Probably climbed before but worth documenting for crowd-avoidance. Go up Easy
Gully to where it splits (the left fork is often used to bypass the steep start of
Curved Ridge). Head instead onto the rib. After 50m the rib becomes a deep runnel
leading to a cave. Exit on the right (or tunnel). Go left onto the obvious rib for
another long pitch to rejoin Curved Ridge.

CHURCH DOOR BUTTRESS:
Templer Knights 150m VII,8 **. I.Small, B.Fyffe. January 2007.
A fine direct line following the crest of the buttress and cutting across West
Chimney. Start just to the left of the toe of the buttress.
1. 20m Climb a wide crack, sometimes on the wall to the left of the crack to a
terrace. Belay on the right below an obvious groove.
2. 40m Climb the groove to a steep exit. Continue up easier ground to beside a
hole/cave. Flake Route comes in around here.
3. 50m Continue up moderate ground to belay by the boulder (above the Arch) on
West Chimney route.
4. 40m Climb a steep groove in the arête just behind the boulder to a shelf. From
the left end of the shelf, climb up a groove to step right at a spike to another
groove. Follow this to a chimney-groove. Climb this to easier ground.

AONACH DUBH, Far Eastern Buttress:
Fraoch 60m V,7. J.Abbott, V.Scott. 30th December 2003.
A winter line in the vicinity of Buckshee Groove. Start just right of the bottom left
arête of the crag.
1. 25m Pull over the undercut base of the crag onto a slab. Make a thin rightwards-
rising traverse beneath the overlap and swing round a projecting nose (crux) to
gain the base of an obvious groove. Climb this to its top.
2. 20m Go up and right to gain a good ledge. Follow this rightwards until
overlooking a chimney. Climb steep heathery rock on the arête and a wall above
to a large platform.
3. 15m The short obvious corner behind the platform leads to snow slopes.

AN T-SRON, East Face:
Perilous Journey 48m E1 5b. R.Hamilton, S.Kennedy. 25th July 2006.
Situated a short distance right of Cornerstone (see SMCJ 2005, p369). Good in
the lower part but the easier arête is a bit dirty although much easier. The base of
the arête is severely undercut by a large overhang which is topped by a slab. A
crack springs up from the right end of the overhang. Climb the crack for 5m.
Place gear then step left onto the slab and make exposed moves across the slab to
reach the left edge. Step left around the edge then climb the arête fairly directly to
the top.

Andrew Fraser on the first ascent of Springs of Enchantment, E1 5b, Point of Snibe, Galloway. Photo: Andrew Fraser.

Petite Arête   85m   II. R.Hamilton, S.Kennedy. 21st January 2007.
Climbs the most prominent ridge on the right side of the upper east corrie (opposite Hidden Gully) starting just right of a narrow gully. This is the corrie to the right of Daytripper Slab and at a higher level. Broad in the lower section with an airy upper ridge. From the base the ridge climb left of centre before moving back right below a slabby wall. Climb a groove on the right to a block belay (40m). Finish directly up the narrow rocky ridge to reach open ground below the summit ridge (45m). Useful when the higher routes are affected by heavy snowfall.

GARBH BHEINN (ARDGOUR):

The following route probably shares part of Bodkin or Poniard at the start, then climbs through the overhangs between the two (it has also been suggested that Bodkin and Poniard may share a start!).

Jambia   80m E2 *. J.Cox, A.Brown. 15th May 2005.
1. 40m 5b A line through the overhangs between Bodkin and Mournblade, starting at the second shallow groove right of Butterknife. Climb straight up until a tricky move left gains a small ramp. Move back right towards the overhangs and across to a prominent block on the lip. From this pull up and left through the roof on small hidden incuts (crux) to gain a shallow groove and easy ground.
2. 40m Scramble to the terrace.

Great Ridge:

Blood of the Son   180m (to base of Great Ridge) IV,5 *. S.Kennedy, A.MacDonald. 9th April 2006.
Basically a variation start to Great Ridge situated on the slabby buttress a short distance left of Great Gully with one short hard section. Some sections correspond with one of the original summer starts but the route described is fairly direct and when combined with Great Ridge results in a more sustained route overall. About 40m left of the foot of GG is a narrow rightward-slanting rake. This should not be mistaken for the more obvious diagonal line above which seems to be the line of one of the summer starts. Follow the rake until it peters out close to the edge of GG. Climb snow slopes on the left to below a short, slabby rock wall. Surmount the wall awkwardly (crux) then climb a groove above. This leads to the obvious left-facing corner/groove on the left which is followed to easy ground just left of the base of Great Ridge.

ARDNAMURCHAN,
Notes from M.Gear:

Achnaha Buttress: Wheest! - Perhaps E3?
Sgurr nan Gabhar: agree with previous SMCJ, Solar Wind does not appear to exist.
Meall an Fhir-eoin Beag: Yir - reference to starting up Minky looks daft.
Meall an Fhir-eoin, Summit Buttresses: Ring of Fire is only 30m. There is a fragile looking flake on the hand traverse which may not survive much more handling!

SOUTHERN HIGHLANDS

BEINN AN DOTHAIDH, North-East Corrie:
Sleipnir III,5. S.Burns, D.Crawford, G.Gray. 21st January 2007.
The gully line to the left of Thor gives an alternative start to Stairway to Heaven.
Climb the gully (60m) in two pitches passing several chockstones to gain the
ridge of Stairway to Heaven. Finish up this route.
Note: Thor (SMCJ 2006) should be IV,6.

BEINN DORAIN:
Due South 150m IV,4. T.Lenehan, A.Ogilvie. 5th January 1997.
The route follows the largest of a group of icefalls which form on the south
facing aspect of Ben Dorain above the Auch Glen at NN 331 381. An easy pitch
leads to the base of an open corner iced in the angle (20m). Climb the icy
corner (40m). An easy terrace leads to the base of a long groove line. Follow
the groove line (90m Grade II) onto open slopes close to the Meall Garbh to
Ben Dorain col.

BEINN UDLAIDH:
Screw Loose 90m IV,4. R.McGibbon, D.Bell. 8th March 2005.
Starts in the bay immediately to the left of Quartzvein Scoop. Follow a steep
corner on the left side of the bay, which then leads to a steep wall followed by
easier ground. This is between Tick Tock (SMCJ 2001) and Quartzvein Scoop.

BEINN IME:
Note: Friday the Twelfth (guide p210) has been re-named Thursday the Twelfth
by the FAists.

SUB STATION CRAG:
C.Moody notes: A hold that 'appeared' on White Meter in the 90s has been
filled with cement.

LOWLAND OUTCROPS

BEN A'N:
Note: In Tom Weir's book, *Highland Days*, there is a description of a fall on the
third ascent of a route just left of The Last Eighty. The route was first climbed by
L.Lovat probably in 1968 and D.Stewart wonders if this was the route Coriander,
predating the current first ascent.

AYRSHIRE, The Quadrocks:
Sweepstake 12m E1 5a. K.Shields (solo). February 2007.
Take the direct line up the face to the left of Vee Groove. Slopey holds but good
climbing. Beware loose rock on first moves.

Numbers Game 10m E2 6a. K.Shields (solo). 27th March 2007.
Start to the left of Vee Groove on top of the boulder. Head directly up the overhang
(beware loose blocks). Small holds at first easing towards the top.

V For Vendetta   14m   E1 5b. K.Shields (solo). 31st March 2007.
Climb the face immediately to the right of Vee Groove, with sketchy moves to good protection at half-height.

Lichen Angel   10m   E1 5b. A.Mallinson. 16th September 2006.
A direct line taking the shallow groove and crack-line 3m left of Big Corner. Ascend the initial shallow grove on small flakes to an undercling. Make difficult moves to continue up the groove, then follow the crack to the top. Led on-sight.

The Dark Side   10m   E4 6a. K.Shields (solo). 19th December 2006.
Climb the face between Big Corner and The Arête, without using either of these routes for bridging etc.

Absence of Hope   9m   E3 6c. K.Shields. 16th September 2006.
At the far right of main crag face, between The Fatal Kiss and an arête. Climb this line direct, committing, protectionless and with potential for a very bad landing.

End of the Line   10m   E2 6a. K.Shields (solo). February 2007.
From the corner at the bottom of the end of The Traverse, take the direct line up obvious pinches and smears, then direct up the slabby face to finish as The Traverse.

Point Proven   10m   E3 6b. K.Shields. 26th July 2006.
Start at the bottom of the large boulder below The Traverse Finish. Bridge off this and move left. Climb to the good rest and place the only bit of available pro. Make a tricky layback right, then continue up technical climbing. Committing.

The Calling   10m   E2 6b. K.Shields. 26th July 2006.
At the left edge of Sunburst Red, climb the lower face to gain the boulder arête. Bridge left to place gear in a crack. Gain the top of a boulder and climb the tricky and committing left face.

Spite yer Face   10m   HVS 4c. A.McDonald. 25th July 2006.
Takes the direct line The Nose should take. Immediately below the overhanging broken arête, climb by jamming an open flake (very loose!) and finish up the hanging crack above. Protection is limited due to the loose nature of the rock and may improve with traffic and bring down the grade a little.

G-Funk   8m   E2 5b. A.McDonald. 25th July 2006.
Slightly up and right of Sunburst Red is a small buttress with a prominent break at half-height. The route climbs the black crack straight up on good holds but sparse protection to the break. Small brushed holds and zero gear take you through an exhilarating finish.

GALLOWAY HILLS, DUNGEON OF BUCHAN:
Jailhouse Rock   45m   HVS **. A.Fraser, I.Magill. June 2005.
At the top of the crag and 100m right of Cooran Gully is a triangular wall, highest at its left side where a prominent crack slopes left up a headwall. The headwall is visible from the top of Cooran Buttress and the climb is best accessed by a straightforward abseil from its top. Start at the lowest point. Climb a boulder, then

a tricky bulge above, followed by a delicate toe traverse left into a ledge in the corner. Climb the corner to a cracked bulge (possible belay – 20m 4c). Surmount the bulge, then follow cracks to the top. These give sustained and delicate bridging in a great position (25m 5a).

CRAIGNAW, Memorial Crag:
(NX 458 833)   Alt 600m   West facing:
This small crag of impeccably clean granite sits immediately below the summit of Craignaw and overlooks Loch Neldricken. Just below the crag is a memorial to two US Airforce pilots who were killed in a plane crash there in 1979. On a sunny day it is an idyllic spot with wonderful views. It is, however, also a long way from anywhere and can be approached (by the ultra enthusiastic) either as for the Dungeon of Buchan, or from Glen Trool (2hrs 30mins minimum). However, from a campsite on the shore on Loch Neldricken, the crag could be easily reached in 30mins. Although the routes are short, a double rack of Cams up to size 4 should be considered the minimum, whilst wires are of little use.

Main Wall:
Main Wall is very steep, and home to some of the hardest routes in the Galloway Hills. At the left end of Main Wall are easy angled slabs leading to a grass ledge below a steep headwall.

Mij's Slab   10m   Difficult. J.Biggar. 2nd June 2006.
The slab can be climbed anywhere to a walk off left, or continue up Mij's Chimney on the left which is steep to start (8m Very Difficult). This was descended immediately beforehand (solo) by Mij the Border Terrier (in full control) much to the astonishment of the rest of the party! Mij's Chimney added by S.J.H.Reid, J.Biggar, 15th June 2006.

Just left of centre of Main Wall is an obvious slightly left-slanting crack system.

Captains' Crack   22m   E1 5b **. S.J.H.Reid, J.Biggar, L.Biggar, S.Baxendale. 1st June 2006.
Steep and strenuous, but juggy, and well protected with Cams. Follow the crack system to awkward moves to overcome a bulge and gain a grass ledge. Move up to a smaller grass ledge on the right and finish up the left-slanting cracks above.

Memorial Wall   22m   E2 5c ***. C.King, S.J.H.Reid. 15th June 2006.
Excellent steep, strenuous and well-protected climbing up the centre of the wall. Start in the centre of the wall, just left of Dynamics Direct. Climb a short layaway crack and swing left to a flat jug. Climb up slightly leftwards to an illusory rest and then make hard up rightwards to grab a hollow horizontal spike and gain a narrow ledge. The short wall and crack above hold interest to the last.

Aerial Combat   22m   E1 5b **. C.King, J.Biggar, S.J.H.Reid. 15th June 2006.
Another fine well protected wall climb. The next obvious feature, some 5m to the right, is a short left-facing groove that leads at 4m to a long, almost horizontal, crack leading rightwards. Climb the groove and gain the ledge at the start of the horizontal flake, then climb up leftwards via hollow flakes to a block. Move left and climb the wall above trending rightwards to a hard finishing move.

General Dynamics   25m   E1 5b **. J.Biggar, L.Biggar, S.J.H.Reid. 1st June 2006.
A great route, mainly HVS but with a puzzling and reachy crux. Start as for Aerial Combat. Climb the groove and hand traverse the crack rightwards with a long thin reach to gain a good hold on a block. Commit to this to make a wild swing right into a shallow groove up which the climb finishes.

Towards the right side of Main Wall are two grooves capped by overhangs.

The Murder Hole   14m   E2 6a *. C.King, S.J.H.Reid. 15th June 2006.
The left-hand groove gives a very sustained and technical route. Climb the groove up to the roof and make tenuous moves up and leftwards to finish up the last few moves of General Dynamics. Hard for the grade.

Granny Eggface   12m   E2 5c *. C.King, S.J.H.Reid. 15th June 2006.
The right-hand groove is also quite a toughie. Step up rightwards from two blocks, then move left to a slot. Pull directly over the roof with difficulty and continue with more difficulty leftwards to the top.

Aardvark   10m   VS 4b. J.Biggar, S.J.H.Reid. 2002.
Immediately round to the right of Main Wall is a short left-leaning slab with a crack on its left side in the upper half. Climb the poorly protected slab.

Back to Bax   10m   Severe 4a. S.Baxendale, L.Biggar. 1st June 2006.
Just right of the slab of Aardvark is a short trench-like groove/crack system. Climb this to a ledge, then make a hard move up right to finish. Better (and harder) than it looks.

Unnamed   15m   VS 4c. L.Biggar, J.Biggar, S.J.H.Reid. 1st June 2006.
Down and left of Back to Bax is a cleaner parallel line. Climb this to an exit right on to a grass ramp, or continue direct (harder). Finish up the wall above the ramp.

Zebra Wall:
To the right of Main Wall is a short wall below a long grass ledge and above this is a more attractive and slightly larger wall. The following climbs lie on the upper wall, just left of the scramble up to the grass ledge.

F-111   8m   VS 4c. J.Biggar, S.J.H.Reid, C.King. 1st June 2006.
A wide crack on the left side of the wall becomes easier after a hard start.

Zebra   10m   VS 4c *. L.Biggar, J.Biggar. 15th June 2006.
Start towards the left side of the upper wall and climb a prominent left-slanting crack system with a hard move near the middle. A good sustained route.

Craignaw Corner   15m   E1 5b *. S.J.H.Reid, C.King, J.Biggar. 15th June 2006.
Just right again is a smooth left-facing corner. Bridge strenuously up the corner, then tackle twin cracks in the headwall. A good wee pitch.

Just right again are twin crack systems.

Cameater Crack   15m   VS 4c. J.Biggar, S.J.H.Reid, C.King. 15th June 2006.
The left-hand crack soon eases off.

Sword of Damocles 15m Severe 4b *. J.Biggar, S.J.H.Reid. 15th June 2006.
The right-hand crack is more sustained and interesting. The sword, which was of an impressive size, was removed by the second en route and can be inspected at the foot of the crag.

CRAIGNAW, Scotland Slab:
This slab lies low down on the north-east end of Craignaw, just a short detour from the approach to the excellent crags on the Dungeon Hill. Approach as for the Dungeon crags, in about 30mins across the Silver Flowe from Backhill of Bush bothy. The slab is named for the resemblance of the upper slab to a map of Scotland and is a nice relatively low angled granite slab. It steepens from roughly 35° at the base in deepest Cumbria to nearly 50° in Sutherland. Protection is very sparse, but the belays are good, 60m ropes recommended. The route still has some lichen on the easier sections, but the hardest moves have been cleaned. The slab will need several days to dry after heavy rain.

The Road to Wrath 100m Hard Severe 4a *. L.Biggar, J.Biggar, J.Kinnaird. 25th June 2006.
1. 50m 3c From the lowest point of the slab climb easily up and right to cracks and runners at 30m (The Border). Continue straight up between two grass patches, then traverse leftwards to belay on the lower rocks of the upper slab, just west of Glasgow.
2. 50m 4a Step over the overlap and traverse further leftwards to reach a thin crack through the steeper slab above. Climb this crack for a few metres before a traverse can be made back right to Inverness. Make a tenuous move to a good pocket here then up diagonally left to Cape Wrath. Belay using a cracked block a few metres up and left. (The direct line up the A9 from Glasgow to Inverness is also good, but a very unprotected lead).

CRAIGNAW, Point of the Snibe (NX 465 815):
The rocky south-eastern tip of Craignaw consists of a number of clean buttresses of premium-quality granite, unaccountably overlooked in the past. The crag is south-facing and has all day sun (with a consequent lack of midges).
Approach: Either from Craigencallie up the Backhill of Bush Road until directly opposite the crag at NX 478 817 in an area of recent felling, at which point it is possible to cross the Cooran Lane and approach the crag directly. The location of faint goat tracks across the moor tend to indicate the best places to cross the otherwise deep and sinister Cooran Lane (1hr by bike, 1hr30mins on foot); or from Loch Trool by way of Loch Valley (1hr30mins).
The cliffs consist of five main areas. These, and the climbs on them are described right to left.

The Seven Pillars:
The right edge of the crag is marked by a rib, steep at its bottom and with a series of pillars on its left side. The rock is excellent and the climbs are easier than they look.

Swamp Fever 13m Severe 4a. A.Fraser, I.Magill. 20th August 2005.
A pleasant climb up the bottom of the rib. Start up the boulder at the bottom left of the rib, then follow the arête above, on its left side where necessary.

The following routes take the series of pillars on the left side of the rib.

McKinlay Murmerings   5m   Very Difficult. R. Pontefract. 24th July 2005.
Climb the first short rib.

Denali De-Brief   10m   Hard Severe 4b *. R.Pontefract, I.Magill, A.Fraser. 24th July 2005.
This climbs the first of the larger pillars, starting up cracks on its right side, then when the angle eases, climbing cracks up the centre.

Cleanliness is Next to …   12m   Severe 4a **. A.Fraser, A.Gillies. 14th May 2005.
Lovely steep climbing on huge holds. To the left of Denali De-Brief is a vegetated area, then a steep buttress above a large boulder. Climb this on its right side, then to the left of a prominent detached block.

Goatliness   12m   Hard Severe 4b *. I.Magill, R.Pontefract, A.Fraser. 24th July 2005.
Another steep route with surprisingly cooperative holds. Start at the left edge of the same buttress as the previous route. Climb slightly right, then back left till feet are in the wide horizontal crack near the top. Traverse left into the chimney and up this to finish.

Burning the Goats   10m   Hard Severe 4b *. I.Magill, R.Pontefract. 24th July 2005.
Immediately left of the previous route is a blanker pillar, which nonetheless provides a good route at a reasonable grade.

Arabian Nights   10m   Very Difficult. R.Pontefract, I.Magill, A.Fraser. 24th July 2005.
Left of the previous route is an area of more broken ground then a paler buttress. Climb the pale buttress then the groove above with surprising ease.

The Uncarved Block:
To the left of the Seven Pillars is a cracked wall.

Pointless of the Snibe   9m   Severe 4a. A. Fraser, D.MGimpsey. 24th July 2006.
The rounded rib at the right edge of the wall, unsatisfactorily requiring use of the turfy blocks on the right of its lower section. Continue up the wall above if desired.

Timorous Cooran Beastie   10m   E1 5b **. A.Fraser, I.Magill. 17th September 2006.
Superb sustained climbing up the right-hand crack. The easiest line on the top section is not obvious.

Springs of Enchantment   15m   E1 5b ***. A.Fraser, I.Magill, R.Pontefract. 24th July 2005.
A classic route which climbs the disjointed cracks in the middle of the wall. While it dries quickly after showers, drainage from farther up the hill emerges at the crux, meaning that it is rarely dry earlier in the season. Worth waiting for!

Ram Attang   16m   VS 4c *. A.Gillies, A.Fraser. 14th May 2005.
A wider right-sloping crack 5m left of Springs of Enchantment gives a fine sustained climb. Start direct by a 5b boulder problem or as for pitch 2 of the following route. Pitches 1 and 3 of the following route can also be added for taste.

Silver Sand   41m   VS 4c **. A.Fraser, A.Gillies. 14th May 2005.
Another good route in a fine position. Down left of the main wall is a lower buttress with two parallel cracks at its left side. Climb the left one (9m 4b). Climb

the crack up the left edge of the main wall to the heather terrace (20m 4c). Continue up past a higher heather ledge. Move left to gain and climb a final friction slab (12m 4b).

The Arête:
Across a vegetated gully from The Uncarved Block is the soaring Arête, the longest feature on the crag.

The Call of the Weird 45m VS *. A.Fraser, I.Magill 20th August 2005.
This route takes cracks on the right side of The Arête. Although the start is mediocre, the crux is a not-to-be-missed piece of climbing. Scramble up to gain and climb the crack on the right side of The Arête. Go up this till it becomes vegetated, at which point a hitherto hidden series of foot ledges leads memorably left across the wall to gain, then climb The Arête to a large heather ledge (25m 5a). Climb the crack behind the belay, exiting right at its top to climb a right-sloping gangway. Continue directly to the top (20m 4b).

The Arête 50m VS *. A.Plumb, S.Aird. 1987.
Some excellent climbing, improving with gradual vegetation removal. Start on the left side of the arête and climb short walls to gain a corner just left of the arête. Climb the corner (not the cleaned crack to its left) exiting left onto a large heather ledge (22m 4b). Easy cracks lead back to the crest of the arête at a heather ledge. Follow the crack behind the ledge, exiting left onto a ramp. Follow this with difficulty to the very top, ignoring the cleaned crack near the end (28m 4c).

Walk on Hot Coals 47m VS **. A.Fraser, I.Magill. 17th September 2006.
The meat of the route is the improbable slab crossed by the ramp of The Arete's top pitch. Follow The Arête to the foot of the corner on its first pitch, then climb the cleaned crack on the left wall of the corner (22m 4c). Move left to climb a crack at the right end of the slab, traverse left for 4m to gain a crack and gear, then move slightly back right and commit yourself to the centre of the slab. Follow this to the ramp of The Arête, which is followed left until it is possible to finish up a crack on the right wall of the ramp (25m 4b).

Cornarroch Walls:
The following climbs are on the walls, which run up to the left of the Arête.

Cat Goat your Tongue? 25m VS 4c *. A.Gillies, A.Fraser. 14th May 2005.
About 10m left of The Arête is a black left-facing corner. Climb this, then move up and left to gain and climb cracks on the right side of a prominent large overhang. Follow the easier upper buttress to the top.

To the left are two vegetatious chimneys.

Cornarroch Chimney 21m Very Difficult. A.Fraser, K.Donaldson. 23rd May 1978.
Climb the left-hand chimney to the heather terrace, traverse this up and left until a right-sloping crack can be climbed to outflank the overhang. Finish up the buttress above.

Original Route 20m Difficult. A.Fraser, K.Donaldson. 23rd May 1978.
This is 3m to the left of Cornarroch Chimney. Follow the easiest line up a shallow corner to gain the heather terrace. Cross this and climb the jug-infested upper buttress to the top.

Man the Lifegoats   9m   VS 4c *. I.Magill, A.Fraser. 17th September 2006.
At the top of the wide grassy gully to the left of the Cornarroch Walls is a tower
with a conspicuous steep crack on its left side. This gives steep climbing on good
holds.

The Philosopher's Stone:
Down left from The Arête is a blank wall with intermittent cracks. Below this is a
short lower tier of slabs.

Beltie   15m   E3 5c ***. D.MGimpsey, A.Fraser. 24th July 2006.
Good climbing up the cracks in the centre of the wall. Low in the grade, the grade
being merited by its sustained nature.

Lower Slabs:
The following three routes are on the slabs underneath the Philosopher's Stone.

The Goat, the Bad and the Ugly   7m   VS 5a. D.McGimpsey, A.Fraser. 24th July
2006.
An awkward little blighter, taking the groove at the right side of the wall.

Let the Goat Times Roll   8m   VS 4c *. A.Fraser, D.MGimpsey. 24th July 2006.
A fine climb up the cracks left of centre.

Kids Play   8m   Moderate. A.Fraser. 24th July 2006.
Delightfully easy climbing up cracks on the left edge.

The Pearly Goats:
Left again, at the left edge of the crag, is a two-tier buttress, the upper section of
which is marked by wide parallel cracks.

Rivergoat Gambler   28m   VS 4c. I.Magill, A.Fraser. 17th September 2006.
Much better than appearances suggest. The right side of the buttress is a vegetatious
gully, capped by a fine corner. To the right of the gully are two stepped ribs. Climb
the scoop between these, then continue up left to the fine corner. This is climbed
until it is possible to escape onto a ledge on the left. Follow the rib above (crux),
avoiding the easier cracks on the left.

The Alchemists Dream   35m   E1 ***. I.Magill, A.Fraser, E.Magill. 29th August
2005.
A powerful line giving steep jamming up the right-hand crack. Start up the right
crack on the lower buttress, moving left into the scoop at mid-height, then continue
up the centre of the buttress to the heather terrace below the upper wall (10m 4a).
Sustained and excellent climbing up the right crack leads to a rightward-slanting
scoop and cracks which are climbed to the top (25m 5b).

Juniper Cracks   32m   HVS *. A.Fraser, E.Magill I.Magill. 29th August 2005.
Climb the left crack on the lower buttress (9m 4b). The third crack from the right
is Y shaped with much juniper in the right branch of the Y. Climb a combination
of the next crack to the left and the left branch of the Y until it is possible to move
right above the juniper to gain a groove. Climb this groove to a heather ledge then
climb the short wall above (23m 5a).

Little Egypt   30m   VS *. A.Fraser, E.Magill I.Magill. 29th August 2005.
Five metres left and down from pitch 2 of Juniper Cracks is a recessed cracked

slab. Climb cracks at the right side of this, before moves lead up left across the slab to gain the thank god grass ledge at its left end. The steeper wall above is liberally endowed with holds and provides very agreeable climbing to the top.

The Faa Side 45m Very Difficult. A.Fraser, E.Magill, I.Magill. 29th August 2005.
The ridge at the left end of the crag. The second and third tiers are climbed on the left side by a crack and slab respectively. The climb includes the slabby buttress of clean rock lying just above the main ridge.

CRAIGDEWS:
Pushing the Goat Out 62m VS *. A.Fraser,I.Magill. 19th July 2006.
A sustained and interesting slab climb. Another series of rightward-sloping slabs lies 15m right of the start of The Dark Side. Start at the right end of the blank lower slab. Climb 8m to a small grass niche, then move 2m up and right into a shallow niche. Leave this on its left side and continue up for 6m to a ledge from where it is possible to move 3m up and right to another ledge. Climb the left side of the slabs above to gain the upper slab. Traverse 3m right and pad the slab to exit just right of a prickly bush. Continue up right to gain and climb the arête above (47m 4c). A steep wall lies 4m to the right. Claim the central nose of this, finishing to the right of the nose (15m 4c). Exit by scrambling up the ramps to the right.

CLIFTON CRAG:
Elders Traverse 12m Hard Severe 4b. S.Reid, S.Baxendale. 24th March 2007.
A mini girdle. Start at the bottom of The Esplanade and follow a wiggly hand/finger traverse (2m below The Esplanade) leftwards across the wall, crossing Muckle Knob and Elders Crack, to finish up the final crack of The Arête.

Little Clifton:
This is a short outcrop under the descent ramp, between the Red Slab Area and Twin Cracks Buttress. Belays are well back.

Gorilla Warfare 10m VS 5a. J.Biggar, L.Biggar. 3rd May 2006.
The clean narrow slab on the left side of the buttress. Start just before a step down in the path under the crag, above two blocks. Use a pinch grip to make an awkward start and then continue up the right side of the arête, moving right to a crack towards the top.

The next routes start in a pleasant grassy bay up and to the right.

Gordon Bennett 10m VS 4c. S.Reid, S.Baxendale. 25th May 2006.
Towards its right-hand side, the upper wall is dominated by a hanging shield of rock; the main aim of this climb. Start 4m left of this and climb a slim clean(ish) rib to a huge flat block. Stand on the block and traverse rightwards, step down off its end, and make a long stride out right to stand on a small protruding block under the shield: then climb the shield (bridging out right is cheating!).

Chimpish 8m Hard Severe 4a. J.Biggar, K.Berry. 3rd May 2006.
Start towards the right-hand side of the grassy bay, under the hanging shield of rock. Climb rock and grass in equal quantity, leftwards and then back right to gain a ledge. Finish up a crack to the left of the shield.

Piece of Cake 8m VS 4b. L.Biggar, A.Brooke-Mee. 3rd May 2006.
Just right of the hanging shield is a slim red slab - climb it (quite bold).

GALLOWAY SEA-CLIFFS, Meikle Ross, Fox Craig:

Left Arête   10m   VS 4b **. L.Biggar, J.Biggar, D.McNicol. 7th June 2006.
Climb a diagonal finger crack to reach the juggy arête left of Rez Route.

Twin Cracks   10m   Severe 4a *. D.McNicol, I.Cameron. 2002 or 2003.
Twin cracks just left of the corner groove of Sharks Tooth.

Burrow Head, Camp Site Walls:

Diagonal Crack   20m   Severe. D.McGimpsey, B.Davison. 31st May 2006.
The prominent right to left diagonal crack mentioned in the guidebook description.

Opening Gambit   20m   HVS 5a *. B.Davison, D.McGimpsey. 1st June 2006.
Two metres right of Left-Hand Crack and 4m left of a rock island exposed at most
states of tide in calm seas is a diagonal fault running up right to a shallow groove
at the top of the wall. Climb the wall around the narrow crack and enter the shallow
groove above (crux); follow this to the top. The base is only accessible at low tide
Variation: High Tide Start   20m   E1 5a. B.Davison, D.McGimpsey. 31st May
2006.
A high tide start from the top of the exposed rock island to the right. Climb up
diagonally left to a squarish recess and then to a ledge a metre above, poorly
protected. Hand traverse the ledge leftwards, then move up and diagonally leftwards
to finish up the shallow groove above.

Delilah   15m   VS 4c *. D.McGimpsey, B.Davison. 1st June 2006.
The obvious crack-line at the left-hand side of the wall about 4m in from the left
arête is only accessible at low tide. Climb the crack with an awkward move at
two-third height.
Note: The two existing routes (Goblin's Eyes and Killer on the Loose) are closer
to 20m than the 25m in the guide.

Portobello, Mare Rock (Partially tidal, South facing):

A steep crag which forms a long wall in a cove south of Portobello. The cliff has
a steep crack at its landward end, a left-trending ledge at two-thirds height in its
central section, and a compact wall at its seaward end. The rock is sound, but very
compact and less gear-friendly than Portobello. No nesting birds. The climbs are
on the seaward wall.
Approach: Park as for Portobello and follow the coast south for about 1.5km
(20mins), the cliff coming into view once it is passed.

Horse to the Water   15m   HVS 5a *. A.Fraser, I.Magill. 2nd June 2006.
At the left end of the cliff an easy, leftward ramp leads up from the boulders at the
foot of the crag. At low tide climb this (at high tide start at the top of the ramp by
scrambling down the end of the crag). From here climb the rightward trending
crack, then move leftward over the bulge. Continue directly to the top

Dancing White Horses   15m   E2 5c ***. I.Magill, A.Fraser. 2nd June 2006.
A superb sustained outing through some intimidating territory. It climbs the centre
of the seaward wall, starting from the largest of the sea boulders, and climbing
directly to an obvious spike above the overlap. Micro friends and nuts required,
but easy for the grade.

ROSYTH QUARRY: As a fairly popular venue, some of the lines are likely to have been climbed before.

Poison Dwarf 7m E1 5c. R.Wallace, A.Wallace. 5th February 2006.
The steep wall immediately right of Andy's Route has a line of sidepulls leading to a thin flake-crack. This gives a great wee bouldery eliminate route.

Forth Bridge 10m HVS 5a. R.Wallace, A.Wallace. 4th February 2006.
Just right of Hands Off is a wide open groove, often damp. Bridge up this till it steepens and narrows, then stand on a hanging block to the right. An undercling and a crack gain easier ground.

Fog on the Forth 10m E1 5b. A.Wallace, R.Wallace. 5th February 2006.
Climb directly up the front of the pillar, over the roof and onto the top of the block. Finish up the previous route.

Gumball 3000 10m HVS 5c. R.Wallace, A.Wallace. 17th June 2006.
Climb easily up the right side of the pillar, onto the block. Move up to gain a short left-facing arête. Layaway the arête to gain a good ledge, then jug haul to the top.

Named and Shamed 15m Hard Severe. R.Wallace, A.Wallace. 17th June 2006.
Starting just to the left of Grenville, a few tricky moves lead into a chimney groove. This gives easy bridging to a harder move through a small overhang. Finish over a concave overlap.

Life during Wartime 15m E1 5b *. A.Wallace, R.Wallace. 17th June 2006.
An eliminate but excellent boulder problem start between Grenville and Heathy gains a standing position on the bottom of a wee ramp. Follow the left arête of a steep slab onto a big ledge, then climb up by the left side of a fin to gain a flat jug on the arête. A dyno gains a similar hold directly above before turning the rectangular overhang to the right and finishing up a short flake-crack.

Fire in the Quarry 15m Mild Severe. R.Wallace, A.Wallace. 5th February 2006.
On the left of Corpuscle are two narrow grooves. Start up these, then carry on up a prominent groove system.

FIFE, Limekilns:
Muffintop Blues 13m E3 5c *. C.Adam, P.Ebert. June 2006.
Climbs the arête right of Grasp the Nettle. Start as for Edge of Fear, where this route moves right continue straight up to gear and a rest below a small overlap. Step left and tackle the bulge with fingery moves (crux) right to the obvious hole. Continue straight up the arête boldly but more easily and over a final bulge to finish.

EDINBURGH AREA, Ratho Quarry:
Stupid Boy 20m E3 6a. I.Small. 19th June 2006.
The wall left of Sheer Fear. Climb a clean corner to a ledge, take a crack on the right to an inverted V feature. Undercut from this to the left, gaining a shallow groove, then a flake to reach a triangular ledge. Finish up the top groove of Sheer Fear.

EAST LOTHIAN, Traprain Law:
Sod Dangling 20m Hard Severe 4b *. F.Hughes. 1st May 2006.
Start up Dangle, but trend right following the slab to its top to where it becomes simple to pass the overlap. Trend leftwards towards a thread belay (in-situ tat).

MISCELLANEOUS NOTES

The W. H. Murray Literary Prize.

As a tribute to the late Bill Murray, whose mountain and environment writings have been an inspiration to many a budding mountaineer, the SMC have set up a modest writing prize, to be run through the pages of the Journal. The basic rules are set out below, and will be re-printed each year. The prize is run with a deadline, as is normal, of the end of January each year. So assuming you are reading this in early July, you have, for the next issue, six months in which to set the pencil, pen or word processor on fire.

The Rules:

1. There shall be a competition for the best entry on Scottish Mountaineering published in the *Scottish Mountaineering Club Journal.* The competition shall be called the 'W. H. Murray Literary Prize', hereafter called the 'Prize.'

2. The judging panel shall consist of, in the first instance, the following: The current Editor of the *SMC Journal;* The current President of the SMC; and two or three lay members, who may be drawn from the membership of the SMC. The lay members of the panel will sit for three years after which they will be replaced.

3. If, in the view of the panel, there is in any year no entries suitable for the Prize, then there shall be no award that year.

4. Entries shall be writing on the general theme of 'Scottish Mountaineering', and may be prose articles of up to approximately 5000 words in length, or shorter verse. Entries may be fictional.

5. Panel members may not enter for the competition during the period of their membership.

6. Entries must be of original, previously unpublished material. Entries should be submitted to the Editor of the *SMC Journal* before the end of January for consideration that year. Lengthy contributions are preferably word-processed and submitted either on 3.5" PC disk or sent via e-mail. (See Office Bearers page at end of this Journal for address etc.) Any contributor to the SMC Journal is entitled to exclude their material from consideration of the Prize and should so notify the Editor of this wish in advance.

7. The prize will be a cheque for the amount £250.

8. Contributors may make different submissions in different years.

9. The decision of the panel is final.

10. Any winning entry will be announced in the *SMC Journal* and will be published in the *SMC Journal* and on the SMC Web site. Thereafter, authors retain copyright.

The W. H. Murray Prize (2007)

THE winner of this year's W. H. Murray prize for his article *Bouldering With Ghosts* is first-time contributor John Watson.

Last year's winner, Guy Robertson, had this to say about the winning article: "This was quality mountaineering literature for the bouldering generation – beautifully crafted, vivid and inspirational. For me this piece, like all the best climbing writing, breaks down and even transcends ethical barriers, reminding us all, very neatly, why the people and the places are as vital as the rock itself."

President Paul Brian said: "Fantastic stuff, funny, stimulating and profound. The writer takes us through a wide range of emotional experiences in a very short article. The final passages are thought-provoking and poignant. Altogether a comprehensive, balanced and satisfying piece of writing."

John is clearly a writer out of the top drawer as evidenced by some of the reflective writing in what I would hesitate to call simply a guidebook *Stone Country – Bouldering in Scotland* which he published in 2005. There is a follow-up due out in October, *Stone Play – The Art of Bouldering* which I am sure will be of the same excellent standard.

John was run very close by Gavin Anderson with his tale of a fatal accident in the Northern Corries in the far off days of Jean's Hut. This, I feel, is probably of the 'Faction' genre in that the basis of it is undoubtedly true but the tale has been cleverly crafted to present much more than a simple prosaic account of events.

Ian Hamilton said: "A well-crafted and moving essay which any climber could relate to, the action taking place against a totally monochromatic background due to the combination of menace that is the Northern Corries in adverse conditions and the dank squalor of that least-loved of mountain bothies, Jean's Hut. Elation, sorrow and guilt are well balanced in this piece."

Paul Brian said: "Gripping and exciting writing with a serious purpose. Anyone who has been involved in a mountain tragedy will recognise the feelings experienced by the writer, though few of us have the skills to express them so clearly and with such sensitivity."

Other pieces which drew comment from the judges were Dennis Gray's excellent essay on Patey, *Last Of The Grand Old Masters* which only he could have written and which I feel is a welcome and insightful addition to the archives of the Club.

Past winner of this prize Peter Biggar, in his own inimitable style, gave us an excellent piece, *Untrodden Ways,* exploring what Ian Hamilton described as being "the age-old theme of the master/pupil relationship".

I'm afraid space precludes me from mentioning all the other fine entries that were considered. Congratulations again to John Watson and all who took part, and for all you other budding writers out there – there's always next year.

The winning article, as well as appearing in the Journal, will published on the club website.

Charlie Orr.

SCOTTISH WINTER NOTES 2006-2007

By Simon Richardson

Northern Highlands:

A HIGH pressure over Scandinavia sucking cold winds in from the North, is every winter climber's dream and when it happens in the second week of February after a major snowfall, you know you're in for something special. The Northern Highlands is the place to be in such weather, and this year, as the temperature dropped and conditions came good, several teams raced up to the North-west to put some long, sought-after projects into action.

In the flurry of routes climbed during a frantic week, the standout climb was perhaps the easiest. A winter ascent of *Marathon Ridge* on Beinn Lair had been in many climbers' sights for years, but the 18km. approach had put off all suitors to date. The 3km. long North Face rises up to 400m. in height, and is said to be the largest cliff of schist in Britain. Scattered along its length are a mere 20 summer climbs and the massive approach has kept the number of winter visits to a handful. It's not just remoteness that keeps the crowds away however, because the determining factor is that good winter conditions are rare. The crag is seamed with wet gullies and covered in vegetation, but with a cliff base at only 400m. and lying close to the sea, it is rarely in winter condition.

Dave McGimpsey, Dave Bell, Andy Nisbet and Mark Edwards got the conditions spot on when they walked into the mountain and picked the plum objective of *Marathon Ridge*, which is one of the longest, and most pronounced features on the face: "The line and location are amazing", Dave McGimpsey told me afterwards. "There were some good pitches, especially the wee fissure pitch on the top tower, but there was quite a lot of standard turf bashing too. We thought it was about III,4 – a small number perhaps, but for all of us it was one of our most memorable winter days."

There is enough new route potential on Beinn Lair to keep future generations happy for a long time to come. Unaware of the *Marathon Ridge* ascent, Iain Small and I battled in against a fierce easterly wind the next day, and found *Monster Munch*, a sustained six-pitch VI,6 up the well-defined chimney-groove on the right side of Molar Buttress.

A little farther north, An Teallach saw some attention. Gareth Hughes and Viv Scott were first on the scene and climbed the obvious line of *Crashed Out* (VII,7) up the curving ramp and chimney on the upper part of the wall overlooking *Hayfork Gully* in Glas Tholl. A couple of days later, Nisbet and Farmer went into Toll an Lochain and filled in an obvious blank by climbing the face left of *Opposition Couloir*. *The Upper House* (VI,6) involved some bold climbing leading to a well-protected technical crux.

Nearby, James Edwards, Ollie Metherell and Roger Webb made an exploratory visit to the south peak of Beinn Dearg Mor. This large cliff, which was probably last climbed by Sang and Morrison in summer 1899, is cut by a prominent gully line that leads up to a huge square cave: "The cave was huge," Roger said. "It was big enough to hide a house, but we managed to find an escape on the right that led into a continuation gully. We called it *Filly's Cave Route*, and it's an excellent V,6 that is surprisingly more than 400m." Beinn Dearg Mor is a difficult mountain to approach, with several awkward river crossings, and the 15-hour day was comparable to the Beinn Lair outings. This was particularly impressive as Edwards and Metherell had made the first ascent of *Finlay's Buttress* (V,7) on the Gleann Squaib cliffs on Beinn Dearg the day before.

Ian Parnell had an energetic visit up north and came away with two technically demanding routes. He teamed up with Guy Robertson intending to climb the icy line up the wall left of *Die Riesenwand* on Beinn Bhan. After two very difficult and devious pitches up steep mixed ground and thin ice, they reached the point where the original route traverses back left. The wall above was very steep and poorly protected, so they finished up the original route. Their Direct Start weighs in at a hefty VIII,9 and could possibly be completed to the top in exceptionally icy conditions. Most climbers would be content to rest on their laurels after a route like that, but next day Parnell visited Sgurr an Lochain in Glen Shiel with local guru Martin Moran who pointed him up the series of very steep off-width cracks right of *Flying Gully*. The result was the two-pitch long *The Beast and The Beast* (VIII,8), which was described as unremittingly hard and strenuous, and requires a double rack of monster cams.

Apart from this superb week, North-west activity was relatively quiet. Other notable ascents include the true left edge of *Skyscraper Buttress* at VI,7 by Guy Robertson and Pete Benson, and *Once Bitten, Twice Shy* (VI,6) a right-hand line up the buttress left of *Flying Gully* on Sgurr an Lochain in Glen Shiel by Martin Moran and Andy Nisbet. Otherwise it was the quartzite cliffs of Beinn Eighe that provided most of the action with the Nisbet/McGimpsey team prominent with three new routes, although pride of place went to the first winter ascent of *Olympus* (VII,8) on the Eastern Ramparts by Blair Fyffe and Martin Moran.

BMC International Winter Meet:

The winter season stepped into top gear during the International Winter Meet in February. These bi-annual meets have become established dates in the world mountaineering calendar. This year, 45 international guests from 22 countries teamed up with 30 UK hosts for six days of winter climbing based at Glenmore Lodge. Unfortunately, a major thaw set in a few days before the event began, and winter climbing conditions for the first two days were close to non-existent. Apologetic hosts led bewildered guests up wet rock in the Northern Corries and soggy ice on Ben Nevis, but fortunately, and against all the odds, the weather cooled down at the end of the second day and winter climbing was back on the agenda.

Most teams went to Ben Nevis on Day 3 and experienced crisp snow and ice on the classic routes and frosted rock on the mixed routes in Coire na Ciste. Es Tressider and Rok Zalokar from Slovenia made the second ascent of *Hobgoblin* (VI,7) on Number Three Gully Buttress, and added the more direct Rok Finish (VII,7) up the right edge of the upper wall. Just around the corner, Ian Parnell and Kristoffer Szilas from Denmark made the third ascent of *Babylon* (VII,8), swiftly followed by Freddie Wilkinson and Jon Varco from the US. Canadian mixed climbing ace, Sean Isaac, and I visited Braeriach, another sure-fire venue in lean conditions, where we found a good V,6 mixed route up the buttress between *The Waster* and *The Wanderer* in Corrie of the Chokestone Gully. The route was christened *Slovenian Death Water* after the potent brew that was being passed around the bar later that night.

It snowed heavily overnight, and next morning an Avalanche Category 5 warning was in place. Most people were happy to have an easier day nursing tired legs and hangovers, although a couple of teams succeeded on routes in Coire an t-Sneachda. The weather was kinder the following day, and many parties climbed in the Northern Corries, but the stage was set for a superb final day with a good weather forecast and plunging temperatures.

Again Ben Nevis was the venue of choice, and Coire na Ciste saw one of the most impressive displays of mixed climbing ever seen in Scotland. The pace was breathtaking. Steve Ashworth and Nils Nielsen from Norway climbed the 1990s test-piece *Darth Vader* (VII,8), followed by *The Sorcerer* (VII,8), a new line up the front face of the Lost The Place Buttress, before racing up *Thompson's Route* (IV,4) to warm down! Fellow Norwegian Bjorn Artun and Tim Blakemore had a similarly impressive day with *Albatross* (VI,5), one of the most prized routes on Indicator Wall, followed by *Darth Vader*. Nearby, Stu McAleese and Tomaz Jakofcic from Slovenia climbed *Cornucopia* (VII.9), and Es Tressider and Paul Sab from Germany made an ascent of *Stringfellow* (VI,6).

Two big ascents took place on Number Three Gully Buttress. Ian Parnell and Sean Isaac climbed a line based on the summer HVS *Last Stand*, which takes the blunt arête between *Knuckleduster* and *Sioux Wall*. Parnell has made this part of Nevis his own after the second ascent of *Arthur* a couple of seasons ago and the first winter ascent of *Sioux Wall* last year. This knowledge proved vital in putting together the intricate line of *Curly's Arête* (VIII,8). Just to the right, Freddie Wilkinson and Rok Zalokar made the third ascent of *Sioux Wall* (VIII,8) taking in the final difficult pitch added by Andy Turner on the second ascent, last January.

Next door, Viv Scott and Domagoj Bojko from Croatia climbed the hanging chimney just left of the icicle of *South Sea Bubble*. The route starts up the lower ramp of *South Sea Bubble* and continues up a hidden slot to reach the upper snow funnel: "It's the hardest thing I've ever led," Viv said. "The protection was really poor and holds kept snapping under my feet but the position was really exciting!" *Salva Mea* (VIII,8) is a worthy addition to the half-dozen mixed test-pieces that lie at the left end of Creag Coire na Ciste.

Across on The Comb, Dave MacLeod and Hiroyoshi Manome and Katsutaka Yokoyama from Japan climbed *Isami* (VIII,8), the conspicuous hanging groove to the left of *The Good Groove*. This had been stared at longingly by several teams over the years waiting for the requisite amount of ice, but Macleod solved this problem by climbing it as a thin mixed climb. Also on The Comb, Toby Keep and Kristoffer Szilas made the second ascent of *Lost Souls* (VI,6) and added a new Direct Finish (VII,7), which takes the prominent slot avoided by the original route.

Three new Scottish Grade VIIIs climbed the same day in the same corrie is unprecedented, and says everything for the immaculate mixed climbing conditions that day, and the enthusiasm and skill of the guests and hosts. It was especially pleasing that the Scottish mountains put on such a good show on the final day of the meet, and everyone went home with huge smiles: "Mixed conditions on the Ben were outstanding," Ian Parnell enthused afterwards. "They were perhaps the best I've seen. The BMC winter meet was a superb advert for the chase, both frustrating and rewarding, for the fickle and elusive proper Scottish conditions."

Cairngorms:
The most difficult ascent of the season took place in early March when Guy Robertson and Rich Cross made the first winter ascent of *The Scent* (IX,9) on

Beinn a' Bhuird. The pair had tried this summer HVS two weeks previously but failed at the base of the 'awkward ramp' mentioned in the guidebook, and gingerly abseiled off a number of poorly equalised pieces.

Robertson said: "On the second attempt I sorted my rope work out a bit better. I simply clipped the poor belay as a runner. As predicted, the ramp was indeed hard – very precarious, blind and rounded seams – and it didn't yield any pro at all for maybe 20ft. or so, when I placed a hook in some turf. I'm not really one for big grades, but this is certainly among the most committing bits of climbing I've done. In retrospect it was pretty difficult to justify, so it's well protected crack lines for me from now on! It's a bit of a shame about the boldness in some ways as it's genuinely a really nice, cunning line up an impressive buttress in a wonderful setting."

The most impressive new addition in the Northern Cairngorms was *Rumpeltstiltskin* (VII,8) by Iain Small and Andy Turner. This sustained three-pitch outing cuts across *Poison Dwarf* on Carn Etchachan, and has a spectacular and difficult middle pitch. Next door on the Shelter Stone, James Edwards and Paul Warnock found *Lectern* (VII,8), the steep corner on the left side of *Pinnacle Gully*.

Some good pioneering activity took place deeper in the Cairngorms. Guy Robertson and Es Tressider made a fruitful trip into Coire na Ciche on Beinn a' Bhuird where they made a winter ascent of *Hot Toddy*. Guy had previously climbed the lower part of the route with Jason Currie before finding an easier finish, but this time he returned to make a complete ascent of the summer line at VII,8. Pete Benson and Ross Hewitt were also in the corrie that day making the second ascent of *The Watchtower* (VI,6), the imposing buttress above *Twisting Gully*.

The remote Coire Sputan Dearg on Ben Macdui saw a number of visits and several new routes were climbed. Roger Webb and I probably got the pick of the bunch with first ascents of *Rough Diamond* (V,7) the line of steep strenuous cracks on the left end of Grey Man's Crag, and *Little Gem* (V,6), the well-defined V-shaped buttress nestling between the branches of Y Gully. In late February, Andy Nisbet and Mark Edwards took advantage of icy conditions on the high cliffs, with the first ascent of *East of Eden* (VI,5) in Coire Bhrochain on Braeriach. This takes a groove-line midway between *West Wall Route* and the obvious chimney line taken by *The Lampie*. Nisbet also climbed *Big Foot* (V,5) with Dave McGimpsey, which takes the rib right of *The White Hotel* in Corrie of the Chokestone Gully.

Lochnagar also saw some good, early-season activity, although the mountain failed to catch much snow through the season, and conditions were generally lean. Es Tressider and Viv Scott had a great find on the headwall of Eagle Buttress.

Es said: "We went to repeat *Where Eagles Dare*, but we ended up doing the right arête of the wall instead, as it looked superb. It was great climbing, quite funky and hard to figure out at first, with a burly torque flake farther up"

State of Independence (VII,8) is an excellent addition to this exposed part of the mountain that comes into condition rapidly after a north-westerly blast. In the Southern Sector, James Edwards and I climbed *Ghost Dance* (V,6), the pillar at the left end of *The Cathedral* and *Starlight and Storm*(V,5) up right edge of *The Sentinel*.

Central Highlands:
There were three superb additions to the Central Highlands. High up on Bidean's Church Door Buttress, Iain Small and Blair Fyffe found the superb *Knight's Templar* (VII,8), which takes the left side of the prow of *Dark Mass* and finishes directly up the headwall.

Iain said: "Conditions were excellent. The cracks were very icy and there were a couple of really steep sections. My arms were still aching three days afterwards." Across on Stob Coire an Laoigh , Ed Edwards, Dave McGimpsey and Andy Nisbet climbed the sensationally steep *Some Like it Hot* (VII,7). This takes the right-facing corner in the steep wall between *Jammy Dodger* and *Serve Chilled* and is similar in standard and quality to *Central Grooves* in Stob Coire nan Lochain. A few weeks later, Nisbet and Edwards returned to add *White Heat* (VI,7) which takes the corner right of *Some Like it Hot* before being forced onto the exposed right arête.

A winter ascent of *Stalking Horse* on Raw Egg Buttress on Aonach Beag has been on climbers' lists for some time. I tried the line 15 years ago with Roger Everett, but we made little progress, and were completely baffled by the off-width entry crack and fazed by the overhangs looming above. Rich Cross climbed the off-width pitch several years ago but finished up *Salmonella*, and the complete ascent fell in January to Andy Turner and Dave Hollinger who graded it a modest VI,7. Dave said: "The wide crack proved to be the crux, but those adept in successive can-opener moves should not find it too taxing."

Ben Nevis:
The continuous run of storms in early January was good news for Ben Nevis. As soon as the temperatures dropped, the Ben started oozing ice and many of the mountain's great climbs came into outstanding condition. On the Little Brenva Face, Iain Small and I climbed the broad rib between *Slalom* and *Frostbite* and then continued up the very steep headwall to the right of the icefall of *Super G*. We were expecting difficult mixed climbing, but instead we found the wall was covered in a layer of squeaky plastic ice. The next day it thawed, and *Wall of the Winds* (VI,5) collapsed as quickly as it had appeared.

Big news on the Ben was the first winter ascent of *The Knuckleduster* on the front face of Number Three Gully Buttress. This summer HVS was first climbed by Jimmy Marshall and his brother, Ronnie, in 1966, and had been admired by climbers for several years as a futuristic winter possibility. It came a step nearer to reality when Ian Parnell and Ollie Metherell made the first winter ascent of the nearby *Sioux Wall* (VIII,8) last season. The *Knuckleduster* was clearly going to be a harder proposition, so it was no surprise when it was snapped up by Steve Ashworth and Blair Fyffe. Ashworth is well known for his series of very difficult Lake District routes and Fyffe has had an excellent season with a string of good new routes from Glen Coe to the North-west. They graded the route VIII,9 and Ashworth said it was harder than *Unicorn* in Glen Coe. A few weeks later, Dave MacLeod and visiting US climber, Alicia Hudelson, made the first winter ascent of *Steam Train* at VI,7, a steep HVS on North-East Buttress that has seen very few summer ascents.

In late March, a high-pressure system centred over Scandinavia sucking in cool easterly winds. This is the weather scenario that ice climbers drool over, because the clear skies and frosty nights coupled with warm daytime temperatures are perfect for building ice on the higher Ben Nevis routes. Teams were quick to take advantage of the superb conditions with ascents of *Sickle, Orion Direct* and *Astral Highway*. It was quickly realised that the ice conditions were very special indeed, and some of the Ben's most highly prized thin face routes such as *Riders on the Storm* on Indicator Wall and *The Great Glen* on Gardyloo Buttress saw ascents. The quality of the soft plastic ice was fantastic, with first time placements that gripped axe picks and front points like glue.

Andy Nisbet and Ed Edwards were first on the spot to take advantage of the new route potential with the first ascent of *Unleashed* (VII,6), the steep undercut ice smear to the left of *Vulture* on Number Three Gully Buttress. A little to the right, Roger Webb and I climbed *Wall Street* (VII,7), the ramp and steep mixed groove right of *South Sea Bubble* leading to a hanging ice tongue.

The next day the action centred on Indicator Wall when Iain Small and Blair Fyffe made a very early repeat of the much-prized *Stormy Petrel* (VII,6), taking a more direct variation up a thinly iced groove in the centre of the route. Before setting off, Fyffe tipped off Ian Parnell and Viv Scott that there was a direct start to his route The *Rhyme of the Ancient Mariner* still waiting to be done. Parnell quickly despatched this difficult VII,7 variation that avoided the cunning detour on the original line, and then continued up the original line to make the second ascent. Next day, Andy Benson, Rich Cross and Dave Hollinger repeated Parnell and Scott's direct line and confirmed its superb quality. With three difficult pitches straight up the centre of the wall this is one of the great modern mixed climbs on the mountain. The following day, fresh from his success on *Stormy Petrell,* Iain Small teamed up with me to climb the left rib of *Albatross. Arctic Tern* (VII,5) starts just left of *Albatross*, passes the smooth slab of *Fascist Groove* before climbing a spectacular tiered ramp system and finishing up the upper rib. Small compared it in difficulty to *Stormy Petrell* but said it was not as sustained. It was repeated two days later by Graeme Ettle, Pete MacPherson and Jonathan Preston.

Iain and I visited Indicator Wall again on Sunday, April 1, where we climbed *Ship of Fools* (VIII,7), the pillar between *Riders on the Storm* and *Albatross*. After the introductory rib, this takes the very narrow sinuous groove right of *Riders* to bypass the huge roof in the lower section of the pillar. It then continues up the crest of the pillar via difficult mixed to finish up the vertical ice arête left of the exit gully of *Le Nid d'Aigle*. Iain's lead of the second pitch pulling through overlapping slabs on discontinuous hollow one centimetre-thick ice was one of the finest leads I have witnessed. The pitch collapsed behind me as I climbed it, so this one will have to wait for another season with exceptional ice conditions high on the Ben to see a repeat.

SUMMER NOTES – 2006

By Dave Cuthbertson

LOOKING back over the rock climbing year, and given the generally good weather, there's not a great deal to report where the mountains are concerned. This neglect of the higher crags has been much talked about in recent years (a common tale elsewhere in the UK), and to some extent does concern my prickly little mind.

The consequences are clear to see, dirty climbs being a most common complaint, though, I personally feel this is a reflection of a softer, cleaner society. And there's also a general feeling of quietude in areas where one might have queued to climb in the 1970s and 1980s. Much more worrying is a shift in attitude. A – why bother, when you can go to the wall, go bouldering, or take a cheap flight to sun-scorched venues abroad – approach. Diminishing dirt thresholds aside, my worry is that attitudes without soul or passion will evolve, which may affect climbing in different ways. There have already been attempts to control adventure in the outdoors, the consequences of which could be disastrous, indiscriminate bolting being just one example. I might have been a cog in a wheel that set this whole thing in motion, but at least I care about our heritage. Time will tell. I do feel it's a shame because it never ceases to amaze me just how good, how utterly unique and how rich an experience, climbing on many of the Scottish mountain crags can be.

In a recent conversation with the well-known Lakes activist, Dave Birkett (who incidentally has been visiting the Scottish crags for some years), Dave said that he was completely gob-smacked by a recent trip to Creag an Dubh Loch. This was his first visit. He climbed *The Ascent of Man* (E5) and although it was a little bit dirty, he thought it was brilliant and added that with all the recent developments taking place in the Scottish Highlands there's nearly always somewhere to go if the weather is unsettled.

Anyway enough ranting for now. Rather than detail every event that's taken place over the year, this report more or less highlights a selection of the best and most interesting climbs and achievements. As ever, more details of these and other Scottish climbs can be found in the *New Climbs* section of this Journal. My apologies if I've omitted your finest hour.

THE CAIRNGORMS:

In typically Pateyesque fashion, Julian Lines has contributed a cluster of new routes on the remote crags of Ben MacDui's Coire Sputan Dearg. Julian couldn't have found a more remote venue to court some death-defying experiences, but one has to praise his individualistic sense of adventure – something of a novelty amid today's fashion-conscious trends. To the left of *Sundance* there is a green east-facing slab. This provided a triptych of single pitches, all of which were climbed on-sight and described as worthwhile solos! *Rooibos* (E5 6b) takes a line of blind runnels up the left edge and is said to be bold and absorbing. *Echinacea* (E4 6a/b) challenges the centre of the slab with some 'thin' moves and a bold upper section, while the right-hand line, *Ginseng* (E4 6c) required 'heinous scratching' to reach the sanctuary of a diagonal crease and thus completing an unfinished project from 10 years ago. Julian's unquestionable slab-climbing ability would suggest that these climbs come complete with a government health warning. The centre of the lower tier is dominated by an impressive arête which presented something of a dilemma for Jules who was determined to climb the line on-sight. After two previous attempts, he even considered returning in winter when the evil landing would at least be buried under snow. But in the end he was resigned to a brief inspection on abseil. *Ataraxia* (E6 6a/b) was the outcome and described by Jules as, "Bold but technically straight-forward". On Terminal Buttress (appropriately named on this occasion) *Romontado* (E6 6a) accepts the 'stunning' challenge of the blind crack in the wall left of *Chute*. Climbed on-sight and solo the ascent is described as, "ultra serious and only for those with a death wish". Readers will be pleased to know that Jules has not been sectioned, is alive and well and was last seen enjoying a solitary existence on a North Sea oil rig. On the summit tor of Beinn Mheadhoin *Silkworm* (E3 5c) follows an obvious quartz seam on the West Face while *Classic Crack* (HVS 5a) takes the superb and obvious crackline. Both routes were soloed by Julian.

Every now and then a new kid on the block enters into the Scottish climbing arena. While we generally want to be supportive and err on the side of giving benefit of the doubt, Malcolm Kent's achievements for this year, not just in Scotland but globally, are almost beyond belief. One of his more moderate claims is an ascent of *Origin of The Species* on the Dubh Loch's superb Central Gully Wall. This would make the third known ascent, Julian Lines having made the second a few years ago.

Shelter Stone Crag:
Defenders of the Faith – Ian Small and Tess Fryer, climbed an interesting new line running the full height of *The Bastion*. The route weaves around *The Needle*, sourcing some new pitches on the way but savours its best for the final headwall, which climbs thin cracks and the characteristic pink streak right of *The Needle*. Ian had attempted the line previously but the bold nature of the climbing and dirty rock got the better of him on that occasion. Climbing on-sight Ian returned and armed with an array of small cams, he successfully completed the exposed and intricate top wall to give *The Camel* (E5 6a).

Braeriach:
The unseasonably warm autumn found Andy Nisbet and Jonathan Preston high up on Garbh Choire Dhaidh where they made the first ascent of *Wombat* (VS). The same team also climbed Koala (an existing VS) which they thought to be excellent.

Coire an t'Sneachda:
On the Mess of Potage, Nisbet with Keith Haldane added *Crackpot* (S), which is said to be a fine route thanks to the cleansing process of numerous winter ascents. On Aladdin's Buttress, Nisbet and Preston discovered *Witchcraft* (E2 5b), the result of having inadvertently abseiled the line while descending from *Magic Crack*. Not untypical for these parts, they very narrowly beat Ian Peter and Alan Fyffe who also had designs on the same route.

Coire an Lochain:
Cardiac Arête (HVS) is a worthy addition to Number 1 Buttress. Having spotted the line some years ago, Nisbet remembered that is wasn't until he received a route description for the new winter climb, *Open Heart*, that he realised that there was a way round a line of baffling overhangs guarding the exit to the arête.

NORTHERN HIGHLANDS NORTH:
Most activity has been in the development of the coastal fringes rather than in the mountains. In the far north at Whiten Head, Ross Jones and Rob Reginski added

a companion to the Original Route on Stac Thormaid with *Run-Diomhair* (HVS 4c). This starts up a chimney to the left of the seaward face and involves some bold climbing. Jones reports that despite the original route remaining unreported, it is a fine stack deserving more ascents given its easy access, situation and climbing. Apparently, Mick Tighe and party climbed it in 1993 which is thought to have been the second ascent. Sounds like a must-do for anyone embarking on a Scottish sea stack quest.

At Melvich, Lady Bighouse Rock, Jones this time with Matt Dent climbed a fine 25m. precariously perched stack with *When the Big Lady Sings* (HVS 4c). This starts at a corner on the east face before gaining the landward (south) face to access the top. An abseil followed by a 15m. swim is required on the approach. Jones this time alternating company with John Sanders and Dent accounts for a cluster of new routes at Red Point (reference SMC Northern Highlands North guidebook, p.345), with grades ranging between VDiff and E1.

Tarbert Sea Cliffs:
Steve Kennedy and Bob Hamilton (occasionally joined by Dave McGimpsey and Andy MacDonald) have revisited the gneiss sea cliffs near Scourie. At the Balmy Slabs area – *Violator* (E1 5b) provides a sustained route on the steep wall left of *The Boardmaster* (a steep and well protected E2 (from 2005) which is said to be superb. *Captain Hook* (HVS 4c) – the slab forming the left wall of the deep chimney of *Black Tidings*. Dolphin Crag – *Inshallah* (E1 5b) takes a line up the slabs directly below a 'suicidal downward pointing flake', stepping gingerly onto it before the finish (attempts to remove the flake on abseil were unsuccessful and it is perhaps more solid than was initially thought). *Last Train to Somerville* (E1 5b) takes the slab mid-way between *Meal for a Seal* and *Central Crack*, while *Sneak Preview* (E1 5b) climbs through the jagged overlap left of the former with a thin slab to finish and finally *Solitary Man* (E1 5b) takes a thin crack through a bulge to slab left of *Sneak Preview*.

Rhue:
Having recently entered into the realms of becoming one of the 'older guard', Ian Taylor would appear to have rediscovered hard (or should it be harder, as Ian is no slouch on the rock), with the advent of head-pointing, and why not? Adopting this approach Ian dispensed with a fine new E6 called *Kanga Rhue* (E6 6b) and competing with Rab Anderson for the most cringe worthy route names. This takes the wall and crack to the left of *Rhue Mania*. The latter was climbed with Tess Fryer at E4 6a and follows the steep sculpted wall round to the left of *Cats Whisker*.

Julian Lines added a little gem of a deep water solo by climbing a direct on Tim Rankin's, *How Now Brown Prow* (E2), with spectacular moves through the jutting prow to give *Gung Ho* at E4 5c/6a.

Ardmair:
On Monster Buttress, Ian and Tess dispensed with *Soor Plums* (E5 6a) which follows the thin crack and technical right arête of *Summer Isles City*. Another aspiring oldie, Andy Cunningham has also embraced modern trends to complete a long-term project left of Big Foot at E5 6a.

Reiff:

Stone Pig Cliff

Ian Small and Tess Fyer have added a new line to the left end of this steep wall. Unnamed as yet, the route is E5 6a and more than 20m. long which is pretty big by Reiff standards. The upper wall provides the crux and is described by Ian as a bit 'goey' and run-out but safe.

Rockers Cliff

Ian Small and Ian Taylor have repeated two of Gary Latter's routes here. *Cullach* and *Headlong* (both graded E4 in the guidebook but one was supposedly E5). Small remarked that the E4 (which ever one that is) was 'pokey and worrying', while Taylor who climbed the E5 thought it to be good with better protection. Both of these are thought to be second ascents.

In his quest to find a DWS nirvana, Julian Lines has been putting his recently acquired inflatable dingy to good use, exploring the Rubha Coigeach peninsula. The discovery of the Baby Tiapan Wall has yielded more than a dozen lines – half of which are current projects. The remainder are in the French 6b to 6c category and should be within the grasp of many, assuming you can cope with the long and rough approach. This superb wall (which has been known about for some time) is 15m. high and overhangs by 20°. Aspiring deep water soloists will be pleased to learn that the main difficulties of the routes centre round the lower portion. All the climbs have been nicely documented for Mike Robertson's forth coming DWS guide to the UK (due out later this year). To provide a flavour, here are a couple of descriptions.

Land of Milk and Honey (6b, 30m) – the perfect traverse is tackled with a sequence of jams and stamina. Can be reversed... amazing. *Cyber Pimp,* (6c, 15m.) The fine crackline runs out of a shield, forge past this with vigour, take a rest under the roof and a choice of finishes which includes jumping if it tickles your fancy.

NORTHERN HIGHLANDS CENTRAL:

Beinn Eighe – Far East Buttress

Body Swerve (90m, E4 4c,6a,5b), starts up *Body Heat* before taking to the wall on the right with some bold climbing and was the work of Ian Taylor and Tess Fryer.

Rubha Reidh

Ross Jones and Matt Dent climbed A'Staca Beag with *Silent Wisdom* (HVS 5a) – a short route on the arch of the landward face, while the south face of A'Staca Eilean an Air, yielded a 15m. Hard Severe 4a requiring a simultaneous abseil for descent.

Caithness

Despite nearing maturity the superb cliffs of Latheronwheel and Mid Clyth continue to yield routes of surprising quality at a reasonable grade (Hard Severe to E2), courtesy of Ross Jones and John Sanders. And as ever, locals, Raymond Wallace and Rob Christie have been busy exploring previously untouched stretches of coastline in this area. These two venues together with Occumster and Sarclet offer some of the best low-to-mid grade one pitch climbs, as good as any in Scotland. Each has its own distinct character and style with Latheronwheel being a popular VS venue. For those interested there is also potential for quality, hard new routes in this area. In the Latheronwheel area, Cleit Mor (40m, HVS) is the largest of three stacks and was climbed by Jones via its south face in two pitches of 4c. No evidence was found of a previous ascent though the local farmer had witnessed repeats of Cleit Beag and Cleit Ruadh which were previously climbed by Mick Fowler and party in 1989.

Glen Nevis
On Whale Rock, Dave MacLeod's super crimpfest, *Hold Fast* has been repeated by Dave Birkett, though only after side runners were placed in adjacent routes. The grade of E9 7a reflects the more or less protectionless lead required. But on Birkett's ascent a hold broke and he subsequently fell onto the runners which cushioned his fall, preventing a deck-out. While this is a great effort on Birkett's behalf, the question of side runners used in outcrop climbing has always been a contentious issue. It will be interesting to know a projected grade that includes the 'baby bounce'.

Dumbarton Rock
Alan Cassidy reports of a sport-style ascent of *Requiem,* which brings the known total to six (the second, third, fourth and fifth ascents going to John Dunne, Paul Laughlan, Dave MacLeod and Spider MacKenzie). Alan returned to lead the route placing the gear and is probably the first climber to do so.

Quad Rocks
Kevin Shields has been on a mission here adding another two technical problems with *Point Proven* (E3 6b) and *The Calling* (E2 6b). Both of these were worked then soloed.

SKYE:
The Cullin
On The Bhastair Tooth, Es Tresidder and Blair Fyffe have climbed a logical direct start and finish to *Rainbow Warrior* to produce a much-improved superb pitch at E4 6a. Julian Lines confirms his on-sight solo link-up on the East Buttress of Coire Laggan at E3 5c,5b. The route named *Diura* is said to offer a combination of the best climbing on the crag.

Marsco: South West Buttress
Bob Hamilton and Steve Kennedy have climbed a fine and well protected prominent crackline to give *The Yellow Jersey* (E1 5a) – but aren't all Bob and Steve's routes E1.

LEWIS:
In recent years it would be fair to say that rock climbing on Lewis and Harris has been overshadowed by the Pabbay and Mingulay boom. But for me the former has always been my preferred choice. While there's no doubting the quality and grandeur of climbing in these islands, the beauty of Lewis and Harris is the combination of both mountain and sea cliff. When the weather is bad there's usually somewhere to go, and without the additional Robinson Crusoe syndrome of being marooned on a small island.

A new Skye and Hebrides guidebook in the pipeline has rekindled a pulse of activity among some Lewis aficionados with a number of different groups contributing to the sea cliffs of the west coast. Sadly, it would appear that the magnificent Sron Ulladale and Creag Dubh Dibadale remain virtually neglected. The Sron is remarkable and undoubtedly one of the UK's finest crags. An area transformed by Crispin Waddy and friends in the 1990s. Though Crispin climbed many of the best remaining lines, there is still potential for high quality, challenging new routes.

Uig Sea Cliffs
Visitors, but no strangers to the Scottish scene, Paul Donnithorne and Emma Alsford have been developing an area north of The Painted Wall called Torasgeo. Half-a-dozen routes (up to three pitches in length) between HVS and E3 have been climbed. These include a four and three star E1 and a three star E3. An Aberdonian team also got in on the action repeating routes and adding a few of their own. Rob Durren and party repeated Garthwaite and Anderson's *Puffing Crack* (E4 6a) confirming its grade and superb quality. Rab and Chris Anderson as usual spent their annual holiday on Lewis and despite mixed weather, still mananged to come away with a respectable quarry of 20 first ascents. With the new guidebook in the making however, Rab – surprise, surprise is reluctant to disclose the whereabouts of his new venues until all the deeds are done. Meanwhile, Mick Tighe continues to explore stretches of untouched coastline, some of it apparently of high quality but remains as elusive as ever.

Beannan a Deas
Inland from the Uig area on the south side of this hill, Kevin Neil and Adam Van Lon Lopik have discovered a small, quick drying venue of quality gneiss. The pair climbed half-a-dozen lines ranging between VS and E3 with *Commitment* at E3 5c getting four stars. Though missing out on the discovery of this crag, Rab Anderson was quick in with a second ascent of *Commitment* (suggesting E2) and adding a couple of routes of his own.

THE BARRA ISLES:
Mingulay and Pabbay have potentially received more attention than just about any other crag in Scotland (especially in areas at E2 and above). While the majority of visitors are content to repeat existing climbs, new route activists are on the whole very guarded and secretive regarding their projects. Keeping abreast of new developments therefore is no easy task. Kevin Howett, for example, accounts for 350 new routes on these islands out of a possible 800. Annoyingly, these haven't been officially written up outwith Kev's little black book. So don't be too disappointed if your prized first ascent has already been climbed. But I have my spies Mr Howett. Two Pabbay fishermen just happen to enjoy the occasional climbing holiday with guides in the Alps – it's a small world. But fisherman certainly know these cliff-girt islands. They have to because they drop lobster pots next to them and occasionally they see climbers, such as those noted on the cliffs of Barra – all food for thought.

Pabbay
On The Banded Wall (formerly Banded Geo) Gary Latter and Andy Lole have discovered around eight climbs between VS and E2. The majority of these are located farther south beyond a broken sector where a prominent wide ledge situated at half-height divides a fine, smooth lower wall. Of those that stand out, *Posture Jedi* (E2 5c) and *Run Dafti Run* are said to be excellent. On the South Face, Carl Pulley and Mike Mortimer added three new routes between HVS and E2, and

another by Gary Latter. I'll refrain from highlighting all the various route names which were inspired by a certain young Edinburgh lady, also on Pabbay on a climbing holiday. *Off Wid Emilys Bikini* (E2 5b) sets the scene and is obviously a reference to an off-width chimney up which the climb finishes.

MINGULAY:
Guersay Mor – Cobweb Wall
Situated towards the south east end of the Undercut Wall, Latter and Lole unravelled *Bikini Dreams* (E3 5c,5c,4a). This is a fine addition and follows a line of flakes and grooves via a pegmatite ramp before tackling the upper wall directly.

SANDRAY:
There has been a number of hush-hush trips to this island that date back to the late 1990s. The usual suspects, Grahame Little and Kev Howett were at the forefront of those early developments, and a then young up-and-coming Gordon Lennox. Last year, Lennox and Craig Adam added several fine routes to Creag Mhor – a long cliff of 30m. in height and located on the west side of the south west tip of the island. Climbs range between E1 and E6, but this is really a place for those operating at E3 and above. The most outstanding venture by this pair in 2005 is a four star, wildly steep and aptly named route called *Orang-utan* (E6 5b,6b,5c). But another 10 or so routes were added and at least four of these are three star E4s and 5s. This year saw two teams comprising Ian Small and Tess Fyer, and Alastair Robertson and Johnny Clark who added several routes to La Louvre. La Louvre is one of three small cliffs known as The Galleries, the others are fittingly named The Burrell and Tate. A feature of the climbing here is their quality which has been described as perfect.

La Louvre
Pointillist (E3 5c) takes the line of a discontinuous crack to the left of *First Impressions* while *Art for Arts Sake* (E4 6a) follows a thin crack right of *Dot to Dot*. *Crazy Horse* (E5 6a) – the arête left of *Tormented Textures* via some highly sculpted rock. *Line of Beauty* (E4 6a) is a rising traverse starting at the base of Pointillist and climbing via a quartz blotch, crossing *Tormented Textures* and described as gorgeous.

The Burrell
Life Begins… (E5 6a,6a) is a counter diagonal to *Pastiche,* starting on a sea level ledge below the leftmost black groove and finishing up a hanging corner of right edge. The route has been described as a magnificent line with committing hard moves on the first pitch.

   A contender for one of the best routes of the season in the Hebrides goes to Steve Crow and Karin Magog's *K&S Special* (formerly Firewall) on Creag Dearg Mingulay. The renaming of the climb is a reflection of their shared experiences which started with *The Scream* (E7 6b) back in 2000. But Steve always had designs on a new line in this area and promised himself that he would return to the fray. After a brief inspection on abseil, Steve found himself powering out some 30m. up the line. In a last ditch attempt to keep things clean he started reversing to the sanctuary of the belay but unfortunately failed to make it by one move. Exhausted he handed over the lead to Karin who, climbing on Steve's beta alone, was able to top out. It was a great effort. However, there was a nagging formality to address and, of course, Steve wanted to lead the route placing all the gear. Two days later he did just that and the climb was done. A monster 58m. pitch with a 5c mantle to top it all off. The climb is E6 6a and well protected, although a bit of scouring to find placements is required. Steve regards the climb as one that he is most proud of.

ORKNEY:

Yesnaby

Tim Rankin and Neil Morrison have picked up the pieces from last year and added yet another cluster of high-quality climbs to this small, but attractive venue. It's worth noting that not all the climbs in this area are in the upper echelons and grades vary between E1 and E6, with some even easier climbs nearby. *The Orkney Session* (E5 6b) takes the fine wall between *Ebb Tide* and *Gardyloo Gold* and was climbed on-sight with Tim in the lead. *Dragonhead* (E6 6b) has been described by Tim as 'stunning' and among the very best of its type and grade in the country. The climb links cracks in the wall left of *Skullsplitter Groove* and required a wee bit of practise before it was lead. *Lost in the Desert* (E1 5b) is the result of a failed attempt on the fine crack in the pillar of *One Winter's Day*, up which this route finishes. *Peedi Breeks* (E4 6b) is a short but tough excursion with fiddly pro on the wall between *Up Tae High Doh* and *The Cog*.

For those of you unfamiliar to this part of Orkney, Yesnaby is home to a very fine sea stack graded E1 (by the normal route), and also features a Fowler creation (E3 6a) which follows a fine crack on the seaward face. This is a lovely stretch of coastline with potential for some interesting new climbs and well worth a visit, either in its own right or in combination with a trip to The Old Man of Hoy or Rora Head.

SHETLAND:

Rock climbing in the Shetlands is rapidly becoming a must-do alternative to the Barra Isles and is easier to get to (by air at least). There is a good-grade spread and the climbs of Esha Ness are considered to be of truly outstanding quality, ranking with the best anywhere in the UK according to Gary Latter. Gary said that climbing on Esha Ness and Da Navir alone is enough to justify the considerable expense in getting there. There are also numerous outlying islands that offer plenty of alternative sea cliff and stack adventure. The island of Fowla for example with it huge red sandstone walls which are as high as any in Britain.

In late May, early June, Ross Jones enjoyed a productive fortnight completing 40 new routes. Of adventurous slant, Ross covered a lot of ground, exploring a variety of different venues. On Saint Ninian's Isle and climbing with Simon Calvin, he christened Loose Head Stack with *The Cheesegrater* (VS 4b). On the Prophecy Wall of the Faither headland he climbed *The Oracle* with John Sanders. This takes the left arête by some bold initial moves. *The Faither Prophecy* (E1 5b) is said to be outstanding and follows a slanting line of weakness through hanging roofs up the wall. Ross and friends account for several more routes in the immediate area. The climbs of Lunning Head located at Lunnastin have been described as a venue best reserved for a day when the west coast is subjected to high seas, being short, sheltered and on good quality gneiss. Jones, climbing at times with Peter Sawford and Paul Whitworth, climbed all in all approximately ten routes ranging in difficulty between V. Diff and E1.

On Ronas Voe, Hollinders Crag (low crag in the SMCJ) is a granite outcrop set back from the sea. As with the majority of crags already described in this area, most of the development is attributed to a small number of both local and visiting climbers. Sanders and Whitworth together with Ross Jones added fourteen routes varying between V. Diff and E1.

Ronas Hill Crags
These granite outcrops are located a few miles north of Ronas Hill in the area of Hevdale Water. Currently, there are somewhere in the region of 40 routes. The climbs are short, up to 10m. and range in difficulty between V. Diff and E2, most of which are the work of Paul and Al Whitworth with Sawford and Jones contributing half a dozen routes between Severe and E1.

So there you have it – get yourself up there!

SPORT CLIMBING:
In the Gairloch area, Paul Tattersall has been developing a small, but pleasant, sport climbing venue named Grass Crag. Not the most inspiring name but apparently worthwhile, with an all important sunny aspect. Climbs range in difficulty between 5+ and 7a, with the best around 6a-6b+. Creag Nan Luch has proved to be a great success, with the lower tier especially receiving traffic. There are a dozen or so climbs on this sector, up to 20m. long and between 6a+ and 7b+. The Upper Tier is a bit more hardcore with several climbs at around 7c'ish. Work is still in progress here so I'm sure we'll be hearing more about their development soon. As a winter playground, Am Fasgadh is definitely one to earmark. The Central Wall remains permadry and, coupled with a sheltered southerly aspect, climbing just about all year round is possible. The best routes here are between 7a+ and 7c+ though a newly developed sector has yielded a crop of easier routes. These venues are worth bearing in mind when in the north-west and are between 45 and 65 minutes drive south of Ullapool. For more information, visit 'Wild West Topos' website.

On a different note, a recent conversation with Paul revealed that he was saddened by the clinical response of some climbers who it would seem have a sweet disregard for the creator of sport climbing venues. I can empathise with Paul. But we have to bare in mind that climbers as a generalisation can be notoriously selfish. I don't think it's always in our nature to stop and spare a thought for the visionary or creative mind responsible for these venues, not to mention the sheer hard work involved. That goes for trad. too. And don't expect a pat on the back either. The only feedback you're likely to receive is that the bolts are too far apart!

So how important is the creator of a venue versus the first ascentionist. Elitist that I am, ground–breaking first ascents obviously deserve recognition. (But then again one person's 5+ is another person's 8c). I suspect all that Paul is looking for is a wee thanks and a bit of respect.

Moving on, and this time much closer to the Central Belt, where there is a new venue in the pipeline. Initially, paranoia lingered in the air and I was sworn to secrecy but its whereabouts is now out in the open (I hope!). I'll pass on the heated differences between the two main activists, but the crag is known as Robs Reed and although it's not quite Ceuse this will be a welcome addition to Scotland's esoteric sport climbing scene. Scott Muir was the man responsible for the crag's initial development, and established around 10 routes before work commitments at 'Extreme Dream'. Neil Shepherd then took over the driver's seat as its main protagonist. Neil (and others) had visited the crag before but wrote it off. But for some reason Neil changed his mind, adding 20 new routes. The crag comprises a long barrier type wall, 12–15m. high and,in the main, vertical and gently overhanging. Grades vary between 5+ and 7b+. The rock is sandstone and split by a band of conglomerate in its lower half which makes for some interesting climbing.

In the Arrochar area (Lochgoilhead), The Anvil is receiving positive feedback. But other than a couple of routes graded 6c+ and 7a, this is a hardcore crag. I use the term 'crag' loosely but really it's a huge block of mica schist that appears to have been dropped from outer space. For those of you who haven't been there before, essentially it is divided into three facets – a short south face of impending, quality rock, providing half-a-dozen routes. Of these *Spitfire* (solid 8a) and *Crossfire* (7c+) – both Dave Redpath creations – get rave reviews. The west face features a fine 7a, and is the only reasonably graded climb on the crag. In the angle between the west and north-facing facets, a fine prow yielded what is perhaps the route of the crag with *Shadowlands* (7b+), courtesy of Mike Tweedley. The undercut sector is reserved for the bionic, being bouldery, power–endurance terrain (and has even inspired Malcolm Smith to take note). The only two routes to date are needless to say, the work of Dave MacLeod, *Body Blow* (8b+) was climbed earlier last year, while *Body Swerve* at 8c (climbed in October) is currently Scotland's hardest offering.

While on the subject of Dave MacLeod, I have to say that I've enjoyed watching his recent success (and his rise to fame over the preceding decade), and wondered where he would take his climbing next. Is *Rhapsody* the pinnacle of his career or just the beginning?

Once the high (following a great climb such as Rhapsody) has run its course and the little gnawing rat has had its fill, euphoria is so often replaced by an emptiness or vacuum. A sense of where do I go from here. In Dave's case he returned to sport climbing (after big plans to climb in the Alps fell through) and who can blame him after the huge physiological strain imposed by a route such as *Rhapsody.*

I concluded that Dave is quite unique and yet the result, or a product if you like, so endearingly Scottish. His European counterparts are red-pointing 9a or 9a+ and on-sighting 8b+, and achieving great things in the Alps and Greater Ranges. Are Dave's achievements in Scotland every bit an equal? His success in Scotland is attributed to an ability that builds upon and draws from a homeland apprenticeship, and modern influences with roots in England and other parts of Europe and America. Achievements that are quite remarkable when we consider how disadvantaged climbers are in Scotland, especially sport climbing resources and a balmy climate. But perhaps that's precisely why we are so motivated.

Dave's climbs on the Anvil are certainly impressive and yet in the wider scheme of sport climbing developments elsewhere, one would have to say pretty average. Sport climbing has not been Dave's greatest strength but he has achieved some huge personal advances in this area. I do believe however, that he has the ability and above all, the motivation and tenacity to succeed on 9a and harder. Achieving this level can only further support his greatest attribute which is head-pointing. Finding projects of this calibre close to home is problematic, and *Rhapsody* in this respect worked very much in Dave's favour. Trips abroad are an option but they are so often fraught with cost and time implications that prey heavily on the psyche of most climbers attempting a hard route. There are however projects at this level in Scotland and a good starting place for Dave would undoubtedly be *Ring of*

Steall, an open project in Glen Nevis that has recently been labelled a contender for 9a.

So is *Rhapsody* the pinnacle of Dave's climbing? I believe this to be a sort of mid-way point in his career. If he can succeed on 9a then E12 is not beyond the realms of possibility, but ultimately a human being can only endure climbing at this level with all its inherent risks for a very limited period. Good luck Dave.

Tighnabruach
Andromeda (8a+) a MacLeod creation from 2004 received its second ascent from an on-form Alan Cassidy, who also went on to make a rapid ascent of *Shield of Perseus* (formerly 8a but now 7c+ by general consensus). This received another ascent by Robin Sutton who flashed the route. MacLeod reinforced his dominance with the crags hardest yet – *Apollo* (8a+), another super roof problem that involves all sorts of trickery and cunning knee bars. And finally, Tweedley succeeded on his 15m. roof project with *Elysium* (8a), a pre-dawn start being a key factor in his success (an alpinist at heart!). Its second ascent came only minutes later from MacLeod (who held his ropes). Dave confirmed the grade as solid and a contender for Scotland's best route at that grade. Not that there are that many routes of 8a to compete with.

Dunkeld
At Cave crag I was saddened by the appearance of an eliminate (graded 8a) squeezed in between *Silk Purse* and *Marlina*. While I understand one's quest for a route of this grade, my gripe is purely from an aesthetic standpoint. The wall is already peppered with bolts and with this new addition it has become a real eyesore. No doubt I'm in a minority but I'm hopeful that such a blinkered approach will not spread like an unwanted rash to other quality crags such as The Tunnel Wall.

Glen Ogle
Niall McNair sends in details of two worthy second ascents – *Solitaire* was completed after a swift couple of hours work. Originally graded as soft touch 8b by MacLeod, Niall found a completely new sequence (lurking beneath some dollops of moss) reducing the grade to 8a+. Niall confirmed the climbs high quality. Niall also accounts for the second ascent of *Ceasefire* (8a+) on The Diamond and said it was the first time he spent more than a day working a route. I apologise for sticking my nose in here but Niall's comment did bring a smile to my face. *Ceasefire* is an abandoned project which was equipped by Duncan Macallum back in the early 1990s. It's projected grade at that time was 8b. In between shifts I had a play and after two attempts top roped the route after about an hour's work and guessed 8a+. So Niall, if it's the first time you've spent more than a day working a route, it's about time you put your talent to good use.

Dumbuck
Voodoo Magic has been repeated by McNair who settled for 8a+. This climb has something of a chequered history. It was originally climbed by Andy Gallagher in the early 1980s and graded 8b. MacLeod repeated the route after a large percentage of the climb's holds had been pulled off. Dave confirmed the grade but was of the opinion that in its original state it was overgraded. The climb continues to receive attention with a corresponding loss of holds, and the most recent ascent by Niall only came after another hold was pulled off and glued back in place by someone else working the route.

Mountain Rescue Committee of Scotland
Incident Report 2006

Summary of mountain incidents and accidents in Scotland:

Table 1

Year	Incidents	Fatalities	Injured	No Trace	Persons assisted
2006	306	25	138	1	430
2005	313	25	167	7	435
2004	310	18	161	1	424
2003	259	17	142	3	347
2002	273	19	140		433

This report is only an interim one as there are a few outstanding incidents still to be completed by teams.

Summary of non-mountaineering incidents:

Table 2

Year	Incidents	Fatalities	Injured	No Trace	Persons assisted
2006	100	16	21	3	102
2005	105	15	28	10	110
2004	84	17	14	3	80
2003	86	14	20	13	83
2002	81	14	14		77

THIS report has been compiled with the assistance of Dr Bob Sharp who is in the process of publishing an academic paper on Mountain Accidents and who has been invaluable to me for advice and professional comment. In addition Mike Walker, who is our Systems Manager/IT specialist, keeps the system running despite my best efforts as a 'computer dinosaur'. The following are trends that seem to be prominent:

1. Since 1990, there continues to be a downward trend in mountaineering incidents. This trend mirrors a rise in participation in mountaineering over the same period. It would be safe to say that that the incident rate is falling. Very few instances of poor equipment/clothing are now noted, the common problem, historically proven, is that poor navigation is, and continues to be, a key factor in accidents. The idea that GPS is the absolute answer to navigation is a fallacy and several accidents/ incidents have been attributed to GPS failures.
2. The number of people injured or who have suffered fatal injuries also follows an overall downward trend. It should be noted that, over the past 10 years, some 25% of all fatal accidents are the results of males suffering heart attacks.
3. As in previous years, the vast bulk of incident callouts are to search for people who are lost/overdue (33%) or to rescue people who have slipped or fallen (38%) Also, in previous years, lower leg injuries are the most common (43%) with 34% of all resulting in fractures.

4. The number of non-mountaineering incidents is slightly down on 2005 but still much higher than previous years. This may reflect the growing use of teams by the emergency services. This shows that the diverse ability of MRTs is now widely recognised. A small number of teams are used extensively for local incidents and non-mountain searches.

5. More than one-third of incidents are initiated by mobile phone, although this is less than reported by English MRTs. Many involve team leaders/team members talking to casualties who are 'lost'. These 'lost souls' are invariably talked down safely by teams. I would like to thank all teams for their continued support.

6. Helicopters are involved in nearly 40% of our evacuations, not just the Military and Coastguard SAR Helicopters, but also Air Ambulance and Police Helicopter involvement is increasing. This will involve a change in practices in certain situations and will need careful liaison between all agencies to ensure that the right asset is sent to the correct situation.

Note: As you are aware Mountain Rescue information has been absent from these pages for some years and there has been a lot catching up to do. This is now nearly completed and it is hoped that by next year I will be able to report all mountaineering incidents in narrative form and in areas as per SMC District Guides.

D. (Heavy) Whalley.

Ruminations of a 20-Watt man.

I AM TOLD that a physically fit adult is capable of working at the rate of 70 Watts all day long. I came upon this piece of information while pedalling an exercise bicycle at St. John's Hospital sports injuries clinic. The bicycle recorded my output in watts. I was at the time 75 years of age and quickly discovered that I was no longer a 70-Watt man. In fact I was now a 30-Watt man. This merely quantified an impression I had already arrived at, and which showed up in my rather slow progress up hill. I was tempted to find what my short-term maximum output was and, to my agreeable surprise, I topped out at 250 Watts, then sank back exhausted and breathless.

Three years later, I was leading the final pitch on *Agag's Groove*, which members will recall has a vertical section, which, though full of holds, does require clinging on. My heart beat, not through nervousness, but through effort rose sharply, suggesting that my short-term maximum had also diminished. I was forced to pause at the top of this section to get my wind back and let my heart-beat subside.

Thinking back to earlier, fitter times, I wondered just how high an output of effort is needed to, say, climb an overhang. Much would depend on how sustained was the move. I learned that one rower in the Cambridge team in a recent boat race against Oxford was recorded as having an instantaneous output of 700 Watts! Do our young hard men have that sort of fitness and ability?

Being now a 30-Watt, or possibly even a 20-Watt mountaineer, adds an hour or two to bagging a Munro. The analogy is using a 10hp engine to drive a heavy truck. In low gear it's possible, but it all takes longer. The trick for we geriatrics is not to stop climbing, not to stop hill-walking, but to pace ourselves, and avoid ever getting into a position where survival means an output of 250 Watts. I suspect Bill Wallace's untimely end was just such a reason.

Malcolm Slesser.

THOSE JMCS BUS MEETS

THESE gatherings have received ocasional mention in the *Journal* since their effloresence over the early post-war years. We now reprint an impressionistic account of them, (style much impressed by the relentless 'Tiger's Prose' just then issuing from the chewed pencil of Robin Smith, whose 'Bat and The Wicked' came out in the same issue.) it is a reprint from SMCJ XXV11 pp 153-156 (1961), featured here again in memory of James Russell (obituarised in this issue, a great upholder of such gatherings and who contributed much to their quiet and continuous success.)

Sir, – When they began it was a long time ago in times not credible, when the Old Men were men and the new men were new, when Russell carried an ice axe and Smith a sewn-on waterproof, Slesser, they say organised the first one; that is likely. They were needed then for the war had just gone and the petrol not come and everyone wanted to get back to the hills and eat and sleep and whoop and fry amongst them. Day trips were no good, just picnics, and trains had their own rules; buses were the answer and soon every club had buses and they would race and glower at each other all the way North, fighting for the single chip stop. But it's the JMCS buses we must think of, for things are different now, there are birds and birdwatchers and meccano-men. In those days it was pure. There'd be a lot of people sitting on the kerb at Waterloo Place, rucksacks and axes and boots on the pavement and maybe a couple of groundsheets hung up where Cairns was changing his breeks and old *Daily Mirrors* lying about with pieces of Wally's piece in them. This Wally was a character; he even got put in the SMC but didn't pay, he went to New Zealand and got hitched instead, a real smasher. He had one adjective and two or three nouns and a great beaming face and spectacles and a superb stammer that got him many victims: he had a great wit and used to quote Moses in the dark. Others that turned up would be G., he'd no other name but two of everything else, two watches, two axes, clinkers and trikes just to make sure; and Russell tightly packaged, though the other half Donaldson wouldn't get on till his own house: he lived on the Monadhliath side of Saughtonhall and never seemed to be there anyway until just before it was too late, probably because he was sideways on and not easily seen; these two had a famous tent, the Slum, Slum 1, it was eaten into and out of again by various animals in hard winters but served these two until well before they stopped climbing. MacLennan was not there at first, he was not readily thought of but probably existed, they always do. About that place, too, Hewitt got on, packed with cans and kettles and knives and hatchets and bundles of twigs, travelling light being fond of tea and striking matches; he drummed up on his sticks and bark, paper, straw, sheep dung and braziers on Gargantuan variety but never on a primus. He had a favourite expression as he tripped up over the step coming in, dear and familiar to us all as the white tops above Callender and as eagerly awaited.

In Callender there was a cafe, the Rex, that had a good place upstairs where they put people from buses, in Strathyre on the way back was a wonderful pub where everyone was happy and the barman roared at Hampton's jokes and they sold crisps. All gone now. And there was a good place in Perth open all night with sausages, peas, egg and chips at tables at 2 in the morning after waiting for some fool to get lost in the Gorms, but any stop was good at night, the smoke and smell and noise came different. Our own smoke, we had Grieve who burnt herbs, he burnt rosewood, wormwood, dogsgrass and shrubberies, we pitched them out of the window one time stove and all, and there was Hampton, he had asthma, he used to smoke black Egyptians, coughing up their mummy dust and going blue; he breathed in a cat one night at Lazarus', so thick the fug, that raked his tubes a bit. Lazarus' is gone too, in a blaze of fire, the jewel of Kinlochleven, a Far-West doss-house crossed with a Naffi: cheap and teeming at all levels of life. Youth Hostels we never liked much, they were like trains but slower and wanted their wardens sweeping out. Ritchie's loud genealogical salute to the four-eyed one at Crianlarich who liked dancing stills warms up all Old Men. This Ritchie was just the same then but stopped talking once when a ski hit him on the neck over a bump from the roof rack; he sat nearer the window next time so that he could yell at the polis and throw streamers. Marshall was there, a wee laddie and polite, Hague, Hood, Cole, Rodgie, Scott, Millar, Tait, Bulbous and more, sundry musicians on mouth organs, combs, jugs and alimentary tracts, a varied horde, and when all these were emptied onto a stricken landscape together they drained into the night at once, like swill down a gutter, tentless ones trotting helpful and effusive and friendly, gloomy grubhunters like Dutton, furtive behind, undeterred by stones; these parasites clutching dogsbowls for alms, wandered from tent to tent till suitably undernourished, then crawled into dubious heaps of their own for the night. And all this time the driver was backing his 32 seats alone in the dark down a 10ft. Highland waterway with no lights no help and 32 dead lemonade bottles clanking behind him.

The nights were good, real nature communions, earth and soup and stones and paraffin and pine needles and no prickers, tents fuzzing in the dark, green or orange or grey, or khaki number 2, and inside boots and mud and smoke and sleeping bags and outside tin plates, rinds, spoons and scrapings, and those great black beasts sitting all round humped up to God's cloud and snow that all the fuss was supposed to be about. And you put on jerseys and balaclavas and extra socks and pulled the string and died in your bag and forgot the feet and the snores and the drystane dike beneath. And in the morning it was raining. And people went off and did things.

"We push attack and foray, over ridge and peak and corrie."

And when they came back it was dark and raining and there was no time to cook anyway and the tents had to come down and the guys were twisted, so they must have been, but they all came down together, even Donaldson's who had lost his milk into his rucksack. MacLennan's weekend sarcophagus, and the immaculate villas of Ferrier and Watt who always camped tidily, dovetailed tentpegs and levelled spirits, serene beyond the bacon gobs and skewed single-enders of the immature.

All bundled into the bus and the driver'd had a bad night so we helped him reverse and the usual fools were late, sweating blood and blisters, look, so hard had they run. And we moved off somehow and squeezed our feet and tried to get warm and the songs started up. Grieve was tenor and Brown about bass and the rest filled the gaps. And the songs roared all the way from Kirriemuir to Gleann a' Chaolais, there and back, smut and slop from all tongues, great lungfuls that steamed up the air and rivered down the windows, so thick they choked out the diesel and the tyres. It was great. But it was a black distance and there were hours and hours and miles and miles and we stopped and drank and had to stop again and the step was narrow. But it was a black distance and when we got back after all the stops there were more stops because people had to get off, they lived near here. That was alright as usual for Slesser who lived first, but what did it matter anyway, for every rucksack got rucked up, frames with straps with boots with tents together and well wedged down between the seats and up to the roof at no angle of rest. And the dawn got nearer. When they were all out they jolted and rattled away under the lamps with boots and rucksacks into streets of bare disbelief. And the buses went home last, with an axe or two and somebody's wallet.

And of all this lot some went abroad, some really died, some joined the SMC and a few forgot. SMC, we had some of them but they didn't look it and before them the first SMC we'd ever found it was George Elliot, and he was walking in a daft-shaped hat under the Pap of Glencoe shaped just like his hat, and there was snow on the Pap down to 1800ft.; and there was snow on George's hat down to 1800ft.; and if you'd squinted you couldn't tell the difference except that the Pap stayed still and George's hat went up and down and up and down and up and down, and that was the SMC.

Yours etc.\
ANON ANON

The present success of the Club in weathering the post-war social changes is in great measure due to the activities, deliberate or involuntary, of those mentioned in this extract.

G. J. F. Dutton.

Slesser's 80th – Porters and all!

A LONG straggle of walkers buffeted by the wind and drenched by the rain forged upwards towards the CIC hut. October 28, wet and wild.

Here came 16 panting figures, spanning every age from three to 83, to celebrate Malcolm Slesser's 80th birthday. The burn before the hut was swollen and the crowd milled around looking for a dry way to cross, then Malcolm hoisted Rosie, his grand-daughter, onto his shoulders and strode through the torrent. Lesser mortals followed.

A master of expedition organisation, his skills honed in Greenland, the Pamirs and the Himalayas, Malcolm had bribed some climbers from the Fort to act as porters and the table groaned with leg of lamb, salmon mousse, trifle, birthday cake and enough wine for a wedding. It had the makings of a great weekend and so it proved. Songs and stories, some old and some new. Of course, even the old stories acquire new threads and if they don't, the decline of memory with age makes them fresh. Tales of epic proportions – of climbs and voyages, of rescues and near calamities, of old friends departed, of expeditions so long ago and others being planned. Bothy ballads, Gaelic songs and even one composed for the occasion followed the feast, competing against the banshee wind generator.

Gradually, the copious wine took its toll and the bunks began to fill, and peace descended on the hut, apart from the obligatory snoring.

To the regret of some, but not of course Slesser, nor Smart, nor the Simpsons, the Sunday dawned bright and clear and off we slouched with no excuse, to gain the summit by the Arête. To those who had never gone up or down this way without the benefit of snow, it proved a trial but the reward was glorious views down into Glen Nevis and a huge respect for the energy of the octagenarians. The descent was eased by champagne and pate which dulled the pain of the slog back to the hut by Lochan Meall an t-Suidhe. Gear gathered, the party made its way down to the Aonach car park.

A wonderful weekend, a remarkable man and a privilege to have celebrated his 80th. Lang may his lum reek and his ice-axe bite.

Robin Shaw.

The Professor's last ice climb

THE arrangement to rock climb with Malcolm Slesser as he approached his 80th birthday was thwarted by the copious amount of rain that descended on the Langdale meet last September. As an appeasement I suggested that we might manage to arrange an ice climb together during the 2007 winter as I had heard tales of Malcolm's 'Last Ice Climb' intentions.

At the Dinner in Fort William it was decided that an attempt on *The Vent* in Coire an Lochain would be a suitable objective.

Winter had failed to materialise by the time Malcolm was heading off to France for a skiing holiday in January and the situation had not improved on my return in mid-February from thawing Austrian ice curtains.

Malcolm's 'Last Ice Climb' was in serious doubt until a heavy snowfall on March 17-18 prompted a series of phone calls which resulted in me arriving late in the evening of Friday, March 23 at Malcolm's accommodation at Rothiemurchus.

The forecast had been stating overnight temperatures down to -5° and this was confirmed as the path to Coire an Lochain on the morning of Saturday, March 24 was frozen solid with blue skies overhead and any remaining snow underfoot took our weight. Our six o'clock rise had paid dividends, as it was only when we stopped for an adjustment to one of Malcolm's crampons as we approached the climb that we were overtaken by a party heading for the same route.

As we waited for our overtakers to vacate the initial pitch we could see that the walls of the route were sheathed in verglas and that rock belays would be at a premium. Their second second man was obviously having difficulty, even with the most modern of ice axes, and asked if I could remove one of the runners that his leader had placed.

Once I was tackling the impending pitch, I could see that it was not in straight-forward Grade II,III condition. A mushroom shape had formed above and below it and a shell of ice gave way to soft snow where there should have been good left foot support. I hacked out what turned out to be a bulldog ice anchor from deep under this mushroom then placed my own ice screw in the remaining good ice that was about a foot wide and adhering to the right wall. This ice was virtually vertical and I found climbing this short pitch very strenuous. The ice was like concrete, picks barely penetrating and I was panting heavily as I emerged above the mushroom.

An old peg on the right wall suggested a belay as it went through my mind that

Malcolm might not manage to ascend the ice as he had stated earlier that he "...probably should not be here"! Once clipped onto the old peg and a dodgy block, I summoned Malcolm to start climbing and with a good tight rope and a few 'offs', a smiling Slesser was at the stance, remarking that he had heard my heavy breathing from his belay. An amazing effort for a man in his 81st year.

Establishing himself at the stance Malcolm dropped a glove and, looking down to see where it had gone, I could see a chap in a yellow cagoule about to ascend the nasty wee pitch. I asked if he had seen the falling glove and remarked that the pitch was at least Grade IV, adding that the two of us, being pensioners, would be some time on what remained of the ice above. Fortunately, Malcolm had a spare glove in his rucksack and I was able to set off up the ice and placed another screw, still amazed at the hardness of the ice itself.

Once up at a belay I placed two good nuts and shouted for Malcolm to ascend. I couldn't see him on this pitch and, once climbing, I heard the command: "Keep a good tight rope." I duly obliged until a grinning Malcolm appeared, explaining that his picks were bouncing off the ice and that the saving grace had been a hole in the ice at the point when he had to make a straddle move. As Malcolm moved up and round to a better stance we witnessed a yellow vision waving to us from the plateau with Malcolm's glove in hand.

All that remained of *The Vent* was a full run-out on good snow to a belay, then Malcolm completed his 'Last Ice Climb' with a short ascent to a sun drenched rocky plateau. Handshakes, photographs, off with the gear and crampons, some lunch in the warm sun, then down to the Goat Track descent where crampons were required again until under the bare cliffs of Coire An T-Sneachda.

As we headed down to the carpark I remarked to Malcolm what a wonderful day we had enjoyed, while also thinking to myself, would I still be able to climb ice in 15 years!

Douglas Lang.

No Snow Survives

No snow in Scotland survived 2006. Despite a snowy March 2006, less snow than usual fell during the winter as a whole, and the number and size of patches in summer was well below the long-run average. Mick Tighe found none left at Ben Nevis on September 13 and the last snow seen was observed by Davie Duncan at the foot of Sphinx Ridge in Garbh Choire Mor of Braeriach on September 26, when it was down to less than 3m. long and melting rapidly. We judge that it finally vanished before September 30, and visits in early October revealed none. A detailed account with photographs has been published (A. Watson, D. Duncan and J. Pottie, 2007, *No Scottish snow survives until winter 2006/07*, Weather 62, 71-73).

Adam Watson

Arthur W. Russell's Walking Diaries

ARTHUR RUSSELL joined the Club in 1896. He had climbed since 1890, and was a prodigious walker, whose only rival in this sphere was Frank Goggs. Last year, thanks to the generosity of his grandson George R. Russell, we received – together with other interesting material – his diaries covering the period 1891 to 1912. Russell's *annus mirabilis* was 1897, in which he recorded what may be the first continuous traverse of the four Cairngorm 4,000ft. peaks, and the first traverse of the Aonach Eagach ridge. A sampler of the highlights of the diaries, and a brief account of Russell's life and career, will be prepared for next year's Journal. In the meantime, I give below a brief description of the objects received. These have all been added to the Club deposit in the National Library of Scotland. They are held under a separate Accession code – Acc.12690 – in the Manuscript Department of the Library, and may be consulted there.

Six photograph albums, as follows:

1. 10.5ins. x 13.5ins., containing photographs from the 1890s and 1900s, inscribed 'The Cairngorms and Skye/Arthur W. Russell/15 Strathearn Place/Edinburgh'.

2. 9ins. x 12ins., containing family photographs from 1929 onwards (first part), and mountain photographs from the 1890s and 1900s (last part)

3. 8ins. x 5.5ins., containing undated and unannotated small photographs of various subjects.

4. 9.5ins. x 6.5ins., inscribed 'To Arthur from Madeline and Robert/6th July 1893', and containing photographs of various subjects from the 1890s.

5. 5ins. x 6.5ins., inscribed 'Glencoe/A.W.R. 1895'.

6. 5ins. x 7ins., inscribed 'Scotch Mountain Views/A.W.R.'.

Eleven diaries describing walking and climbing expeditions, each approximately 5ins. x 3.25ins., as follows:

1. Inscribed 'Walking Tour in the Summer of 189/David Reid, Robert and Myself/ from Dunkeld to Stronlacher via Blair Athole, Dalwhinnie, Loch Laggan, Fort William, Ballachulish, Glencoe, Kingshouse Inn, Tyndrum, Crianlarich, Tyndrum, Inversnaid', followed by a 'List of Ascents' from 1890 to 1907. Recently numbered '1' on front cover.

2. Inscribed 'Journal/of the/First Visit paid to Alassio/in 1892/as well as of/A fortnight's trip to Rome/April 9th – June'. Recently numbered '2' on front cover.

3. Inscribed 'Walking Tour in/the Summer of 1893/David Reid, Robert and Myself/ from July 26th – Aug 2nd/Dunkeld to Kirriemuir via Tummel Bridge, Rannoch, Loch Garry, Dalwhinnie, Lynwilg Inn, Braemar, Clova'. Recently numbered '3' on front cover.

4. Inscribed 'Walking Tour/in the/Spring of 1894/by A. R. Wilson & A. W. Russell/ Expense for 9 days £4 : 2 : 10/Route: Comrie, Strathyre, Tyndrum, Dalmally, Taynuilt, Glen Creran, Glen Coe, Inveroran, Dalmally'. Two photographs enclosed.

5. Inscribed 'Ascents of 1895/The Cobbler … Ben Dothaidh … Ben Doireann … Aonach Dubh … Aonach Eagach … Bidean nam Bian/A. W. Russell/76 Thirlestane Rd.' Two photographs enclosed. Recently numbered '4' on front cover.

6. Inscribed 'Ascents of 1896/Stob Garbh …. Cruach Ardran …. Creag MacRanaich …. Ben More …. Meall ant Seallaidh …. Stuc a Chroin …. Ben Tulachan …. Creag na Leacainn …. Cairn an Lochain… Braeriach …. Ben Macdhui …. Cairngorm/Arthur W. Russell'. One photograph enclosed. Recently numbered '5' on front cover.

7. Inscribed 'Arthur W. Russell/76 Thirlestane Rd./Edinburgh/1897'. Containing accounts of visits to 'Aberfoyle, Cairngorm, Ben More, Cairngorms, Aviemore,

Glencoe, Pentlands and Arthur's Seat'. Four photographs enclosed. Recently numbered '6' on front cover.

8. Inscribed 'Arthur W. Russell/76 Thirlestane Rd./Edinburgh/1898'. Contains a 'List of Ascents' for 1898 and 1899, and accounts of (1898) 'Lomond Hills, Salisbury Crags, Pentland Hills, February Trip with Robert, Good Friday excursion, Spring Holiday, Cairngorms in June, Skye, Speyside, South' and (1899) 'Guislich at Spring Holiday, Braeriach at Queen's Birthday, Autumn Holiday at Ft. Wm.' Recently numbered '7' on front cover.

9. Inscribed 'Arthur W. Russell/76 Thirlestane Rd./Edinburgh/1900 – 1902'. Contains a 'List of Ascents' for 1900, 1901 and 1902, and accounts of (1900) 'New Years trip at Loch Awe, Inveroran in March, Good Friday on Ben Bynac, Sunrise on Sgoran Dubh, Skye in August and ride there, Speyside in August and ride there', (1901) New Year at Loch Awe, Braeriach on Good Friday, Spreyside at Spring Holiday, Sunrise on Ben Muich Dhui, and (1902) New Year at Tarbet, Aviemore and Dalwhinnie with R., Glencoe in June, Ben haluim from Camp, Arrochar in October'. Recently numbered '8' on front cover.

10. Inscribed 'Arthur W. Russell/18 Learmonth Gdns./Edinburgh/1903 –1906'. Contains a 'List of Ascents' for each of 1903 to 1906, and accounts of (1903) 'New Year at Killin, Braeriach in September', (1904) 'Spring Meet at Aviemore, Easter at Strathyre with Ara., Cruachan in September, Arrochar in September', (1905) 'New Year Meet at Loch Awe, Strathyre in March, Easter at Tyndrum, Ben Lawers in June, Norway in July, Rannoch Moor in September', and (1906) 'New Year Meet at Tyndrum, Killin March, Aviemore in June, Arrochar in September, Arrochar in October, Ben Lawers in July'. Recently numbered '9' on front cover.

11. Ring-bound loose-leaf notebook, some pages misplaced. Short descriptions of visits to Cairngorms (mostly) in 1906–1912. Recently numbered '10' on front cover.

A *letter* of four-and-a-half pages, dated August 21st, 1890, addressed to 'My Dear Madeline', and headed Portree Hotel, Portree. The letter describes a journey to Skye with Robert, with a visit to the Quiriang planned, and then an excursion to Staffa and Iona from Oban. Signed off 'With much love to Papa/ & yourself from your loving brother'. The signature is clipped, but it seems to have been signed with full name (!) 'Arthur Russell'.

Robin N. Campbell.

The First Ascent of the Great Tower

LAST year I was hornswoggled by Ken Wilson into writing something about Tower Ridge for a new version of *Classic Rock*. This led me into reading accounts of early visits to the Ridge.

The first account is the note by John Hopkinson in Volume 17 of the *Alpine Journal*, pp. 520–1, a third-person narrative giving minimal details. The Hopkinson party visited the ridge in September 1892, and their first effort was to ascend "…as far as the point where the ridge is broken by a well-defined perpendicular face, which they endeavoured to turn by traversing slightly on to the western face, and ascending a narrow chimney, but were stopped by a high pitch", whereupon they presumably made their way back down the ridge. On the following day they climbed to the summit, then "…descended the same ridge from the summit past the cairn, well seen from near the Observatory, marking the farthest point previously reached in descent, as far as the chimney on the west face of the ridge. Descending this to the pitch before mentioned, and then by a short but difficult traverse, they reached a small rock platform, from which they regained the ridge below the rock face, and completed the descent."

Clearly, the cairn referred to pre-dated their visit, and it is a reasonable inference that they must have been told about this earlier exploration of the upper part of the ridge by the Observers or some other local source. It is also a reasonable inference (made by our guidebook writers) that they were stopped on the first day on the western side of the Great Tower.

The second account is Norman Collie's Bunyanesque *Divine Mysteries of the Oromaniacal Quest* (SMCJ, vol. 3, pp.151–7), describing the first ascent of the ridge in March 1894. When the party eventually "…climb sagaciously upwards to the summit of the great tower" they find "…a heaped-up accumulation of stones, a mystic pyramid, set there doubtless by a former seeker in the work, to the end that true searchers might not despair, but continue the matter of the work with fresh hope and industry". When I read this passage many years ago, I assumed that this cairn must have been left by the Hopkinsons in1892, but John Hopkinson's account makes no mention of building any cairn, and again it is a reasonable inference that this is the previously-built cairn mentioned by Hopkinson.

The third account is by William Naismith (SMCJ, vol. 3, pp.231–3), who climbed the ridge with Gilbert Thomson in September 1894. Describing the Tower Gap, Naismith mentions a 'curious anecdote': "It seems that the builder of the first cairn on the Tower conceived the brilliant idea of making the peak inaccessible; and accordingly, on his way back from the Tower, which he had approached from above, he either manufactured the cleft, or at least deepened it considerably, by throwing down a lot of loose blocks."

So all three accounts are consistent, and together they imply clearly that before the explorations of the Hopkinsons in 1892, the Great Tower was reached from the summit plateau, and a cairn built there. In confirmation, there is a postcard view of the Tower by Valentine's of Dundee, which is dated 1885, and shows a cairn on top of the Tower. A digital image of the card, identified as JV-5391[A], may be viewed in the St. Andrews University Library Photographic Collection. As to who made this enterprising climb, I have no idea.

Robin N. Campbell.

100 Years Ago: The Club in 1907

THE 18th Annual Meeting and Dinner took place on Friday, December 7, 1906 in the North British Station Hotel, Edinburgh, with John Rennie presiding. Treasurer Napier announced a balance of £208-19s., which, together with the Life Membership Fund, brought the Club's total funds to £437-8s.-5d. Secretary Clark announced seven new members, and Librarian Goggs reported the addition of 60 books (mostly now vanished, like the members). William Garden proposed the production of Library and Slide Catalogues, and the first was agreed to. New Club Rules (much as we know them today) were adopted.

The New Year Meet was held at the Corrie Hotel on Arran, and attended by 18 members and three guests. Conditions were wintry throughout, with deep new snow, and heavy snowstorms. The only climbs achieved were Pinnacle Ridge of Cir Mhor (Goodeve, McIntyre, Ednie), the A'Chir Traverse (Goggs, Ling, E. B. Robertson, Unna), and numerous descents of the Witch's Step. Raeburn injured his knee badly on his only outing, walking to the Saddle.

In early March Goggs and Euan Robertson walked from the Bridge of Lochay

Inn to Fearnan, traversing all the peaks of Ben Lawers en route. Goggs complained that "…the only peak on the whole range requiring an ice-axe" – An Stuc – was "not considered worthy of a place in the immortal list". On the following day, they walked back to Bridge of Lochay, passing over all the peaks of the Carn Mairg range, and crossing the Lairig Breislich. A prodigious walk, but nothing to Goggs, as events later in the year showed.

The Easter Meet of 17 members and one guest was held at Inchnadamph, with a subsidiary Meet of six members 'joining the classic pursuits of a Glasgow holiday throng' at Arrochar, and a well-attended unauthorised Meet of 13 members and four guests led by Gilbert Thomson, discomposed by the prospect of the 3a.m. start for Inchnadamph, gathered at the Alexandra in Fort William. Inchnadamph saw the reappearance of Sandy Mackay after his terrible leg injuries on Arran in January 1903. On Friday, along with Gillon and Euan Robertson, he climbed Suilven by Pilkington's Gully and traversed it, getting there and back directly from the hotel over the north-west shoulder of Canisp (what a day!). On Saturday he traversed Stac Polly, and on Easter Monday he took part in the famous ascent of the Barrel Buttress of Quinag along with Raeburn and Ling. Mackay's leg function seems to have been adequately restored.

On the Cobbler, Naismith explored the north side of the South Peak unsuccessfully. The Fort William Meet was distinguished by brutal walking expeditions, notably Goggs' and Russell's journey to the Meet from Corrour via Binneins Mor and Beag. Edred Corner had an Easter Meet all of his own, along with medical colleagues Drs. Johns and Pinches. They explored parts of the Western Highlands and Cairngorms, and – equipped with several aneroids and a scientific approach – made a careful survey of the peaks and passes of Ben Wyvis. "It is… obvious that the range… can be divided… into two mountains… [and that] the composite ranges of Liathach, Beinn Eighe and An Teallach can be subdivided in a similar manner". This has happened to the latter three, but not, alas, to Ben Wyvis.

In early April, James Greig's party encountered an electric storm on Beinn a' Ghlo before discovering his useful eponymous Ledge on Crowberry Ridge, and the Walkers and 'a friend' made a winter ascent of Rose Ridge on Sgoran Dubh. In May, Glover and Ling made the first climbs on An Teallach and Beinn Dearg Mor. In early June, Gibbs, Mounsey and Edward Backhouse climbed the Eastern Buttress of Coire Mhic Fhearchair. However, the second famous expedition of the year fell to Goggs and Raeburn, who explored the Shelter Stone Crag in mid-June. At 7 p.m. on the 15th. they left Kingussie on bicycles and used these to a bothy on the north side of the Lairig Ghru, arriving at 8.40pm. After a few hours 'rest', they rose at 1.30a.m. and left after an hour for Creag an Leth-Choin. They then rounded the head of Loch Avon to reach the top of the crag at 6a.m., descended the crag by the ridge on its left (Castle Wall, 600ft. Difficult) to the Shelter Stone, completing their lunch there by 7.30a.m. They were back at the foot of the crag by 9.15a.m. and climbed the prominent buttress on the left-hand side (Raeburn's Buttress, 650ft. Severe), arriving at the top just before 1am. Taking the shortest route to their bicycles, they were back at Kingussie by 4.30p.m., allowing Raeburn "ample time for a bath and a meal before catching the 5.16 for Edinburgh". It is one of many disgraces that only a vague trace of this ferocious day remains in our current climbers' guidebook. I doubt whether there is any party in the present Club capable of repeating it.

In the summer, members struggled with bad weather in Norway and the Alps. Robert P. Hope managed Finsteraarhorn, Schreckhorn and Grand Dru despite encountering storms on all three peaks. His legendary Alpine exploits along with W. T. Kirkpatrick (guideless, with featherlight equipment – even the handles of toothbrushes were sawn off to save weight) were collected by Kirkpatrick in *Alpine Days and Nights*, published in 1932. Ling and Raeburn were twice repulsed by storms on La Meije, then moved to Isäre where they made long traverses of peaks in the Vanoise and on the frontier ridge before proceeding to the Gran Paradiso, where they were both struck by lightning on the summit. Their holiday ended with a traverse of Mont Blanc from the Sella Hut to Chamonix. Despite a severe storm at the summit, they found their way down the ordinary route 'in dense mist and driving snow'. Tom Longstaff spent three months in the Garwhal Himalaya with Major Bruce and A. L. Mumm and three Alpine guides, climbing Trisul (23,406 ft.; Longstaff and Borochel) on June 12, the first 7000m. peak to succumb.

The Journal for the year contained many fine things, some – such as Raeburn's account of Green Gully, Edred Corner's disorderly wanderings in the misty hills of Ey, and Douglas's confession of navigational incompetence on Beinn a' Bheithir – relating to 1906. The anonymous 'Knees of the Gods' is a well-turned dream of the future by John Buchan (see his obituary by Stair Gillon in J. 22, 200-5 for evidence of authorship). The climber dreams of a Sligachan in which smoking is banned (confirmed 2006), and also alcohol (next year). The Alps are festooned with railways and summit elevators (not for a while, perhaps), and a standard expedition on Skye is the night traverse of the Ridge in winter (well, why not?). The whole of the September issue (not even a scrap of small print) is taken up by Douglas's wonderful guidebook to Skye, the basis of all subsequent Skye guidebooks and a model for guidebook writers everywhere, supplemented by a Three and a Half Inch version of the Six-Inch map with red-inked paths and approaches marked – a far better map than the ugly Priestman map hawked by the Club for so many years subsequently. This heroic effort by Douglas was quickly complemented by the publication of Ashley Abraham's racy alternative guide – *Rock-Climbing in Skye*. Even though no new climbs had been recorded there, 1907 was a good year for Skye.

Robin N. Campbell.

Metric Mountains
By Michael Götz

BRITAIN 'went metric' in the early 1970s. I vividly remember, during family holidays, bill boards, public announcements and a sense of excitement about the imminent connection of Britain to the rest of Europe: a virtual bridge well before the tunnel. The excitement was short-lived: teenagers today continue to weigh themselves in stones, ham goes by the ounce, milk is sold in pints, and radio announcers translate temperatures into Fahrenheit.

Friends and colleagues have been subjected to long monologues about units of measurement for many years now. There is nothing inferior (or superior) about single units of imperial or other measurement systems when you consider them on their own – the inch is a convenient way of measuring the thickness of a plank of wood; the pint makes sense in a pub; the ounce goes well at the butcher's; the metre is a stride. The imperial system, however, is disadvantaged when we want to relate one unit to another: knowing that one litre of water weighs one kilogram, that one gram of water has a volume of one cubic centimetre, that one square kilometre contains one million square metres is a thing of beauty. How much does a gallon of water weigh? And the concept of a $^3/_8$th fraction of whatever unit of measurement is frankly bizarre to anybody not born in Winton-on-the-Ouze: a bit more than a quarter? How much more?

You know where we are heading for: the hills and tops of Scotland. Munros are Munros and shall remain Munros. We will not touch their tradition and integrity. There are, however, about 150 tops in Scotland which are higher than 1000m. What a splendidly round figure; one kilometre. A neat number of hills which can be bagged, just like the Munros and the Corbetts.

I propose all hills and tops in Scotland above the height of 1000m. to be called Götzes. One could be fanatical and demand that only those who head for the hills specifically to climb the Götzes deserve the title Gotzist; having collected them by serendipity as part of a Munro bagging venture, one could argue, shouldn't count. I suggest to be less rigid: anybody who climbed all the hills and tops in Scotland above 1000m., who declares a lifelong allegiance to the metric system and who from henceforth promises to pour scorn on miles, pounds and gallons deserves the title Götzist.

SCOTTISH MOUNTAINEERING TRUST – 2006-2007

THE Trustees met on February 3, June 10 and October 13 2006.

During the course of these meetings support was given to the Jacobites Mountaineering Club for Hut Renovations; the Jonathon Conville Memorial Trust; the Junior Mountaineering Club of Scotland for Renovations to a Hut called 'The Cabin'; the Scottish Council for National Parks; Lorraine Nicholson for a Course for the Visually Impaired and for Training for the Visually Impaired (Alpine Skills Training); to the SMC for the scanning of W.N. Ling's Mountaineering Diaries; to the SMC Journal Editor for a new computer; to the British Trust for Ornithology for a Ptarmigan Survey; to the Nevis Partnership – Mick Tighe Collection; to the Mountaineering Council of Scotland – access and conservation; to the Dundee Mountain Film Festival; to the Oban Mountain Rescue Team; to Douglas Scott for an Exhibition entitled *A Life of Photography*; to the Bill Wallace – 'Go and Do it' fund to be administered by the John Muir Trust; to A. H. C. Chalmers for the Borders Forest Trust – native tree planting.

The present Trustees are A. C. Stead (Chairman), R. Aitken, R. Anderson, R. J. Archbold, D. A. Bearhop, P. V. Brian, D. Broadhead, C. M. Huntley, C. J. Orr, and R. J. C. Robb. J. Morton Shaw is the Trust Treasurer.

The present Directors of the Publications Company are R. K. Bott (Chairman), K. V. Crockett, C. M. Huntley, W. C. Runciman, M. G. D. Shaw and T. Prentice (Publications Manager). C. M. Huntley is both a Trustee and a Director of the Company. R. Anderson is the Convenor of the Publications Company and attends Company Board meetings. Both provide valuable liaison between the Company and the Trust.

Peter MacDonald retired by rotation as Chairman of the Trust in December 2006. His contribution as Chairman of the Trust was very much appreciated and the Trustees wish to take this opportunity of recording their gratitude to him for his services to the Trust.

The Trustees also wish to record their appreciation for the contribution made by Andy Tibbs who has now retired by rotation.

The following grants have been committed by the Trustees:

Scottish Mountaineering Club – Scanning of W. N. Ling's Mountaineering Diaries	£500
Scottish Mountaineering Club – Journal Editor – computer	£500
British Trust for Ornithology – Ptarmigan Survey	£2500
Nevis Partnership – Mick Tighe Collection	£2000
Mountaineering Council of Scotland – Access and Conservation	£12,000
Dundee Mountain Film Festival	£1000
Oban Mountain Rescue Team	£5000
Jacobites Mountaineering Club – Hut Rennovation	
(as grant)	£5000
(as loan)	£3000
Jonathon Conville Memorial Trust	£1222
Junior Mountaineering Club of Scotland – renovations to the Cabin	
(as grant)	£6000
(as a loan)	£4000
Scottish Council for National Parks	£5000
Lorraine Nicholson – Course for the Visually Impaired	£3000
Lorraine Nicholson – Training for the Visually Impaired (Alpine Skills)	£305
Douglas Scott – A Life of Photography	£1030
Bill Wallace – 'Go and Do It' Fund	£10000
A. H. C. Chalmers – Borders Forest Trust	£1600

James D. Hotchkiss, Trust Secretary.

Dibden Bequest

WE WOULD like to take this opportunity of recording our grateful thanks to Brian G. Dibden, who lives in Stirlingshire, for his very generous donation of £5000 that he wishes to be used towards the work of maintaining footpaths in the Scottish mountains.

The Trustees, Scottish Mountaineering Trust.

MUNRO MATTERS

By David Kirk (Clerk of the List))

ANOTHER good year of hill stomping has taken place and I thank everyone who has written to me to register a Compleation, or to amend their original entry. I continue to be amused and touched by the anecdotes your letters contain. The total new Compleaters for the last year is 227 (who registered between April 1, 2006 and April 1 2007).

The Munro Society continues to flourish and, as usual, I have appended a report to the end of Munro Matters by their president, Iain Robertson. I was lucky enough to be invited as a guest to their Dinner in Fort William in the autumn, celebrating the 150th anniversary of Sir Hugh's birth, and enjoyed good food and wine, and excellent company.

I would like to mention again the SMC Website. I would urge everyone on the List who hasn't yet done it, to dig out that old final summit photograph of yourself, and send a copy or the original along with a SAE to Ken Crocket. Your summit picture can then become part of the SMC Website Munroist section and be recorded for posterity. Website enthusiasts may point out that I myself have still to do this! – this is a personal aim for 2007.

As before, the five columns are number, name, then Munro, Top and Furth Compleation years.

3543	William A Macleod	2006		
3544	Gordon A McDonald	2006		
3545	Andy Sutton	2006		
3546	John Frame	2006		
3547	Barbara Frame	2006		
3548	David Bowden	2006		
3549	Ewen D McKinnon	2006		
2550	Ken Keith	2006		
3551	Alan Gilkison	2006		
3552	Martin Richardson	2006		
3553	Bob Calvert	2006		
3554	Lindsay Butler	2006		
3555	Max Munday	2006		
3556	Chris Dodd	2006		
3557	Peter Clifford	2006		
3558	Ernie Hailwood	2006		
3559	Anthony Rigby	2006		
3560	June A. Chappell	2006		
3561	Nigel E. Simmonds	2006		
3562	Andrew Johnstone	2006		
3563	Gordon Gair	2006		
3564	Malcolm Simmonds	2006		
3565	Douglas Herdman	2006		
3566	Roger J. Stevenson	2006		
3567	Russel Wills	2006		
3568	Clare Aldridge	2006		
3569	David George White	2006		
3570	Julian Foot	2006		
3571	Anne Marie Foot	2006		
3572	Richard Butterworth	2006		
3573	Stephen G. Lee	2006		
3574	Karen Lowde	2006		
3575	Graham J. Foster	2006		
3576	Gavin Clarke	2006		
3577	Michael Alexander	2006		
3578	Gordon Fearns	2006		
3579	Derek Banks	2006		
3580	Paul C. Gulliver	2006		
3581	Kevin Hesketh	2006		
3582	Marian Hesketh	2006		
3583	Chris Budd	2006		
3584	Stuart Smith	2006		
3585	Anthony Harper	2006		
3586	Tony Welsh	2006		
3587	Ian D. Pascall	2006		
3588	Albert Duthie	2006		
3589	Bruce Cockburn	2006		
3590	Bruce Bricknell	2006		
3591	Joseph Scott	2006		
3592	Ian Johnston	2006		
3593	Ambrose Gillham	2006		
3594	Leslie D. Nuttall	2006		
3595	David Long	2006		
3596	John M Tweedle	2006	2006	
3597	Billy Urquhart	2006		
3598	Sandy Anderson	2006		
3599	Ian Cameron	2006		
3600	Ian J. Hawkes	2006	2006	
3601	David Laddiman	2006		
3602	Jan Campbell	2006		
3603	David J. Brown	2006		
3604	Lindsay Harrod	2006		
3605	Conan Harrod	2000		
3606	Neville Fernley	2006		

Tom Weir. Photo: Carl Schaschke.

Douglas Campbell. Photo: Duncan Campbell.

3607 Tom Sutherland	2006	3664 David A. Gilchrist	2006
3608 Alice Sutherland	2006	3665 David S. Gilchrist	2006
3609 Darryl Campling	2006	3666 David Burns	2006
3610 Albert Mackenzie	2006	3667 David McGill	2006
3611 Anna Mackenzie	2006	3668 Mike Neale	2006
3612 Brian Slater	2006	3669 Matthew Rendle	2006
3613 Dave Snodgrass	2006	3670 Jim Shanks	2006
3614 Graham Thompson	2006	3671 G. Urwin Woodman	2006
3615 Brian Milne	2006	3672 Dawn Griesbach	2006
3616 John Downie	2006	3673 John Bulloch	2006
3617 Craig Saddler	2006	3674 John P.F. Saunders	2006
3618 Iris Cheshire	2006	3675 Willie Matheson	2006
3619 Phil Rees	2006	3676 Alan D. Barlow	2006
3620 John D. Peel	2006	3677 Bob Ainsworth	2006
3621 Margaret Elphinstone	2006	3678 Robert Murray	2006
3622 Stewart Orr	2006	3679 Christopher J. Cooke	2006
3623 Andrew Thompson	2006	3680 Peter John Herman	2006
3624 David Parkinson	2006	3681 Lesley A. Bryce	2006
3625 Victor Marrone	2006	3682 Malcolm Clark	2006
3626 Elaine Marrone	2006	3683 David Bradshaw	2006
3627 Colin Donald Walter	2006 2006	3684 David S. Cargill	2006
3628 David I. Barlow	2006	3685 Hein Hogenhuis	2000
3629 Karl Proctor	2006	3686 Ken Murray	2006
3630 Thomas Kaald Olsen	2006	3687 Dave Coustick	2006
3631 Gordon Roberts	2006	3688 Alan Watt	2006
3632 Tom Gameson	2006	3689 John Watt	2006
3633 Maureen Lang	2006	3690 Brian Delaney	2006
3634 Paul Harrison	2006	3691 Morag Macgregor	2006
3635 David J. Lappin	2006	3692 Garry Walker	2006
3636 Margaret Cameron	2006	3693 Kenneth Allan	2006
3637 Douglas Cameron	2006	3694 Paula Drollet	2006
3638 Mike Duncan	2006	3695 Richard Adlington	2006
3639 Derek Mitchell	2006	3696 Roger H. Barr	2006
3640 William Mather	2006	3697 Arthur Finlay	2006
3641 Jim Coyle	2006	3698 Ruth McWilliam	2006
3642 Greig Whitton	2006	3699 Jean S. McAndrew	2006
3643 Ann Walder	2006	3700 John McAndrew	2006
3644 Peter Branney	2006	3701 Kenneth M. Fallas	2006
3645 W. Alan Johnston	2006	3702 John Hands	2006
3646 Susanne L. Johnston	2006	3703 Simon Birch	2006
3647 Julie Cameron	2006	3704 Judith Campbell	2006
3648 Diane G. Morgan	2006	3705 David Mitchell	2006
3649 Jon Meeten	2006	3706 J. Brian Harrison	2006
3650 Jim Linnell	2006	3707 Mark Tulley	2006
3651 Jack Addison	2006	3708 Douglas Fordyce	2006
3652 Mike Levy	2006	3709 David F. Bird	2006
3653 Robert Allan	2006	3710 Iain D. Brown	2006
3654 Nan Hargreaves	2006	3711 Norman Smith	2006
3655 Jill Turner	2006	3712 Geoffrey Hill	2006
3656 Rob Soutar	2006	3713 William Thomson	2006
3657 Michael J. Morrison	2006	3714 John Ambrose	2006
3658 Michael Hartley	2006	3715 Len Trim	2006
3659 Brian Purves	2006	3716 Annette Hood	2006
3660 Michael Williamson	2006	3717 Colin Johnson	2006
3661 Jacqueline McCulloch	2006	3718 Stephen M Marlow	2006
3662 Diane S. Beveridge	2006	3719 Stephen Lunt	2006
3663 John A. Greig	2006	3720 Fraser Hardie	2006

Dunmore Hotchkiss. Photo: James Hotchkiss.
George Bruce. Photo: D. Whalley.

3721	Philip Tinning	2006	3746	Adrian O'dell	2006
3722	Debbie Cockburn	2006	3747	James Cockburn	2006
3723	Neil Cockburn	2006	3748	Catherine Pearce	2006
3724	Graham Williams	2006	3749	Charles Harmer	2006
3725	Yvonne Cuneo	2006	3750	Val Belton	2006
3726	John Willioner	2006	3751	Mark Elder	2006
3727	Douglas Johnston	2006	3752	Eric Derwin	2006
3728	Zefiryn Kazmierczak	2006	3753	*Robert McMurray	2006
3729	Gordon Anderson	2006	3754	Paul Todd	1993
3730	Peter Jackson	2006	3755	James Tweedie	2006
3731	Andrew Thow	2006	3756	Toby Green	2006
3732	Colin McPherson	2006	3757	Douglas Brown	2006
3733	David Hand	2006	3758	Derrick Smith	2006
3734	Barbara Hand	2006	3759	Ian Sutherland	2006
3735	Anne M.M. Ross	2006	3760	Dr P. McCue	2006
3736	Patricia R. Cook	2006	3761	John A. Parks	2006
3737	Hans van Dijk	2006	3762	Robin Stevenson	2004
3738	John Mitchell	2006	3763	Alan H. Hughes	2003
3739	Brian Cook	2006	3764	Moira McPartlin	2006
3740	Mary E. Haddow	2006	3765	Hank Harrison	2006 2006 2006
3741	Jim Cochrane	2006	3766	Seth Armitage	2006
3742	Donald Macleod	2006	3767	Alan Hinchcliffe	2006
3743	Kevin Mallett	2006	3768	Alan King	2006
3744	Gill Martin	2006	3769	Jacob A. Roell	2007
3745	Jean Ramsey Smith	2006			

As ever, the tales of the various triumphs and antics of this year's Compleaters make interesting reading. Final summits are usually happy occasions, but it was the smell of fear, which was in the air when David Bowden (3548) summited on Sgurr Mhic Choinnich. As his companion raised himself from a table-sized block, the whole thing slid away and crashed down the hill.

It was at 1.23pm. on 4–5–6, that the imaginative Martin Richardson (3552) topped out on Ben More on Mull (he had thought of knocking off his final 'beastly' hill on 6–6–6). He had previously completed the English and Welsh 3000ers. as a night hike, which spanned two centuries!

After Ian Pascall's (3585) son had been injured on Ben Lui, Ian decided to do that hill himself. He did it, but got back down to find further bad news – his car had been vandalised. Although this wasn't his first Munro, it was what got him started. Russel Wills (3567) achieved his first Munro during a school trip from Surrey. Travelling by coach, train, Mallaig lifeboat and dingy, he finally climbed a snowed-up Great Stone Shoot in ex-army boots to reach Sgurr Alasdair.

Malcolm Simmonds (3564) was glad to find that Stob Coire Rainach had a 'noble' cairn, but even happier when he found under the top- most stone, a playing card picturing a naked woman!

Compleating all hills together were Kevin and Marian Hesketh (3581 and 3582). They started as 19 year-old students, and finished 33 years later. On Slioch, walking down into a thunderstorm, an unknown walker took a photo of them. They later found the picture as a full page spread in *Classic Walks*. Jean and John McAndrew (3699 and 3700) also compleated all their summits together, and raised money for the Ayrshire hospice. Starting and finishing together were Billy Urquhart (3597) and Sandy Anderson (3598). They started with the four 4000ers, and finished exactly fifteen years later with Seana Braigh. Graham Foster (3575) also started with the Cairngorm 4000ers., aged sixteen. On the subject of the 4000ers., Chris Dodds (3556) reported his hardest day was when he did the first traverse of all the Scottish 4000' Munros (i.e. both the Lochaber and Cairngorm areas), in 23 hours in July 1980. He compleated on Slioch.

Seana Braigh is becoming the new Beinn na Lap as far as compleations is concerned. Malcolm Clark (3682) compleated on it via the An Sgurr scramble. At 25, Malcolm is one of the youngest people to record with me, but Derrick Smith (3758) who completed on Seana Braigh via Strath Mulzie complimented this nicely, as he was 70 at the time. Only one year older, at 71, James Harrison (3706) completed on Schiehallion. He had suffered from asbestosis, but felt that his hillwalking had expanded his lungs.

Conan Harrod (3605) spent two hours on the summit of Ben More at Crianlarich with 65 people and barbecues. He'd done Everest only a month earlier after breaking his leg on a previous attempt at 8550m. His wife Lindsay (3604) had met Conan during a trip to Skye, whilst he was using the pseudonym 'Survivor'. At the Munro Society Dinner, which I mentioned earlier, I met David and Barbara Hand (3733 and 3734). The day after the Dinner, they gathered 37 people and completed on Geal Charn at Drumochter. Gathering a good group can be one of the most special things about that final summit, indeed Gavin Clarke (3576) got his local Ceilidh band up Schiehallion! Gary Walker (3692) got 24 on Wyvis, where he made the announcement that he was planning to get married. One of his summit group was an 81-year-old who lost his walking poles on the way down, and had to retrace his steps quite a way to get them.

I must give special congratulations to Mike Duncan (3638) and his companion Derek Mitchell (3639), who compleated on Beinn a Bhuird and Ben Avon respectively during the same outing. Mike is our local Postie in Banchory-Devenick, and has been delivering all the compleation letters for numerous years now. He was able to hand deliver his own one!

Torstein Kaald Olsen feels he's probably the first Norwegian to compleat. I'm sure he's also the first person based in Banchory to compleat all the hills in welly boots! Also this year, we've had Jacob Roell (3769) who managed to compleat on January 2 on Luinne Bheinn, with a group of nine from the Nederlands; and his countryman Hein Hogenhuis (3685), who completed within a four-year period. Also finishing was Australian, Yvonne Cuneo (3725), who is part of the Findhorn Community. Her celebrations took place simultaneously in Scotland and Sydney.

Andrew Thompson (3623) from Surrey was taken up Cairngorm by his parents in 1956 aged 14. He begged to go on to Macdui. His parents let him go, but declined to go themselves. As they didn't want him to go alone, they told him to take along and look after his younger brother – changed days indeed. Andrew's other favourite memory from his round was watching his 61-year-old wife's first attempt at abseiling, off the Inn Pinn.

On Nan Hargreaves (3654) final summit, she was presented with gifts from both the Forfar and Friockheim Hillwalking Clubs. These bore the clubs mottos – 'Far i wi noo?' from Forfar and 'Abune then a' from Friockheim.

David A. Gilchrist (3664) offered his son, also David (3665) £5 for every Munro climbed as an incentive when he was aged 10. His son is now £1420 better off.

Peter Herman (3680) finished his last 10 in a bit of a campaign during the last two weeks of August 2006. He packed in such hills as Lurg Mhor and Mullach na Dheiragain, and achieved two visits to Knoydart (by both boat and foot), and had a night at Carnmore stable. He had epics including a friend breaking an ankle and being helicoptered out. He eventually got to Mull for his final hill.

I had one continuous round reported in 2006. This was by Graham Williams (3724) going from Ben Hope to Mount Keen. He had weekend support from his girlfriend, and some food parcels along the way. He also managed to squeeze in two weddings during his Round! Arthur Finlay (3697) on the other hand was more into reps. He had notched up 384 ascents of the Cobbler and 216 of Ben Narnain at the time he completed on Beinn Sgulaird.

To finish off, its always interesting to hear about the embarrassing things done to Munroists, or near Munroists. Alan Hughes (3763) and Nigel Hewlett compleated one week apart. In both cases, their friends tried to assist by lightening their sacks to which they tied large heart shaped helium balloons.

And so moving onto the Amendments, these are as follows. As before, the columns are number, name, then Munro, Top, Furth and Corbett Compleation years:

AMENDMENTS

The following have added to their entries on the List. Each Munroist's record is shown in full. The columns refer to Number, Name, Munros, Tops, Furths and Corbetts.

Number	Name	Munros	Tops	Furths	Corbetts
3061	Nigel G Thackrah	2003	2006		
2084	Elspeth A Smith	1999	1998	2006	
		2006			
		1996			
455	Laurence A. Rudkin	1986	1991	1989	1995
1623	Mike Dales	1996	2006		
		2006			
		2004			
		2000			
		1998			
		1996			
1040	James Gordon	1992	1994	2006	1998
3282	Ray Thompson	2004	2006		
3283	Paul Conroy	2004	2006		
2075	Martin G Hinnigan	1999	2001	2006	
		2004			
494	Terry Butterworth	1987	2004	2006	
		2005			
		1995			
		1988			
279	Jim Wyllie	1982			
1050	Frank A. Mellor	1992	1992	2006	
1051	Jennifer Mellor	1992	1992	2006	
		2000		2006	
		1994		1998	
2494	**Rhona B.I. Fraser	1984	1995	1997	1990
345	John Burdin	1984	1993		
		2006			
1225	Jeff J. Burgum	1993	1993	1993	
		2006			

602	Irvin John Cushnie	1988	1988	1991	1994
		2006			
2096	Jerry Ubysz	1999			
2351	Brian Maguire	2000	2006		
1635	Eric Young	1996		2006	2001
1821	Phil Eccles	1997		2006	
		2006			
466	James Byers	1986		1989	
2795	Maria R. Hybszer	2002			2006
1711	Stewart Newman	1997	1998	1998	2006
1056	Simon Bolam	1992	2006		2006
671	Mike Paterson	1989	1989	1989	
1143	Stephen P. Evans	1993	1997	2006	
587	Harry Robinson	1988		1990	2006
2397	Edith Anne Ross	2000			2006
		2000			
		1992			
364	Brian Dick	1984		2006	
2432	Brian Kerslake	2000	2006		
		1997			
258	Iain R. W. Park	1981			
		1993			
		1986			
112	Peter Roberts	1973	1975	2003	
		2002			
1059	Alexander R. B. Taylor	1992	2006	2006	
2750	Peter Goodwin	1995	2006	2005	
2620	Gerald Davison	2001	2006		
3614	Graham Thompson	2006			
		2006			
118	Diane Standring	1973	2006		2004
3630	Thomas Kaald Olsen	2006			
1625	Thomas Paton	1996		2006	
3194	Gail Crawford	2004		2006	
846	Arthur C. Custance	1988			1999
2606	Colin Crawford	2001	2006	2001	2006
2004	Chris Wright	1998		2006	
		2006			
256	Hugh F. Barron	1981	1997	1988	2002
1558	Andy Heald	1996	2006		
2172	Ian Clark	1999		2002	2006
2173	Alan Clark	1999		2002	2006
2506	Walter C. McArthur	2000			2006
2003	Bob MacDonald	1998	2006	2006	
		2006			
1911	M. J. Almond	1997	1997		
796	David Stallard	1990			2005
904	Martin J. B. Lowe	1991	2006		
989	W. A. Simpson	1988	1993		

After six years in the job as Clerk of the List, I have decided to put away my quill, drain my ink-well and pass the Great Dusty Book (well disguised as an Excel spreadsheet) onto Dave Broadhead. People who wish to register a Compleation or an Amendment and who would like to receive a certificate for either Munro or Corbett Compleation should send a letter with an s.a.e. (A4 size) to the new Clerk. (David J. Broadhead, Culmor, Drynie Park North, Muir of Ord, Ross-shire, IV6 7RP.)

I've very much enjoyed being the Clerk of the List and will miss all your interesting anecdotes.

Have a Great Day on the Hill.

David Kirk

Clerk of the List (retired)

The Munro Society

Now in its fifth year, the *Society* has become an established feature of the British mountain scene. The most important event in the current year was the celebration of the 150th Anniversary of the birth of Sir Hugh T. Munro. The Society took the view that this was an event which should involve as many climbers of Munros as possible and anyone wishing to pay tribute to Sir Hugh was invited to climb a Munro over the anniversary weekend, October 14-16, 2006. More than 450 names have been recorded and these, along with the many complimentary comments about Sir Hugh and the joys of climbing Munros, are now held in the Society's Archive.

It was decided that Driesh, being the nearest Munro to Sir Hugh's home at Lindertis, should be given special prominence and Society members maintained a presence there over the three days.   During that time they welcomed more than 250 well-wishers who 'signed in' at the top. Apart from Driesh many other mainland Munros were climbed and the tributes were recorded with the Society by mail and e-mail. The oldest participant was aged 80 and the two youngest were aged five, one of whom was Sir Hugh's great-great-grandson.

The weekend following was that of the Society's annual dinner and, in memory of Sir Hugh, the event was more formal than usual with SMC President, Colin Stead and Clerk of the List, David Kirk, as official guests. The guest speaker was Dick Balharry of the John Muir Trust. We foresee no further celebrations of this nature until the centenary of Sir Hugh's death in 2019.

Forthcoming during 2007 will be publication of the first number of *The Munro Society Journal.* An eclectic selection of articles has been assembled from both members and non-members, dealing with various aspects of the mountain scene. Depending on how well the first effort is received, it is hoped that further numbers will follow, though not at this stage at regular intervals.

The Society's DVD, *In the Beginning,* has proved very popular. Produced by award-winning director, Jim Closs, it involves interviews with five of the earlier Munroists recalling their experiences on the Scottish hills during the middle years of the 20th century. The narrative is interspersed with some fine shots of the mountains being discussed and the whole is most entertaining. Copies are available from the Society at a cost of £11 including post and packing (cheques should be made out to The Munro Society).

Membership of the Society has now reached the 200 mark, but we are always keen to recruit new members, not least those who compleated sometime in the past. One of the Society's principal objects if to 'Give something back to the mountains' and we continue to seek ways in which this may be done.

Communications should be directed to: Secretary, 12 Randolph Court, Stirling, FK8 2AL or e-mail themunrosociety@usa.net

Iain A. Robertson.

IN MEMORIAM

THOMAS WEIR j.1945

I FIRST met Tom on an expedition to Greenland in 1960 when we shared a couple of weeks studying an Arctic tern colony on a small island of red basalt below the seaward end of the Stauning Alps. The weather was mixed. I remember Tom describing Greenland as "a land of soot and whitewash!" It can't have been that bad because he brought home a fine collection of photographs.

In Scotland we used to meet for a week each year around Easter and carry a camp in to some remote area, usually around Loch Maree, the Fionn Loch or the Fannichs from their north side. From him I learned much about Scotland and the people he had met. He had a wide and growing knowledge of so many things and he had talked to many interesting people in all walks of life. A few days with Tom and you came away more educated about people and places. He broadened my mind.

He was a talented lecturer; he had the gift of turning a slide of a landscape projected onto a flat screen into vivid three dimensions, if not four, because there was usually a piece of history as a highlight. I remember he told me he gave slide shows to the Blind Institute. Tom said that the sea of attentive faces brought out the best in his wit and descriptive powers. He enabled the blind, if not to see, at least to realise something of the vast world we live in.

Tom was an uncontrived enthusiast for the world in all its variety. He had the knack of bringing people out of themselves. I have watched him make the dourest people forget themselves and crack a smile. He was not always sunny. He enjoyed being provocative and when the mood was on him he could be irascible.

During the war he was stationed on the south coast of England, gun-laying against the expected Invasion. As a surveyor his task was to work out the ranging of his batteries for bombardment of the likely landing sites so that fire could be directed on these vulnerable spots without delay and, if necessary, at night. He had the presence of mind to give his home address to the army authorities as 'Glen Brittle House, Isle of Skye.' In this way he gained two extra days leave and a travel warrant to this desirable location. Skye was a restricted area during the war and Tom must have been one of the few people who had the freedom of the Cuillin during those years.

His greatest exploits were the post-war expeditions to the Himalayas with Douglas Scott, Bill Murray and Tom MacKinnon. They were bold men in three senses. First an expedition organised from Scotland was a rarity. We were very much a province in those days; everything was supposed to be done through London; it was bad form for anything to originate in the provinces. Secondly, with the exception of Tom MacKinnon they had to burn their economic boats. When Tom asked for three months unpaid leave of absence from the Ordnance Survey, they said: "No deal – you must resign." Remember, in those days social security was minimal and grudgingly given. Also, leaving your job was a sign of unreliability: it gave you a bad reputation. Times were hard and Tom had to work at his journalism round the clock to make a bare living for fees at first were miserably small. I remember his first car – a ramshackle old Morris van – passengers sat in the back on a spare tyre. (Vans, even small ones, in those days were restricted to an upper limit of 40mph; in return for this restriction less Purchase Tax was exacted – the rebate was recouped later when you were fined for speeding.)

The third boldness was the actual mountaineering when the party finally got to the Himalayas after a three-week sea voyage.

Tom climbed a lot of hard stuff with Len Lovat. It was great to sit and listen to them after a climb. Len was a Procurator Fiscal in Glasgow and a raconteur of legendary skill and Tom had his own fund of stories from his own roots in real life. Their conversation was for me (an unworldly academic) a window into how the world actually works. Tom also climbed with Tom Patey. I wish I could remember his stories of some of the extraordinary outings and conversations he had with the great Patey.

Tom was dedicated to Scotland and like so many of us he hoped that Scotland would grow strongly from her own roots into an independent, self-respecting country with its own individuality. None of us suspected that in the end we would founder in the morass of a global sub-culture in which the chief end of man is to maximise profit.

Tom's greatest achievement on behalf of Scotland was leading the opposition to the proposed hydro damn at Glen Nevis. It was a close-run thing. It was Tom's ability to galvanise public opinion that tipped the balance. He has no successor of comparable clout to provide similar leadership against the present subsidy scam being perpetrated on our countryside by the international windmill industry.

Tom also climbed a lot with younger generations, notably Roger Robb and Ken Crocket. With them he did some memorable climbs when well into his 70s, if not 80s. He also had a number of seaborne expeditions with the Great Tiso – to North Rona, the Flannans, the Monach Isles and other remote locations. I could go on reminiscing about Tom for pages and pages. There was a second trip to the Himalayas… and one to Kurdistan with Douglas Scott…and the time he was smuggled off Stob Gabhar after the party was avalanched out of the Central Couloir…and his remarkable complete recovery from a fractured pelvis after a fall on Ben A'an in the Trossachs.

My favourite memory of Tom is of a time we were climbing something steep on Carnmore crag under a full March moon. He was leading. I can see him now silhouetted against the sky and hear him saying: "This is great! You're really going to enjoy this." The other night in the small hours I woke up and couldn't get back to sleep, so I switched on the radio and Tom's voice came over describing the view from the top of Duncryne. His voice was young and enthusiastic and his descriptive gift brought the scene into sharp focus. I rose up from my bed and walked (metaphorically, of course). I was with him there on Duncryne looking north over the woods to the blue waters of the long loch of islands that divides mighty Ben Lomond from the green Luss hills. It was, of course, a recording of the young Tom in his prime. So much of Tom remains on audio and video tape that he has gained immortality in this world as well as the next.

Iain H.M. Smart.

I THINK it must have been the Campsies that set Tom off on a life of climbing and discovery. Perhaps the shock of seeing for the first time those snow-capped crags was what did it. For in the late 1920s there was little sign of the great popular movement that was yet to come and no adventure schools to take you to the hills. You just went and inevitably met someone doing the same thing. I first met Tom in the early 1930s on the Campsies. He had already found someone, Mat Forrester, also a natural climber and an expert birdman. They had just done a climb on Slack Dubh and Tom was bursting with enthusiasm. He had been inspired early by a delight and interest in bird-watching and had learned a lot from Mat. Tom introduced me to Posil Loch in Glasgow, a fine place for birds and the little woods he had made his own.

Photography was an early interest for Tom. I remember admiring his shot of a tree creeper at its nest and was most impressed to hear it had been used with an article he had written. That was about the start of a great and life long commitment to photo-journalism.

With limited holidays and short weekends time was precious – and so was cash. But climbing was extended with buses and special train fares. The best times were rewarded with his ultimate praise: "That was a day of days."

By 1930 Tom must have explored most of the mountains in Scotland and climbed half the routes then in the guide books; that was also the year that he gave up his job with the Ordnance Survey – a bold thing to do in the hungry 1930s – to allow more time for his flare for writing.

In the post-war years he went on many expeditions and recorded his adventures in books. *The Ultimate Mountains*, the story of one of the first Scots and British expeditions, *Camps and Climbs in Arctic Norway* and *East of Katmandu* are all sought-after classics. An interesting trip we shared was in the remote mountains of Eastern Kurdistan. Those were the early days, later many great things were done by Tom – one of them was getting married to Rhona

Douglas Scott.

IT WAS on a JMCS Novice Meet in February,1957 that I first met Tom, and although on that occasion I didn't climb with him he soon had my address and where I worked. Tom lived at that time in Springburn on the north side of Glasgow, the centre of the Scottish railway locomotive construction and maintenance industry. Serving my apprenticeship in that industry in Springburn, Tom would look out for me at the end of the working day or hear on the radio that industrial strife was to occur, enabling him to make plans for us to go into the hills. From these small beginnings a lifelong friendship developed. Initially, I was very much the novice; Tom had the great gift of putting one at ease and also passing on his knowledge of climbing and his passionate enthusiasm for the Scottish hills and for Scotland.

In those days, Tom had a wee fawn-coloured Morris van, a great asset when the ownership of a private vehicle was rare, but necessary for Tom to gather material to build his career as a writer and photographer and to travel the country giving talks. That same wee van took Tom and I on many a venture, the camp kit packed in the back. More often than not, we headed up the Lomondside road to Glen Coe or the Arrochar Alps.

Rock and winter climbing equipment was very basic in these days, just a rope and a few slings, but that didn't stop Tom taking on climbs in difficult conditions. He was always concerned for the safety of others in the party if conditions proved particularly difficult. It wasn't unusual when conditions were marginal, the rocks wet and greasy, for Tom, determined to finish a climb, to get the spare socks out of the sack, fit them over his boots and continue up the climb.

Tom loved to talk to the people he met, especially hill and rock enthusiasts and when ever the opportunity arose, he would strike up a conversation, finding out what climbs and hills they were doing, what was new to the hill scene and the crags that were being explored. This was the Tom who loved to be immersed in climbing and countryside issues and valued what people had to say about what was happening in the Highlands, especially if it was new.

When the weather was particularly poor for climbing, Tom always came up with something and always managed not to be stuck indoors. An example of this was a mid morning in Torridon, the clouds well down in the glen, the rain hammering on the hut windows: "Not a day for the high hill today," says he "but I know of a chasm up on Sgurr Dubh that would give us an interesting scramble in this sort of weather." After a short walk we arrived at the foot of the sharply defined chasm, water cascading down its sidewalls into an already swollen burn. Very soon, we had forgotten how poor the day had started out as we scrambled up the chasm, water pouring down on us from its walls, navigating round some of the heavier falls or traversing the walls to avoid some of the larger pools in its bed. We emerged from the top of the route several hundred feet above the start quite soaked but satisfied that we had got out despite the weather.

A favourite pastime of Tom's was birdwatching, and I and many others, owe much to him for his knowledge and enthusiasm for 'birding'. Many a day on the hill, be it wet or dry, the field glasses would come into play to identify a bird – maybe just a quick call from a secluded perch – and Tom would announce the bird's identity without breaking step or conversation.

Tom loved nothing better than being among hills and hill people. There was a day we had in the Arrochar Alps when Glasgow and most of the Central Belt were covered by a thick sulpherous fog. We only broke through it on the highest tops, emerging into clear skies and warm sun and were met a solitary climber, Joe Griffin emerging out of the fog as if through an opening door.

Roger Robb.

W. ARNOT W. RUSSELL j.1948

WHEN Arnot Russell joined the Club in 1948 he was already a mountaineer of some distinction. From his native Monifieth, his first sorties into the Angus glens had led him on to greater things and as a student at St. Andrews he climbed extensively in Lochaber, Glencoe and other parts of Scotland. After only a year at University he received his call-up papers and was posted to India where he served with the Black Watch for the latter part of the war. In 1946, rather than coming straight home he went on an expedition to the Western Himalaya where his most important ascent was the South Face of Kolahoi (17,799ft.), the 'Matterhorn of Kashmir', by a new route. He returned to St. Andrews to complete his Chemistry degree, becoming President of the Mountaineering Club there and a golf blue. He was also a member of the Himalayan Club, but an invitation to re-visit the big hills had to be turned down because it coincided with his final exams.

It was on Ben Nevis, though, that he left his most important mark. In the summer of 1943 he took part in the first ascent of *Route II* on Carn Dearg Buttress, the first climb to breach the frontal slabs of that tremendous cliff and now a well-trodden classic. He had been at the CIC Hut with a party from St. Andrews when the legendary Brian Kellet arrived, looking for a climbing companion and Arnot joined him for the ascent. Although Kellet led the climb he needed a strong companion because of the long traverses which the route entails and its intimidating exposure. He could not have picked a better man, for Arnot was steady as a rock in all situations. They probably found the climbing easier than they had expected, but the exposure no less impressive especially as light rain began to fall and they had to climb in socks for better friction. From the top, they descended *Route I* and then climbed the Direct Start to North Trident Buttress to round off a good day's work.

Other climbs followed during that summer including an ascent of *The Long Climb*, also with Kellet.

The CIC became a regular haunt of Arnot's in the late 1940s and early 1950s, especially at Easter and many of the classic routes received his attention, in both summer and winter conditions. In July 1949, with J. H. Swallow, he made the second ascent of *Left-Hand Route* on Minus Two Buttress – a grade harder than *Route II* and another climb of superb quality. Although technical standards have moved on since then, there were not many people climbing routes like this during those early post-war years. He had several Alpine seasons and there is a splendid photograph of him in Bell's *Progress in Mountaineering*, standing with J. D. B. Wilson in front of the Obergabelhorn.

In 1950 he was appointed to the staff of Trinity College, Glenalmond, where he was to remain until his retirement. He continued to climb for a few years and he served on the Club Committee from 1953 to 1956, but he began to concentrate more on skiing and golf, both of which he pursued with the same, boundless enthusiasm.

He took school parties on skiing trips to Glen Shee, in the days when winters were winters and just getting up the Devil's Elbow was a challenge. Uplift facilities were minimal, there were no piste grooming machines and these outings were more in the nature of ski-mountaineering – or as he would say: "Proper skiing." Another regular destination was Ben Lawers where the only form of uplift was Arnot's own drive and leadership and countless pupils followed his tracks up and down the slopes. He was a housemaster at the school for 14 years and he was also in charge of the Combined Cadet Force, for which his army experience naturally qualified him, with arduous training in the Cairngorms an indispensable part of their activities.

In 1958 he married Virginia Kemp, who also worked at Glenalmond. They retired to Crieff where Arnot continued to enjoy his golf and he achieved the satisfaction of 'playing his age' in seven consecutive years.

He died in April, 2005 and will be remembered for his great zest for life, his encouragement of the young and his big, infectious smile. He is survived by Ginny and their three children, to all of whom we offer our sincere sympathy.

Peter F. Macdonald.

JAMES RUSSELL j. 1950

JAMES RUSSELL died in late 2006 aged 86. Active on the hill until his last year or so, he epitomized those members joining the JMCS immediately after war service and then climbing on from 'Those JMCS Bus Meets' (cf. article in this issue).

Russell was on the Scottish hills climbing most of their popular, less demanding, routes in winter and summer, and almost every weekend for many years, mostly at first with Charlie Donaldson. These two invariably camped in a small experienced tent, referred to by them most unkindly as 'The Slum', though boulders and caves could be utilised at times; it was a familiar part of the climbing scene.

He was a remarkably neat, calm and collected climber (and camper) blessed with many self-preservative skills learned earlier in the Scouts and in the combined operations of H. M. Forces. He never scrabbled but seemed to drift up without effort on the grades he favoured. I climbed and camped with him myself after Donaldson moved to the Borders and marriage, and benefited greatly from his imperturbable good humour. Pretty well every weekend we assaulted the Scottish hills in all weathers. We took on skiing, Russell effortlessly, and enjoyed descents that (especially now) make me shudder: heather, replaced by scree and icy crust on many evenings, down to a celebratory cider; he and I tailored ascents to the weather, utilising outstretched anoraks and a strong following wind for many of the tilted summit plateaux.

He was outstandingly generous, and when I was forced to move from the usual cramped Edinburgh digs by the need for overnight research, he offered me a bed and the room he was brought up in, an act of courage much admired by all. My habit of unwittingly introducing mice from previous dosses was regarded benevolently. Ever practical, he oversaw the brushing out of old cheese pieces from my disorderly baggage. I hung on, as long as was decent, to his hospitality but moved out at my marriage; an event he skillfully recorded at my request on camera.

His camping was equally neat but was not an obsession *per se* ; it served whatever he intended to do: fish remote burns, begin a climb right on the first pitch, or just to be among the hills without housewifely fuss. In this course his procedure was not ranked highly by the conventional campers from the original Scouting fraternity, who shook communal heads when Donaldson and he were on the hill one day and returned to find their tent and its contents eaten into and out again by some entrepreneurial fox.

More serious, and attracting great sympathy, was the remarkable Baking of his Flat, occasioned by a cracked chimney flue and unwisely active stoking the previous night. It was too hot to burn anything, and the firemen, alerted by the unusual fumes, discovered next day that every stitch of their clothes and boots were brown and brittle; jackets, and breeks fell from their hangers in heaps. His splendid collection of slides and photographs, extending over years, was of course ruined. Like the fox through his tent, all this was taken philosophically.

Our joint ploys grew rarer when I moved north but he and his flat were always available for refreshment after Edinburgh meetings, and we lost touch very gradually.

About that time, I did notice evidence of other interests; living in the stony centre of Causewayside, he had a yen for the trees he camped among, and a weird collection of bottles, bowls and old pans accumulated in the window recess at his flat, which enjoyed a passing glance from whatever Edinburgh sun briefly escaped from clouds and the overweening shadows of Craigleith masonry. He loved watching the seasons progress across his micro-forests and groves; spring and autumn were always celebrated with appropriate malts. His skill at bonsai resulted in him being elected secretary of a Scottish bonsai society; he was amused by a photograph showing him in deep conversation with the cloud-piercing office-bearers of some Scandanavian bonsai group: his 5ft. 3ins. or 4ins. clearly impressed the tiresomely – 6ft. Swedes: "He is a Real secretary of a bonsai club."

His friendships were wide, and included many of the opposite sex. One companion of many climbs, a highly-competent LSCC member, was drowned by a Cairngorm burn in spate, trapped by a rucksack on the way across. With a later companion, Frances, he shared a house and a happy 'evening of his days' just outside Edinburgh. They shared also many weekends on the Scottish hills, and holidays in the Alps – where he skied, walked and was hoisted to the summits into his eighth decade, dispatching many fresh peaks; and postcards illustrating his success.

G.J.F.D.

DUNMORE HOTCHKIS j.1930

DUNMORE HOTCHKIS was born in Paisley on December, 19, 1909. After school he went to Oxford University where in 1931 he graduated Bachelor of Arts. Thereafter he joined a law firm in Leith and did a legal apprenticeship with that firm attending Scots Law evening classes at Edinburgh University, graduating LLB in 1933. He joined the Writer to the Signet Society in 1934.

While at University, during the holidays and while working in Leith, he went to the hills in Scotland with members of the SMC. He kept a most interesting diary during a period of about 10 years prior to the outbreak of war in 1939. One first ascent on Ben Nevis is recorded, namely a route in summer to the right of *Slingsby's Chimney* leading to the North-east Buttress somewhat above the First Platform. He was particularly keen on rock climbing in Skye and did many of the long scrambles and climbs.

He volunteered for His Majesty's Forces before the outbreak of war in 1939 and he served with the Cameronians for six years spending three of those years abroad. He took part in the invasion of Sicily and Italy and later in the final push into Germany.

After the war in 1946 he returned to the legal profession and took over the law firm of his uncle James Napier Hotchkis in St. Andrews. He continued to walk and climb in the Scottish Hills. He married Betsy Dishington Scott in 1953 and had three sons. He imparted to his sons his love of the hills, wild places and his abiding interest in the environment, birds, wild flowers, geology, astronomy and history. He was an elder at Holy Trinity Church, St. Andrews and became the session clerk to fill in on a temporary basis and remained the session clerk for more than 20 years. He was widely read and remained mentally extremely alert into old age.

He enjoyed going to the hills and particularly the Cuillin with his sons and did short sections of the Cuillin Ridge into his early 80s. He dealt stoically and bravely with failing sight in later years. Dunmore is survived by his wife, Betsy, and sons James, Robert and Michael.

James Hotchkiss.

NEIL MATHER j. 1983

NEIL MATHER died peacefully, aged 78, in his beloved Strathspey, after a long illness.

His part in the resurgence of British Alpinism in the 1950s earned him a place on the 1955 Kanchenjunga expedition. There it was characteristic of Neil to establish and man the top camp (26,900ft.) with Charles Evans, the leader, and to maintain it while George Band and Joe Brown, then Norman Hardie and Tony Streather, reached the summit on successive days. It was equally characteristic for Neil to agree, modestly, with Charles that success had been achieved and support for everyone's safe descent was more important than a third summit bid.

Neil started his long and varied climbing career from Bury Grammar School and his village Scout troop. His old friend and climbing companion, Les Radcliffe, describes it as "very *Scouting for Boys* – style", camping and exploring the Pennine Moors. Their first climbing experience was on Coniston Old Man when their Rover Scout crew camped at Coniston under Fell and Rock Club leaders.

Neil and Les went on to become regular visitors to Widdup gritstone outcrop – sometimes working through the routes in winter and "disappearing back into the darkness and the moor".

After school, Neil entered the still vibrant Lancashire cotton industry studying for his textile manufacturing qualifications, and later lecturing at Bolton Technical College and the Shirley Institute.

There was little time off but Les and Neil frequently climbed in the Lakes and occasionally North Wales. With K. Hargreaves visits were made to Glencoe and Skye for old classics. There Neil acquired his taste for our Munros.

Neil joined the Rucksack Club in 1949 and it was mainly with club members that he went to the Alps. His alpine record done in short holidays included: 1949 – Strahlhorn, Allalinhorn, Zmutt Ridge of the Matterhorn. 1950 – Les Droites, Geant, East Face of the Grepon., Requin. 1951 – Zinal Rothorn, Obergabelhorn traverse, Lyskamn traverse, Weisshorn by Schalligrat and East Ridge. 1952 – Dent Blanche, Charmoz-Grepon traverse, Pain de Sucre, first British guideless of the Peuterey Ridge of Mont Blanc with Ian McNaught-Davis. 1953 – East Ridge of the Plan, frontier Ridge of Mont Maudit, Rochfort-Mont Mallet (solo), Forbes Arête of the Chardonnet. 1956 – Mayer-Dibona on the Requin, Aiguilles du Diable, Mont Blanc de Tacul, South Ridge of the Aiguille Noire du Peuterey with Albert Ashworth. 1957 – Punta Gamba, Cima de Brenta.

In the 1980s he went to the Oberland with Donald Bennet, climbing the Monch, Jungfrau, Finsteraarhorn and the Gross Grunhorn. On another occasion, with Donald, he climbed the main summits of Monte Rosa and Pollux. He climbed the Biancograt of Piz Bernina with Camillo Kind and then traversed Piz Palu with his wife, Gill, Camillo and his wife. In 1993, aged 66, Neil and John Allen climbed the Aletschorn from the Mittel-Aletch hut in superb conditions, after a stormy retreat the previous day. Then they went to the remote Aar bivouac hut to climb the Lauteraarhorn – a wonderful expedition. Then it was off to the Britannia Hut and the Strahlhorn where Gill joined them for John's last Swiss 4000m. peak.

In 1957, Neil married Gill and, looking for a mountain activity they could share at the same level, learned to ski which led to more than 40 years of ski-touring and downhill in the Alps and Scotland. Then living in Yorkshire, Neil changed from the Rucksack Club's propensity for immense hill-walking challenges to long-distance fell-racing. He regularly entered the Three Peaks race and more than a dozen Lake District Mountain Trials. His best result in the Karrimor two-day event was fourth. What pleased him most some years later was to come second, with Gill, to 'two young men' in the Veterans' class.

Neil and Gill, in 1971, moved to Cork where in two years they introduced orienteering to a mixed non-denominational group which was regarded as a considerable social as well as sporting achievement. Whilst there he completed his Furth Munros and wrote the chapter on Macgillicuddy's Reeks for *The Big Walks*.

He came to Fife in 1971 to work and joined the Scottish mountain scene. As vice-president of the Scottish Ski Club he met John Wilson, Douglas Scott, Donald Bennet among others. He became a regular guest at the 'Aberdeen' table at SMC dinners.

Neil speedily completed his Munros in 1980 (including the Cuillin Ridge, the 11 Mamores and the A'mhaighean round in fast, single-day outings). He continued his hill-running with Scottish enthusiasts. Besides many long Scottish winter days, his Alpine ski-tours included: 1967 – The Haute Route, 1971 – Otztal Rundtour. 1972 – Stubai Rundtour. 1980 – Vanoise tour with SMC members and, later, several tours with Alpine guide, Claude Rey.

In 1983, he joined the SMC. With the further withering of the British textile industry, Neil moved to Edinburgh to exercise his management skills with Lothian Council.

At this time Neil and Gill acquired David Grieve's secluded 'bivouac' caravan, near Aviemore, which became a meeting place for many hill friends. A notable occasion was entertaining a group of mature Swiss ski mountaineers after a hard day, who voted fish suppers and malt whisky the best hut food ever. This meeting led to many reciprocal visits including Neil and Gill completing the 20th Engadine Ski Marathon.

Neil retired in 1991 and moved to Kincraig from where he completed his second Munro round and accompanied Gill on her completion; Alpine and Scottish ski tours were pursued, and he experienced modern climbing gear with young Club members to his great satisfaction.

Neil experienced a remarkable range of mountain activities and adventures about which he kept pretty quiet. Difficult and brave moves were played down in favour of gentle, funny reminiscences about his companions. Among these were excitements with spicy cars and motor-bikes. He told a great tale of stormy crossings of the Alps on the back of Mac Davis's smooth-tyred bike in order to climb the Peuterey. Less happy was the losing of the 1953 season by being knocked down by a van in Kent, his AJS being wrecked and Ted Dance, his climbing companion riding pillion, badly injured.

In 1995, along with Gill, he joined the trek to Kanchenjunga base camp to celebrate the 40th anniversary of the ascent. This was very enjoyable, but to those of us whom Neil joined immediately afterwards for a late season Alpine ski-tour, it appeared he had suffered some illness which curtailed that trip for him and from which never regained his old high level of health and fitness.

In the last few years of his life, Neil enjoyed the social life of Kincraig and Kingussie with many new friends and old climbing comrades from far and near, as well as gentler climbs and walks in the Highlands, Tuscany and lower Alpine valleys. He continued moderate skiing well into his 70s.

In the summer of 2005, Neil had a last adventure when Gill arranged a light aircraft flight from Inverness to North Wales for the 50th Kanchenjunga anniversary, in the place where the team had done their preliminary training. He enjoyed that immensely.

Chamonix 1953: Tom Patey and I were going up to the Envers des Aiguilles hut when we met two finely-equipped English alpinists coming down – Neil Mather with Geoff Piggot. Neil chatted with friendly enthusiasm with two scruffy Aberdeen students. Tom had received Cambridge comments about pre-dawn porridge making on hut terraces, remarked as we parted: "That's the nicest guy we have met here."

Fifty-two years later Neil's friends, overflowing Insch Kirk, would have understood.

J.M.T.

GEORGE BRUCE j.1974

I FIRST met George Bruce as a very young 18-year-old lad when I was trying to join the RAF Kinloss Mountain Rescue Team, the RAF premier team. George was on leave when I arrived at the Mountain Rescue Team Headquarters, I was told to go away – I was too small and skinny. George found out and took me under his wing and gave me my start. George was the RAF Kinloss Team Leader, a God. He was a small, stocky man with a face full of character; he spoke and told tales in the same broad accent as the famous Bill Shankly, stories and tales flowed from him. He was without doubt my hero.

George had outstanding people skills, not learned from any management course, but from life. A Physical Training Instructor by trade, he was also a parachute-jumping instructor, with more than 1000 jumps to his credit. Few people know this because he rarely mentioned it. He had a unique personality and charisma which made him one of the best man managers I have ever met. Unusually, for someone in the RAF, George was never intimidated by rank. He was also teetotal, but seemed to get high on a few cans of coke.

Such were his powers of persuasion that a 10-minute discussion with George could change your opinion on any subject. He could convince you black was white. I have never known him to lose an argument.

George was not a crack climber compared with modern day standards, but he had an aura and tremendous area knowledge. He was the thinker and could walk into a call-out anywhere in Scotland, and hold his own on any incident. Due to his 'people skills' he could talk to survivors of an accident and get the full story of what happened, and deploy the troops with maximum efficiency. George was forthright in what he saw as the correct course of action and many owe their lives to his good decisions.

The Kinloss team was heavily involved in the Cairngorm Disaster in November, 1971, when six Edinburgh schoolchildren and two instructors went missing on the Cairngorm Plateau in atrocious weather. Kinloss and a Glenmore party found two survivors barely alive, who needed immediate recovery to survive. George jumped on to a Royal Navy Sea King Helicopter and after a short brief the pilot agreed to fly the recovery mission provided George was with him. George guided the chopper from Glenmore, up Strathnethy and over Loch Avon in desperate weather, and on moving onto the plateau the pilot lost his ground reference and

Neil Mather. Photo: Niall Ritchie.
James Russell. Photo: Frances Craigie.

landed in a white out. George got out and waded the last mile through the snow to the casualties with the chopper hopping along behind him. The casualties were evacuated and made a full recovery. Throughout this tragic operation his leadership was inspirational and George was awarded 'The Queen's Commendation for Brave Conduct'.

George loved Scotland; the Kinloss area of responsibility is huge and the Team travel all over Scotland every weekend. He had a love for the hills and hill people, making so many contacts among the landowners, keepers and gillies on whose land we trained. This allowed access into remote areas way before 'freedom to roam' was granted. A day with George on the hill would involve a leisurely start, a visit to the keeper or the estate house, usually with tea and a good chat on what was going on. He rarely used a map: "a sign of no confidence" in your mountain knowledge and had such knowledge of wildlife, especially bird's, flowers and the wild land we trained in. The day would end with us doing a wee job for the estate and maybe getting some venison or fish and of course a wee dram to end the day. This was priceless local knowledge, invaluable in callouts, allowing us – as a MRT – access to climbs and crags by private tracks accessible only to a few.

In my first winter with the team, 1972, we set off from Ben Alder Lodge where we were staying in the garages next to the great house. The plan was to climb Lancet Edge on Sgor Lutheran, near Ben Alder, a classic winter ridge, very remote. It was full winter conditions and as we broke up on to the ridge George was in full story-telling mode. I was breaking the snow when we were avalanched 600ft. over a buttress. All I remember was George dragging me out of the snow where I was buried. He lit a fag and said that I should be privileged, to be avalanched with him so early in my career as a mountaineer. He said he was testing my route finding, which he said could improve. We then ran away!

When we remember George we must not dwell on the many difficult and sad mountain rescues that he led. But must remember him for his zest for life and the many amusing stories that he told.

Shortly after the Cairngorm tragedy George participated in an expedition to Elephant Island in the Antarctic. On his return he showed me some photos of eight guys pulling a loaded sledge and George standing in front. He said that as the only NCO he had to be the leader as they were all officers and could not be expected to make sensible decisions, so they pulled the sledge. Once again throughout this difficult expedition he showed outstanding leadership and was awarded the British Empire Medal.

When George arrived at Kinloss in 1968 the team was a wild bunch of hard men who took some handling. Trophy pinching was the game for some. However, on most occasions the item was returned and there was no problem. But on one occasion it all went wrong. Two of the troops lifted a cannon from Onich but before it could be returned it appeared on 'Police Five' on the TV. Unfortunately, it was found by those in authority and a witch-hunt started. The local police were involved, but the culprits would not own up. Although the police were threatening to charge the whole team with theft, the troops decided to call their bluff.

The Station Commander was demented. Anyway, after three weeks of a stand-off things were getting heated. George at this time was the team leader in waiting. The Officer i/c gave a 15-minute talk promising the culprits that if they owned up he would find them the finest lawyer in Forres, equally as good as Perry Mason. With that George asked to speak. Don, the officer, eagerly thinking he was going

Arnot Russell. Photo: Geoff Dutton.
Ian Campbell. Photo: Niall G. Campbell.

to get George's full support, invited him to take the floor: " Don't own up because they will hang you," says George and the saga went on for another three weeks.

In 1973, George was posted to the RAF Outdoor Activities Centre at Grantown as Chief Instructor. Many and varied are the courses run at this unit. One of the courses is for senior officers, really a bit of a jolly for two days. George spent the morning instructing these officers on kit and how to pack their hill sacks and how important all this equipment was. They were instructed to be on the bus with their kit at 1300hrs. for a walk round the Northern Corries of Cairngorm. They were duly boarding the bus when George noticed that the most senior officer had no hill bag: "Where is your hill bag, Sir?" says George. "Do I really need one?" says the officer. The retort from George was: "God and the mountains have no respect for rank." With that the officer scuttled away for his bag.

George left the RAF and became Ranger of the Pentlands National Park, a new career and he loved the job and its people. He called it "his estate". He came regularly to the RAF Kinloss team reunions. He was a natural speaker and could give the most entertaining speeches at the drop of a hat. Here he was in his element as a speaker, without doubt one of the finest, he never used notes and spoke from the heart. He could make any subject interesting and his sense of humour was infectious. He became a stalwart member of the British Legion in Prestonpans serving as treasurer for 14 years and more recently as President for six years. He was a great fisherman and loved the crack at the harbour with the locals.

George was an ardent Glasgow Rangers fan, a season ticket holder following them through thick and thin, whenever possible taking his grand-children to the games. When George was told he had cancer he asked the specialist how long he had left to live: "Will I have time to see Rangers win the European Cup?" Unfortunately, you will not the specialist said. George replied: "I would have worried if you had said yes." Rangers were appalling at the time. What a sense of humour.

George touched so many of us, taught us so much about life, people, the wild land, the animals and its mountains. It was a privilege to be a part of your team and the world will be a sadder place without you, but your memories, stories and jokes will live on.

David 'Heavy' Whalley

IAN MACLEOD CAMPBELL j.1927

THE FIRST chapter of Hamish MacInnes' book on mountain rescues, *Call-Out* describes one of the earliest rescues in Glencoe. It was in 1934. The Elliots, stalkers in Glencoe, and others, had brought in a badly injured climber, having carried him down on a door after a difficult rescue at the foot of the Church Door Buttress of Bidean nam Bian. The Factor went into the room where the seriously injured climber lay. He then came into the living room where Mrs. Elliot was handing out bowls of soup to the exhausted rescuers: "There's no need for your camp bed," said the Factor. "I'm afraid he's gone." However, thanks to the courage of his rescuers and the skill of the surgeon Sir Norman Dott, Ian Campbell was not gone and was to live another 72 years, dying, months short of his 100th. birthday, on April 21, 2006.

In 1979, at the age of 72, he returned to Bidean nam Bian and looked at the scene of his accident: "Looking up at the Buttress," he wrote in the *Scottish*

Mountaineering Club Journal, "I was amazed, humbled and very grateful to all those good people who combined to rescue me in 1934."

Ian MacLeod Campbell was born in Edinburgh in 1907, the son of a lawyer, and went into the family legal firm of Archibald Campbell and Harley. He lived all his life in Edinburgh. His fascination for mountaineering was encouraged by his adventurous and independent Aunt Florence (Macleod), who took him climbing in the Alps when he was a 16-year-old. She was one of the founding members of the Ladies' Scottish Climbing Club and worked as a nurse with Dr. Elsie Inglis in Serbia and Russia during the First World War.

His enduring love of the hills led to his joining the SMC in 1927 at the age of 20. In his application form, he provides a list of Scottish hills, climbs on Ben Nevis and in the Cuillins, as well as some Alpine excursions, such as the traverse of the Petits Charmoz. He was a founder member of the Junior Mountaineering Club of Scotland and he was still hill-walking in his eighties. In a note about his climbing, he records that the SMC *Central Highlands Guide* attributes a climb in the North West Gully of Stob Coire nam Beith to him and Alan Horne but states that he remembers nothing about the climb, other than they were asked to see if it could be done.

He did little substantial climbing after his accident on the Church Door Buttress, when, having broken the length of Beale's Alpine rope connecting him to his climbing partner, he fell 200ft. and fractured his skull and much else besides. However, he got great and continuing pleasure from the Scottish hills and the companionship of his generation of friends in the SMC, particularly Sandy Harrison, Maurice Cooke, Evershed Thomson, Duncan MacPherson and Bertie Martin. He was a regular attender at meets.

A member of the Territorial Army in the thirties, Ian joined the army at the start of the Second World War. He served, first, in the Royal Scots and, then, in the newly formed Special Air Service (SAS) with whom he finished the war as a Major. He was part of the team that had the task of deceiving the Germans with misinformation over the D-Day landings and was in Norway for the surrender of German forces.

Ian's other great interest was Scottish and family history. He wrote a book about his branch of the Campbells, the Campbells of Inverawe. This interest also led to his purchase, in 1960, of Fraoch Eilean, a small island in Loch Awe below Ben Cruachan, and revealing a little known Campbell castle through many visits and much clearance of trees and undergrowth. This interest in family history also led to his involvement, as secretary, in the founding of the Standing Council of Scottish Chiefs, to ensure that armorial bearings were properly used and protected.

In December 1939, he married Jean Gordon Sanderson, who predeceased him. He is survived by a daughter and two sons.

Niall G. Campbell.

IAN Campbell was a man of fine character who had a way of looking you directly in the eye and engaging your attention. There was always a warm welcome at the family home in Inverleith Place and it was there that I first heard of the SMC and devoured the contents of its Journals. Fraoch Eilean was also the scene of many a happy visit, with its little hut where we would spend the night, the old ruined castle and the view of Cruachan from the middle of Loch Awe – a magical place. Ian's last appearance at an SMC function was probably at the 99th. AGM and Dinner on Corstorphine Hill in 1987, at which time he had been a member of the

Club for 60 years. Although his membership lapsed after that he had certainly been one of our longest-standing members and he had given service to the Club as a Committee member from 1933 to 1936 and then as Meets Secretary. He wrote an entertaining account of the 1934 Braemar Easter Meet in the Journal of that year as well as an interesting article on climbing at Fast Castle (near St Abb's Head) in the previous year's edition. We are indebted to his son Niall for providing the main Obituary and extend our sympathies to all the family.

Peter F. Macdonald.

DOUGLAS CAMPBELL j.1949

DOUGLAS CAMPBELL was one of life's fortunate people, blessed with excellent health and a sharp enquiring mind. Born in Dumbarton in 1912, he was raised in Coventry. Overcoming limited educational opportunities, he made a career in electrical and mechanical engineering, later forming his own business.

From an early age, Douglas's enthusiasm for the outdoors led him to the hills and his climbs were extensive both at home and abroad. When wartime came, Douglas and his wife Kathleen spent several years in the Vale of Lorton in the Lake District, later moving to North Lanarkshire. Then, as his children grew, his focus changed to weekend hillwalking as well as caravanning trips in Britain, Western Europe and Scandanavia even travelling as far afield as South Africa and the United States.

After Kathleen's death in 1983, Douglas was undaunted. He remarried the following year, emigrating to USA aged 72 years. Unflagging travellers, he and his wife Jane crisscrossed the lower 48 States, visiting most National Parks as well as countless State parks, nature reserves and historical sites. They also travelled to Portugal, the Galapagos Islands, Costa Rica and Chile. Although Antarctica remained an unfulfilled dream, he did make a road trip to the Andes of southern Patagonia aged 90 years.

Douglas's travel reflected his love for the natural world and concern for its preservation. An ever present camera was the means to share these interests with his family and the wider community. His mountain years were an excellent foundation to a fulfilling life.

DSC.

TAM McAULAY
Creagh Dhu Mountaineering Club (1946-2006)

TAM McAULAY died on Wednesday, September 20, 2006 while on a walking holiday on Rhum. During a river crossing with a companion from Arrochar Mountain Rescue Team, Tam was swept over a waterfall. Members of Arrochar Mountain Rescue Team and Ian Nicolson, a fellow Creagh Dhu Mountaineering Club member, recovered his body on Sunday, October 1, 2006.

Tam started climbing in 1976 at the age of 30 years. Dumbarton Rock was where he became a regular feature in and around the Castle's boulders. Dressed *de-rigueur* in his blue cotton workman's trousers, steel toe-capped boots and black T-shirt, Tam would 'levitate' to the crux, pause, pluck the cigarette from his lips and pronounce: "This must be the hard bit."

Without the aid of chalk, he would deftly dispatch a boulder problem. Then, sounding like a dentist calling his next patient to the chair, he would hail down to the gawking crowd: "Next?"

At weekends Tam regularly ventured to either Glencoe or to his beloved Cobbler, where he excelled on the hardest test-pieces of the day. In May, 1980, Tam was admitted to the Creagh Dhu Mountaineering Club, after his faultless ascent of *Club Crack* on the Cobbler. Tam's background of working class Clydeside Engineer fitted well with the club's ethos. As club secretary, treasurer and librarian, Tam loyally defended the working class values, leftward leaning politics and anarchistic attitude towards the establishment that the club was founded on. He never missed a club AGM in his 26 years of membership. During the final two weeks of his life, Tam was reviewing the club archives. Also, in his final two weeks he contributed his time-served skills and physical effort to digging out and relaying the floor to Jacksonville, the club's hut located below Buachaille Etive Mor in Glencoe.

Tam's passions and interests went beyond climbing. He devoted his time to photography, poetry, playing the accordion, literature, and local history. He was often called upon to contribute to radio programmes about the Cobbler or the Creagh Dhu. Typical of Tam, few people knew that in his younger days he had represented Scotland in cycling time trials.

The most unique aspect of Tam was his ability to maintain the great weekenders' tradition of telling jokes and stories. Anyone who happened to be in Tam's company, very quickly realised they were in the presence of a massively talented individual. He could take the corniest joke and with his perfect timing and immaculate gesturing deliver a side-splitting punch line.

With his traditional values and attitudes, Tam gave modern trends and fads, such as 'management speak' and 'political correctness' a run for their money. One dark evening, returning from a late shift at the Esso Oil Terminal at Bowling where he worked as a maintenance fitter, he noticed a gang of youths messing about with his neighbour's Christmas lights. In one effortless movement Tam vaulted the hedge and grasped the ringleader by the throat with his left hand. The youth just managed to croak out: "Mister, yeh cannae hit me. A've goat rights."

" Aye, well son, here's another right," as Tam delivered an eye watering right jab onto the delinquent's nose.

While snowed-in at Jacksonville in 1984 with Arthur Paul, Dave 'Cubby' Cuthbertson and Davie Paraffin, Tam provided the heat and light from his Tilley lamp. After two days, the talk eventually got round to feats of physical strength and the inevitable pull-ups: "Well Cubby, see if you can do this?" Tam leapt up, pinch gripped the roof joists and with biceps bulging and little puffs of breath, hauled his chin up level to his straining fingers. "Now try this," Tam dropped one arm to his side and with an effortless rhythm, pumped his body up and down in one-arm pull-ups. "…nine, ten! And now the other arm."

Holding his torso up to the beam in a one-arm lock, Tam let go of the joist and seemed to float in mid-air before deftly catching the beam with his other hand. "…nine, ten! Your turn Cubby!"

Cubby tried and tried, but failed to even complete a single pull-up.

"Now look, now look, son." Tam shifted the Tilley lamp so his feet were no longer in the shadow. He then performed the whole feat again, but this time revealing that his own feet had never left the floor.

On one dreich Saturday morning, Tam and a couple of the boys decided to go for a wander on the Bridge of Orchy hills. At the first fag break a bottle of 'travelling sherry' was produced. By the time the bottle was finished, the dreichness had degenerated so much, that it became impossible to even roll a fag. By some magical consensus, it was agreed to get off the hill and go to the Inveroran Hotel for a midday session.

As they left the bar at afternoon closing time, a flock of chickens were clucking around Tam's car. With a bit of careful herding by the Team, a prize rooster was successfully enticed into the back seat of the car. Doors firmly slammed shut and windows wound up, the team plus a newly-acquired avian hostage set off north.

At the Kingshouse Hotel, Colin the chef was busy preparing the dinners for the guests. During one of Colin's frequent fag breaks from the heat of the kitchen, Tam ventured to Colin: "Could you do us a favour.? We don't have an oven in Jacksonville, could you cook a chicken for us?"

"Aye, nay bother, just bring it in to the kitchen."

"Well, that's not possible, it's not exactly your Marshall's Chunky Chicken variety. You need to come to the car."

Colin wandered up to Tam's car to be greeted by a very distraught rooster clucking and ruffling its feathers while perched on the back seat.

"No bother, I'll deal with it. Just come back and pick it up tonight,"
said Colin.

As the team departed for the Ville, they glanced back to see a rather large chef dressed in whites, surrounded by a cloud of chicken feathers.

That evening, after closing time, Colin brought the chicken through to the Public Bar in a roasting tin, accompanied by an Asda carrier bag full of chips. Aye, the Chicken Rustlers had a good feed.

Tam had many rock climbing trips with the Creagh Dhu to the US, the Alps, Sport Climbing 8a+ in France, often in the company of John Maclean and Graham Harrison. In the 1990s Tam took early retirement from work due to a heart condition. He bought and settled in a house in Arrochar, which has a stunning view across Loch Long to the Cobbler. Tam involved himself with the Arrochar Mountain Rescue Team. He provided rescue support to the Lowe Alpine Mountain Marathon. He regularly went weekending, holding forth in the Kingshouse Hotel, Glencoe with his unique patter and wit.

Many people in the climbing and weekending scene have encountered Tam, few will forget his charm and wit.

Members of the Creagh Dhu.

Notice has also reached us of the death of Malcolm Slesser.

PROCEEDINGS OF THE CLUB

The following new members were admitted and welcomed to the Club in 2006–2007.

MARK BOYD, (41), Management Engineer, Dundee.
MICHAEL T. COCKER, (52), Physiotherapist, Wilmslow, Cheshire.
GRAEME GATHERER, (30), General Practitioner, Abernyte, Perthshire.
EMILY B. HOLL, (40), Engineer, Blair Drummond, Perthshire.
ROSS A. HUNT, (21), Student, Kingussie.
PATRICK INGRAM, (40), Rope Access Technician, Inverness.
SUSAN L. JENSEN, (39), Statistician, Inverkeithing, Fife.
JEREMY P. L. MORRIS, (30), Structural Engineeer, Glasgow.
DAVID MOY, (63), Rope Access Technician, Inverness.
JOHN T. ORR, (40), Production Manager, Elgin.
HEIKE PUCHAN, (27), University Lecturer, Dunblane.
BRIAN ROBERTSON, (64), Climbing Instructor, Boulder, Co., US.
ANDREW N. D. SPINK, (40), Outdoor Pursuits Instructor, Oban.
DAVID STONE, (65), Architect, Edinburgh.
DUNCAN P. TUNSTALL, (44), retired, Aboyne.
PAUL WARNOCK, (33), Oudoor Pursuits Instructor, Glasgow.
BRIAN M. WHITWORTH, (32), Business Analyst, Dunblane.

The One-Hundreth-and-Eighteenth AGM and Dinner

THE AGM and Dinner was once again back at the Ben Nevis Hotel in Fort William and again there was no sign of winter snows. Many members took the opportunity to have a walk in the morning and be back at the hotel for the afternoon entertainment provided firstly by Robin Campbell, who showed a short film made by Tom Weir of Marshall and Moriarty making a second ascent of *Yo-Yo* in 1960.

This was followed by Simon Richardson racing though a range of slides of winter climbs from all over the Highlands. Both were very well received by the audience and made a good start to the evening.

Then it was on to the AGM where, among other things, the secretary informed us that we should expect to move with the times and receive our newsletters by email. Of most concern to the members was the CIC hut and the plans for an significant rebuild of the extension. The final conclusion, reached after a vote was that the Huts Sub-Committee was authorised to proceed. Finally, the meeting approved the nomination of Paul Brian as new President.

The Dinner was very well supported with 158 diners, who were well fed and watered by the hotel. Dave Broadhead gave the Toast to the Guests and our principal Guest, Mike Tighe, replied on their behalf. For the first Dinner that I can remember, he even had a 'support act' who were parading a range of historic outdoor clothing and climbing equipment that he has collected over the last 40 years. These he has kept in storage until now when he hopes to get the majority of it permenently displayed in Fort William.

Our out-going President, Colin Stead, finished the evening by thanking all the speakers and we were then free to retire to the bars to continue the craik.

Sunday was wet but this didn't stop a merry band from making their way up to Steal Hut to enjoy tea and cake provided by our new president Paul Brian.

Next year the Committee are likely to take us farther north and east to Strathpeffer. I look forward to it.

Chris Huntley.

Easter Meet 2007 - Inchnadamph

THE meet was held at Inchnadamph Hotel. Members had elected to hold this year's meet on the weekend following the Easter holiday. In spite of, or maybe because of, this change of date the meet was well attended. There had been a couple of weeks of good weather and we enjoyed warm hazy days with only mild winds. There was almost no snow on the hills. Conditions were so good that several members, after they had climbed their chosen hills, adopted Iain Smart's custom of having a relaxing sleep in the heather beside a singing burn. John Hay and Bill McKerrow walked to the meet from the head of Glen Casseley and Mike Fleming cycled back from Seana Bhraigh while Des Rubens and Dave Broadhead climbed four new routes at Flurain.

Members explored new areas and climbing including Slabs of Breabag, Tarsuinn Breabag, Stac Pollaidh, Quinag, Canisp, Braebag, Conival, Ben More Asynt, Meallan Liath Coire Mhic Dughaill, Cranstackie and Beinn Spionnaidh, Strone Crag, Eididh nan Clach Geala, Ben Hope, Ben Klibreck, Meall a Chrasgaidh, Sgurr nan Clach Geala, Sgurr Each and Glas Bheinn.

Those present: President Paul Brian, Robin Campbell, Brian Fleming, Douglas Lang, Peter MacDonald and guest Calum Anton, Bob Richardson, Iain Smart, Colin Stead, Dick Allen, Peter Biggar, Dave Broadhead, Robin Chalmers, Quentin Crichton, Mike Fleming, John Fowler and guest Helen Forde, Phil Gribbon, John Hay, Bill McKerrow, John Mitchell, Roger Robb, Des Rubens, David Stone, Nigel Suess and guest Maureen Suess.

Dick Allen.

Ski Mountaineering Meet 2007

Members present: Chris Ravey, Anthony Walker, Donald Balance, Ewan Clark, Graham Dudley, Bob Barton, Bob Reid and David Eaton, accompanied by guests Gordon Clark, Dave Howard, Ian Crofton and Dave Coustick.

The ski mountaineering meet returned to Base Camp at Mar Lodge over the weekend of February 24-25, 2007. This is at least the third time that the meet has been held here, which reflects the standard of the accommodation and suitability for this sociable event.

Keen to set the pace for the weekend, Reid and Crofton arrived early on Friday and made an ascent of Carn a'Mhaim. Unfortunately, the snow was noticeable only by its absence.

Later on Friday evening the rest of the party arrived. The Internet is a wonderful thing and, by the number of mountain bikes attached to members cars, it appeared that everybody had been researching the recent snow reports and forming their own opinions, namely that the white stuff would be very hard to find.

Following a sociable breakfast, numerous parties set out for the hills on Saturday morning. Needless to say that skis were left behind in all cases. Ravey and Walker opted for a day without mechanical advantage and walked up Carn Damhaireach, making a circular route back by taking in Carn Bhac and Carn Creagach. A few patches of snow were noted but the conditions were generally spring like, although the summits were in the cloud. The mountain hares were extremely conspicuous, their white coats standing out on the green hillsides. Eleven were counted at one time.

Ballance and Eaton made an ascent of Carn a Mhaim. Again, very little snow was seen – just as well since skis had been left in Glasgow. Mountain bikes were the chosen mechanical aid and were used to gain access to the hills. The pair obviously had too much time on their hands in the afternoon as it is reported that snooker was enjoyed in the main section of Mar Lodge upon their return.

Clark, Clark, Howard and Dudley ascended Bheinn Bhrotain and Monadh Mor, fully assisted by bikes, with no snow encountered until 950m. Barton, Crofton and Reid (the elder statesmen of the group), covered 26 miles on bikes plus a misty wet ascent on foot of Carn Ealer and An Sgarsoch.

Reports on Sunday's activities have been hard to come by, although it is reported that Dudley, Clark and Howard made an ascent of Beinn Bhreac, partially assisted by bikes and with virtually no snow seen. The ascent was followed by an ecxiting mountain bike traverse of the Clais Fhearnaig

Following retail therapy and Sunday lunchtime indulgence, Ravey began to feel the full burden of his status as acting meet convener and set out after lunch to find the white stuff. A very brief break in the cloud revealed linked snow patches high on Carn an Tuirc and Cairn of Claise. In optimistic mood he set off with skis, which were donned at 700m., giving 300m. of skinning up to the summit of Carn an Tuirc. Compass work aided in locating the col between Carn an Tuirc and Cairn of Claise (by foot down snowless slopes). Skis were again used to gain the summit of Cairn of Claise. From which a 1000ft. descent of uninterupted spring snow was made down Garbh-choire. An unexpected day!

In summary, a fine mountain weekend was enjoyed by all. However, it is rumoured that there is much talk about holding next years ski meet in Norway. Alternatively, we may just accept our fate and re-name the meet as the Mountain Bike weekend.

Chris Ravey.

JMCS REPORTS

Edinburgh Section: Membership is currently 81 and new members continue to join regularly. Rock and winter climbing remain the most popular activities, but members are also active on the hillwalking, skiing and mountain biking fronts.

Regular midweek meets are held every Wednesday. During the winter, these are normally at Heriot-Watt University climbing wall, and in summer the club visits many of the local outdoor venues; sometimes venturing farther afield to Dunkeld or Northumberland. There is also a regular contingent of members at Alien Rock on Mondays.

Popular summer meet destinations included Glen Feshie, Glenbrittle, Buttermere and our own Smiddy hut in Dundonnel, with the weather being mostly benign. Routes climbed included *King Bee* on Creag Dubh, *Triple Buttress* on Beinn Eighe, The Old Man of Stoer, and the round of Corrie Lagan incorporating The Cioch, King's Chimney, An Stac and the Inaccessible Pinnacle.

Winter meets were not blessed with such good fortune, with a combination of bad weather and poor conditions meaning that at least one meet finished with not a single climb having been completed. The March meet to the CIC hut, however, had excellent weather and superb ice conditions. Routes included *Wendigo*, *Comb Gully*, *Thompson's Route*, *Two step Corner*, *North Gully (left fork) and Green Gully.*

The annual dinner was held at Mar Lodge and was a great success. A good meal was followed by an entertaining speech from Charlie Orr of the SMC. The evening was finished with a game of 'Killer Pool' in the billiard room, surrounded by stags heads and other sporting trophies on the walls.

The club's Smiddy Hut at Dundonnel continues to be popular with clubs from all over the UK and booking well in advance is advisable. The club has also taken a lease on a new building, 'The Cabin', near Newtonmore. Work is currently under way to convert this into a second hut to replace Jock Spot's.

The joint slide nights held with the JMCS and the SMC Eastern Section were well attended by members from both clubs. These are held monthly throughout the winter on Tuesday nights at the South Side Community Centre, 117 Nicholson Street. Talks this year included *Toothpaste in the Arctic*, by Colwyn Jones on his trips to Greenland, Dave Macleod on some of his recent cutting-edge first ascents, as well as subjects as diverse as paragliding and mountain footpaths.

Officials elected: *Hon. President,* John Fowler; *Hon. Vice-President,* Euan Scott; *President,* Patrick Winter; *Vice-President* and *Smiddy Custodian,* Helen Forde (30 Reid Terrace, Edinburgh, EH3 5JH, 0131 332 0071); *Secretary,* Robert Fox (10/3 South Gyle Loan, Edinburgh, 0131-334-5582 e-mail secretary@edinburghjmcs.org.uk); *Treasurer,* Bryan Rynne; *Meets Secretary,* Sue Marvell; *The Cabin Custodian,* Ali Borthwick.

Robert Fox.

Perth Mountaineering Club (JMCS Perth Section): The club seemed to have ditched the 2005 bad weather jinx, starting with a successful meet at Glen Etive in January when Brenda Clough ascended her final Munro, Stob Coire Sgreamhach and champagne was enjoyed at the summit.

More sunshine was enjoyed on the Glen Brittle meet with Skye basking while heavy showers could be seen on the mainland.

The June meet to the remote Garbh Choire of Beinn a' Bhuird was well supported and whetted the appetite for similar trips in the future; after a high camp in the corrie many enjoyed climbing *Squareface* while Graham Nicoll and partner climbed *Slochd Wall* on Mitre Ridge. The atmosphere and the quality of the climbing made this an excellent meet.

The Aonach Eagach provided an excellent venue for the July meet which was very well attended. The weather was dry and warm and luckily the predicted rain did not materialise. For some it was their first experience of a ridge and proved to be an exhilarating day.

A small group attempted a Cross-Mounth Walk in July. The day started off with thick mist but this soon cleared by the time the summit of Glas Maol was reached. A spectacular sight of several hundred deer in one of the coires was enjoyed. The weather improved steadily over the day giving wonderful views and culminated in a stunning evening as the group descended Lochnagar.

Good weather failed us during the Northumberland meet which saw our members getting a thorough soaking and even attempting a climb with an umbrella!

The September day meet to Buachaille Etive Mor was again well attended. The weather started off looking ominous and ended in very heavy rain. However, the day was enjoyed by all with several climbing routes attempted including *Curved*

Ridge, Lagangarbh Buttress and *D Gully Buttress.* The rain did not inspire anyone to hang around on the summit so everyone decamped to the Kingshouse for tea.

The Annual Dinner was held at the Ceilidh Place, Ullapool and was attended by a select bunch. The weekend forecast was horrendous but miraculously we managed to avoid the bad weather and instead enjoyed some great views from various summits. A slight altercation over access rights added to the excitement of the weekend.

Wednesday evening climbing meets were well attended with superb weather in the main and only one evening being called off. Some old favourites such as Polney and Cave Crag were enjoyed as well as some interesting new ones such as Farm Crag. The air ambulance was only called out the once!

PSNS/PMC Joint Lecture was an inspiring and informative talk presented by a team of four Scout Leaders with excellent slides. An overview of expeditions to Elbrus, McKinley, Cerro, Aconcagua and Kilimanjaro was given and the project is to culminate with Mount Everest being climbed in April 2007 which is the worldwide centenary of scouting.

Officials elected: *President*, Donald Barrie; *Vice-President*, Trish Reed; *Secretary*, Lucy Garthwaite, St Ann's Cottage, North Street, Burrelton, PH13 9PB – 01828 670447; *Meets Secretary*: Claire Aldridge; *Newsletter Editor:* Des Bassett; *Treasurer*, Pam Dutton; *Committee Members,* Chris Hine, Phil Taylor, Ray Lee, Irene Macgregor.

Lucy Garthwaite.

Glasgow Section: The 2006 winter season was variable, and as usual it was a matter of being in the right place at the right time. Pre-Christmas 2006, cold weather in November and December allowed some mixed climbing at the higher venues. A JMCS team in Cairngorm's Coire an Lochain had a lucky escape when a large block was pulled off by the leader, destroying the second's rucksack on his back but leaving him otherwise unscathed. Those able to take time off work mid-week found excellent rimed-up crags on the Bridge of Orchy hills.

January and the start of February were generally lacking in snow, but club members took advantage of the odd cold period to climb water-ice and mixed routes. The small amounts of snow meant that the Northern Corries proved popular, with members climbing *The Genie*, *Pot of Gold*, *Savage Slit* and *Central Crack Route*, among others, as well as some 'un-starred classics'such as *Vent Rib Direct* and *Inventive*. The paucity of snow in early February is indicated by the story of one experienced club member ascending the same two routes (Ben Nevis' No. 2 and Gardyloo Gullys) on consecutive weekends because there was no other snow to be found on the mountain! Heavy snow in mid-February followed by a period of cold gave the mountains a wintery appearance but in most places did not consolidate well, so that time consuming deep wading and snow clearing were required on routes. The first heavy snowfall coincided with a club meet in Glen Coe, and members made use of this to climb *Flake Route*, *West Chimney*, *Sphinx* (much longer than the guidebook's 135m.) and for a mass ascent of *D Gully Buttress*. The CIC hut meet in March coincided with disappointing ice conditions, but the attendees made good use of the mixed climbing opportunities, ascending *Observatory Ridge* and *Route I*, among others. An accident in which a member broke his leg falling on *North East Buttress* led to a helicopter rescue, and stopped his climbing activities for most of the summer, but at least kept him off the hills so he could spend more time with his new family.

Finally, towards the end of March good ice conditions started to appear, with several members visiting a busy Creag Meaghaidh for *The Wand, Diadem, Centre Post Direct, South Post, Missed the Post*, and *Smith's* on a weekend which provided the best ice conditions of the year for many. The same weekend saw a mass JMCS ski to, and ascent of, *Deep-cut Chimney* in the Cairngorms. A thaw was followed by another cold snowy period which enabled a last few winter routes to be done in April by JMCS parties on Shelter Stone Crag and Eagle Ridge. So the winter at least provided club members with some climbing in six months of the year, even if not much ice or névé was to be found anywhere.

Two members went ski touring in the Pennine Alps accompanied by two SMC members. Three 4000m. peaks (Weissmeis, Breithorn and Castor) and two 4500m. peaks (Zumsteinspitze and Signalkuppe) were ticked over 10 splendid days. In contrast to Scotland the weather was excellent and fresh powder snow on three mornings added to the experience.

The spring started promisingly with good weather, apart from the Easter weekend when those loyal to Scotland were rained and winded off the hills and crags. The first May bank holiday weekend in contrast was gloriously sunny, with JMCS parties climbing on Aonach Dubh, Caithness sea cliffs, and elsewhere. The Coruisk work meet at the end of May had the traditional wind and rain to wash all the paint off before it could dry.

The cool spring kept the midges at bay for a while, so that midweek evening cragging around Glasgow in May and June was very pleasant. (Two keen club members with a fast car and fit legs included Ben Dorain as a midweek evening climbing venue). Of particular note was a meet at the Whangie with 20 attendees (two of whom were eight months' pregnant), barbeques, beers, and a long walk back in the dark.

The hot dry summer allowed members to tick many seldom-dry routes in Scotland, the Lakes and Wales, including the first ascent of a new two-star route on Grey Buttress, Newlands, Lake District – *El Scorchio* (E1). Shelter Stone's *Steeple, Needle* and the *Pin*, proved popular, one team enjoyed *Torro* on the Ben, and several members were pleased to find the routes on Creagan a' Choire Etchachan dry.

As usual, many JMCS were to be found climbing abroad, mostly in Europe in the summer, but some farther afield. One party visited the desert around Moab in Utah climbing several classics including the *Kor-Ingels* on Castleton Tower, *Ancient Art* on Fisher Towers and *Supercrack* at the jamming mecca of Indian Creek. They report landscape and rock formations "out of this world" and that both climbing and hiking in the region are exceptional. They give two particular pieces of advice for would-be visiting climbers – take three sets of cams and, if you think you can jam well then think again!

The usual suspects' raid on the Alps yielded a number of ticks; In the Dolomites, *Comici* (classic north face) and *Yellow Edge* on the Tre Cime, and *Big Michelluzzi* at Sella Pass; *Luna Nascente* in Val di *Mello*; *Motorhead, Graue Wand* and *Kingspitze NE face* in the Grimsel area; and *Cengalo NW Pillar* and *South Ridge* (Bregaglia).

Later in the year, two groups visited Kalymnos and returned with tired arms but much enthusiasm for the steep rock and pleasant location.

The AGM and Dinner were held in November at the Bridge of Orchy Hotel, and the Christmas meet at Lagangarbh featured the usual eclectic mix of slides and photos of the year's activities.

Club members are not just active climbing. Several members are getting close to the end of their Munros, and the Corbett-baggers are also making good progress. Scottish ski-mountaineering this winter was restricted to just six JMCS-member-days, but would prove more popular with more snow. Mountain bikes are seen on many club meets, helped by the access legislation to allow us to explore hitherto out-of-bounds Highland estate tracks.

The club has welcomed a number of new members this year, and membership now stands at 99. Weekend meets are held fortnightly and are often over-subscribed unless the weather forecast is really poor. Members meet regularly midweek at the climbing wall or crags near Glasgow, and the fortnightly Thursday night pub meet in the Three Judges is ever popular.

Jeremy Morris.

London Section: Like the year before, 2006 was characterised by a wide range of activity – climbing, walking, mountain biking and sailing at home and abroad. The year began with the traditional President's meet at our hut, Glenafon in Bethesda, when the mild weather forced a change of plan from the CIC hut. In February, however, the section returned to Scotland and from the Raeburn Hut there was climbing on Creag Meagaidh and Munro-bagging in the Drumochter hills but the highlight was an overnight stay by seven members in Culra Bothy and a sunny ascent and descent of Ben Alder by the Leachas ridges in good compact snow.

Spring meets took place in the Lake District, North Wales and Northumberland, mainly rock climbing in between showers. Late May Bank Holiday on Skye was, however, a washout. Some went motor biking and others retreated eastwards, eventually finding dry weather in Perthshire. The now annual sailing trip to the Hebrides took place in June with visits to the Shiant Islands, Soay, Canna, Rona and Skye and there was a delightful meet in the Yorkshire Dales in June care of Chris Comerie and a great weekend in Edale in July, with a three-year old seconding one member up a route (prospective members get younger even if the section is ageing).

In early August, several members were active in the Dolomites. In the autumn it was back to North Wales for meets near the Rhinogs and at the club hut – mainly mountain biking and walking and then an enjoyable club dinner at Plas y Nant (thanks again Nigel).

Work is under way to make Glenafon 'fire safety approved' and paid up membership now stands at 35. We have a new President, Steve Senior, and a new Secretary, John Firmin. Thanks to Chris Bashforth for several years' service in this capacity. 2007 holds plenty in store with a group undertaking the Annapurna circuit and Chula East, and an Alpine meet in the Ecrins alongside the more traditional UK venues.

John Firmin.

SMC AND JMCS ABROAD

Western Canada

SIMON RICHARDSON REPORTS: During May, I made a quick visit to the Coast Mountains of British Columbia on the back of a business trip to Vancouver. During several previous visits I had struck up a strong friendship with Coast Range guru, Don Serl. Don is the author of the guidebook to the Waddington Range, so I was very excited by the opportunity to climb with him on his home ground.

The Coast Mountains are infamous for their poor weather, but most years there are good weather windows in May and August. The rise in temperatures during May transforms the bottomless powder of winter into more consolidated snow, making it an ideal time to attempt snow and ice routes. Don was keen to explore some of the mountains in the Remote Group, but as we flew in by helicopter on May 14, it was clear that the weather window had arrived a little later than usual and the mountains were still heavy with their winter coat.

We landed below Mount Remote (3015m.), and next day made the first ascent of the 400m.-high East Face via the striking central couloir that cuts through the wall. The climbing was about Scottish Grade IV, and comprised a mix of snow, ice and mixed. We arrived on the tiny summit early in the afternoon. The mountain had only been climbed twice before, and we were the first people to visit the summit for nearly 40 years. The descent down the original route kept us guessing all the way, with a mixture of down climbing and the odd judicious abseil, but eventually we arrived back at the tent early in the evening after a very rewarding alpine day.

The next stage of our trip was to transfer glacier systems and descend to the Remote Glacier from where we planned to attempt Mount Bell (3248m.). Don's proposed descent was down a steep 1000m. south-facing slope which had been pummelled by avalanches, but this was far beyond my rudimentary skiing skills. After a day recceing an alternative we skied along a ridge and descended to the Upper Remote Glacier. The 800m. ski descent wearing climbing boots and carrying a large pack was one of the most exhausting things I have ever done in the mountains, and I felt much happier once we were skinning uphill again. We camped below the unclimbed north face of Broad Peak, a fine fluted ice face in the classical mode. It was a beautiful evening and Don remarked that we were probably the second party ever to visit the glacier. Next day we skinned over a col to the Remote Glacier and descended to make camp.

Two days later, our attempt on Bell floundered in soft snow and unstable cornices so we flew out next day. The Coast Mountains, pristine, untravelled and still little explored, will keep future exploratory climbers and mountaineers happy for generations to come.

Norway

PAUL BRIAN REPORTS: Last year everyone seemed to be talking about Norwegian ice, so when the Rescue Team announced a week of subsidised training in Norway with the opportunity for some climbing thrown in, I applied right away. I was dismayed to be the oldest by about 20 years but greatly relieved when Noel Williams also signed up, thereby elevating the average age (and average IQ he would claim) to a more respectable level.

Twenty-two of us flew to just outside Oslo, hired cars and drove about four hours to Ryuken. The first couple of days were spent in fairly intensive activity and dialogue with the local team. Understandably, they specialise in technical rescues down steep icefalls and inevitably the discussion turned to lowering devices, clampy things and various other gizmos. Some of our guys work on rope access so the conversation gets pretty complicated and, frankly, catatonically boring. Apart from that it was all good stuff. When access to casualties is difficult, Norwegian rescuers are expected to be able to solo Grade IV. This criterion, if applied to the Lochaber Team would, we reckoned, reduce our numbers to about four people.

Next day involved a master class with three local hard men who demonstrated to us the correct way to climb fragile icicles and overhanging chandelles – (Yeah right – very likely!) At this point Noel took off with one of the locals to tackle a ferocious looking Grade IV. Unfortunately, within minutes his mentor had dislodged a fairly large portion of Norway, which proceeded downwards directly on to Noel's head. One very smashed helmet and minor blackout later, the editor of *Skye Scrambles* found himself inspecting the inside of the local casualty unit. Grogginess disappeared fairly quickly and by the end of the week he was back to normal – leading vertical ice, leaping half-frozen rivers and, on the final day, leading a new route for us all to follow.

The routes come as a bit of a culture shock to your average Scottish climber. For a start, perfect ice is virtually guaranteed from November till the end of April. Most of the climbs are in gorges so one actually walks down to the start – average approach time about 10 minutes. Typically, the routes are one or two pitches long and end up on tree belays or, even better, on the road above. The ice is bomb proof so you get to play with all those whizzo ice screws that you gave yourself for Christmas. There are also some excellent multi-pitch routes higher up the hillsides but they can be avalanche prone after heavy snow. In fact, the day before we arrived, the local team had been called out to rescue a party on such a route. The party had abseiled from ice screws but had run out of hardware after 10 pitches then called for help. Brits of course. There was an unseemly rush to inspect the route next morning.

As a holiday resort Ryuken is pretty dismal. The sun doesn't penetrate to the valley floor mid-winter and the temperature didn't rise above zero throughout the entire week. As it snowed more or less constantly it makes for a fairly gloomy atmosphere, and frankly, I would get pretty depressed after a while. It's largely an industrial town about the size of Fort William and originally the lift up to the plateau was built to enable workers to get some sun and to fight off the winter blues. The history of the town is interesting because this was the site of the heavy water plant which was sabotaged, then bombed, in the Second World War – there is a museum dedicated to these events in the old Hydro factory.

Costs of the expedition were not as horrendous as we had feared. A week, all-inclusive, cost about £500 – less if you can get really cheap flights – but check the baggage allowance. We met some climbers from Newcastle there for a long weekend.

My impressions were favourable overall. It's not like the real thing but it's good safe fun and it certainly helps fitness and confidence. We came back to an excellent spell on the Ben and many of us knocked off things we had long fancied. Even your correspondent knocked off a couple of Grade 5s (Norwegian Grade 3) and actually enjoyed them for once.

If anyone wants details of accommodation, guidebooks etc. please get in touch and I'll do my best to help.

Lofoten Islands

ALAN HUNT REPORTS: I'm sure you will remember that piece I wrote after a circumnavigation in the s/y *Blue Biscay* 10 years ago, (SMCJ 2000) No! Ah well, since then the awful climbing rat has reared its consuming head and land-based activities have once more assumed a priority, in particular rock climbing. Sailing has become marginalised to trips to Brittany, the isles of the north and West Coast and a murky trip to St. Kilda. However, the urge to sail and climb lurked in the back of my mind, but I couldn't rise to Bill Tilman's efforts, or afford a paid crew. Pabay was out because the anchorage is lousy but the word came round that Lofoten might be a possibility. The *Rockfax* web site had some worthwhile information including one of their ubiquitous mini-guides, a visit sounded worth while and that was that. The travel part of most climbing trips is usually by assured means, a choice of planes, ferries, trains, buses and hire cars. Any excuse to bring a sailing boat into the mix has to add an interest to the trip, especially when it involves crossing the Arctic Circle.

So, it was that a club cooperative of three, one each from the SMC, FRCC, and CC, left Inverness with a fair breeze in mid-May making Shetland in good time. We decided that if possible we would head directly up the North Sea with the option of sneaking into the Norwegian Fjords in the event of severe weather. Twenty four hours later we were rushing toward the impressively rock strewn Norwegian coast to avoid a rapidly increasing northerly gale and four days later we were still there.

Eventually, the wind dropped and we carried on up north in very wet and cold conditions dodging the weather by using the 'inside route' amid spectacular scenery. So much unclimbed rock.

We arrived in Lofoten and the sun came out then along came the fog and we had an anxious time locating the entrance to the fishing harbour of Hennigsvaer, our nearest jump off for cragging. The crags were a medium walk or very short bus ride away with much to do on the quick drying close-grained granite and we managed several classics in the few days before the rain came back with a vengeance. *Gandalph*, a four pitch VS 4c was excellent and *Guns 'n' Roses* at HVS 5a , equally fine. It was surprising how many other climbing teams were camped under the crags, among them some Edinburgh students: "Are you the guys who sailed here?"

"Yes."

"How are you getting back?"

The obvious rude reply came from another student:

"How do you think you s…p…"

So we did, reaching Inverness at the end of June. Wish we could have spent more time up there and I wish the beer hadn't been so expensive.

Europe

BRYAN RYNNE REPORTS: Having visited the Cote du Rhone Villages area for two successive spring holidays, I felt that a select group of us ought to step up the grade. The obvious destination for this was Burgundy (there is even some good climbing there, which clinched matters).

An excellent week was had, extensively sampling a carefully selected range of premium cru wines (well, I walked along the aisle with the trolley, grabbing the most expensive wines in the shop). These were all excellent. To go with this, we also found some tremendous local mouldy cheeses. What more could you ask for? Well, climbing I suppose…

Pinnochio IV6+ Mont Blanc du Tacul. Photo: John Baird.

We managed some very good climbing, although several days were curtailed by late afternoon thunderstorms. We also lost one day to rain. Apart from that, the weather was good for climbing – sunny, but not too hot.

The climbing was all bolted sports routes, ranging from steep, technical slabs at Remigny, to long (35m.) vertical corners at Cormot. We were doing French Grade 5-6, but there is lots of harder grade stuff available to anyone that wants it. Remigny had a tremendous looking wall, overhanging at about 15°, full of 7b routes – a thunderstorm drove us off before we got onto this wall.

CHARLIE ORR REPORTS: There are increasing references in this Journal to mountain-biking: in JMCS reports; in Brian Davision's hut-to-hut epics and, in this issue we have Chris Ravey raising the spectre of the club ski-mountaineering meet facing the challenge of global warming in one of two ways – either decamping to Norway or changing the name to the mountain-bike meet.

In September last year I undertook a five-day journey by mountain bike around the base of the Mont Blanc Massif accompanied by members Tom and George Denholm and a friend Wullie Sloan. The ride covers 180km., mostly off road and takes in 7000m. of climbing over six mountain passes. The route starts in Chamonix, proceeds over the Col du Balme (2191m.) into Switzerland, then into Italy by way of the Grand Col du Ferret (2537m.) finally returning into France by way of the Col de la Seigne (2516m.). We organised this trip (dare I say it) through the company MBMB in Chamonix and were picked up at Geneva airport and ferried to our chalet in Les Bossons just outside the town.

The first inklings that there may be some organisational glitches along the way came when there was a prolonged argument between our guide, Nick, who met us at the chalet, and the Spanish driver, as to who was going to pay for the taxi from Geneva. I immediately put on my 'bugger all to do with me look' and started to load my gear into the chalet. The dispute was eventually settled when Manuel grudgingly accepted Nick's exhortations that "Phil will pay". Phil being, as we later learned, the boss of the company, who didn't exactly endear himself to me at the first night briefing by referring to us as 'Scotties'.

At 10am the following morning we gathered in the courtyard of the chalet ready for the off, At which point Phil, here-in-after referred to as Boycie – bearing un uncanny likeness, we thought, to the 'Fools and Horses' character, with his wide-boy London accent and braying laugh – appeared and asked who was going to join his 'elite' group (there were two groups of 11) All the 'Scotties' managed to resist this siren call without too much difficulty and each succeeding day only served to confirm us in what proved to be a very fortuitous choice.

A gentle road ride of two miles or so brought us into the main street in Chamonix where some of the group stocked up on spare tubes and more than a few energy gels. The first off-road riding trended up through the woods by the River Arve to Argentiere and as we entered the village we passed a number of very spaced out (not just distance-wise) competitors in the Mont Blanc Ultra endurance running race, which basically followed our route but in the opposite direction. We later found out that the winner completed the course in about 21 hours, but the guys we saw on their last legs were on the last leg of the race into Chamonix and would narrowly avoid the 48-hour cut-off point.

We continued uphill to the village of Le Tour, the scene of a devastating avalanche some years back which all but wiped out the village. Here we took the only cable

Lofoten Islands. Photo: Alan Hunt.

Skiing on the Hardanger Plateau above the Rjukan Valley, Norway. Photo: Noel Williams.

car of the trip up to the Col du Balme which at 2191m. forms the border with Switzerland. Lunch was taken here before some great twisting single-track across the col where we encountered the one and only snow field crossing of the trip. Once we reached the tree line on the Swiss side we had to negotiate some very muddy, rooty and steep single-track which, after the torrential rain of the preceding days, had been churned up well and proper by the passage of the hundreds of endurance race competitors. One of our number came to grief on this descent sustaining quite nasty facial injuries which necessitated hospital treatment and sadly, he took no further part in the proceedings.

This technical descent took us onto a fire road and then on to tarmac and after a couple of miles of steep climbing, a mixture of trail and road, we reached the Col du Forclaz and our hotel. I omitted to explain that the deal with MBMB included our luggage being ferried between each overnight stop. It is possible to do this tour unsupported and we did see a couple of people doing just that. However, George has a saying that he applies in situations like this involving the words 'nuts' and 'mangle' and in this particular case I would have to agree with him. The freedom of being able to ride unencumbered by a hefty rucksack was well worth the extra cost.

From now on it was nine o'clock starts and when we went off-road the next morning onto grassy single-track there was still a heavy dew about and when I locked up on a steep section the tumble that followed was inevitable. No damage done, we continued down winding track to the main road leading to the Grand St. Bernard Pass. After a mile or so we turned uphill and there followed a steep road climb to the village of Champex where we stopped for lunch. This was the regular pattern to the day and despite taking on board huge amounts of pasta over the week I registered a net weight loss at the end of the trip, it was simply burned off as necessary fuel. Calories in/Calories out is the simple equation here and no matter what winky-wanky diet is followed by people trying to lose weight it is this universal truth that lies behind it. I digress, enough of that particular hobbyhorse. I took the climbing prize by a fair margin – competitive, who me? I'm a 'roadie' at heart and I had the polka dot Tour de France climbers' jersey in my bag but I was making sure of my position before I put it on the following day – sad really isn't it (rhetorical).

The day finished with an ascent of the Val Ferret beneath the famous Amone Slab which features in Rebuffat's *100 Finest Routes*, after which we overnighted in the tiny village of Ferret. All accommodation was in mountain gites, mostly with shared rooms. Only once were we in dormitories, an emergency measure after an administrational cock-up by Boycie.

The next two days saw the hardest climbing of the trip over the Grand col de Ferret at 25337m. overnighting in Courmayeur and over the Col de la Seigne 2516m. – where we experienced falling snow at the summit – and the Col de Roseland the following day, overnighting on the shore of very picturesque Lac du Roseland. The final day was, yes you've guessed it, climbing again up to Montjoie with a final descent to Les Contamines and St. Gervais.

Even with the pampering of no luggage and with hotel accommodation overnight this trip is pretty demanding and, if your tempted, make sure both you and your bike are up to it before you go. I'm not even going to tell you about the travelling masseuse – I can sense enough grumblings of derision as it is!

REVIEWS

Hostile Habitats – Scotland's Mountain Environment. (The Scottish Mountaineering Trust, 2006, hardback, 256pp. ISBN 978–0907521938, £15.00.)

This is an excellent, vacuum-filling new title from the SMT stable that sets out to give walkers and climbers a greater understanding and appreciation of the landscape and species that constitutes the Scottish mountain environment.

The 12 contributors, including the joint editors, Nick Kempe and Mark Wrightham, have well-founded academic, scientific and/or conservation backgrounds and are all regular hill-users. (It is worth reading their CVs before starting out on the book).

Seven of the nine chapters cover geology, shaping of the landscape, vegetation, invertebrate life, birds, mammals, reptiles, amphibians and fish and finally, human traces. Each of them also includes an identification section illustrating the more common features and species to be encountered in the hills. However, these sections are by no means exhaustive, therefore the work should not be regarded as a full field guide, but rather an excellent primer and catalyst for the more curious and inspired to further invest in proper field guides and monographs, as required.

A major criticism of the book must be the presentation of the index, which is less than user-friendly, especially for the novice. Broad subject groupings, from 'Birds' to 'Vegetation' are listed alphabetically, but this means that if you want to source information on, say, Adders and Ticks, you have to find your way to the 'Mammals Reptiles and Amphibians' then to 'Invertebrates' (but not 'Invertebrate, general') sections. Also the page numbers for the photographs and illustrations really should be highlighted in bold typeface – standard practice in publishing. These points will, I am sure, be rectified in future editions of which there are likely to be a number for, by Christmas 2006, most retailers had run out of supplies, with Tiso reporting sales as 'phenomenal'. Interestingly, the book is selling well to those who work, as opposed to play, in the hills – foresters, rangers and instructors.

Hostile Habitats is an ideal companion volume to *The Munros* and *The Corbetts* and the area guides, and is good value for money. The photography is superb, including a nice retrospective of the late Bob Scott of The Derry gralloching a stag on Beinn a' Bhuird.

The concluding chapter, 'The future of Our Mountains' by Nick Kempe, is a concise and thought-provoking account of the status of attitudes towards our mountains and current activity to protect them. Kempe does not preach nor exhort, but asks us to: "…consider the wider questions of what the natural environment, including mountains, is for and what roles humans should play in them". And, not for the first or last time, W. H. Murray's words are borrowed to close the book and to define our responsibilities towards the mountain environment we love: "Land and wildlife have their own being in their own right. Our recreation is an incidental gain, not an end in itself to be profitably pursued by exploiting land where that means degrading it. The human privilege is to take decisions for more than our own good; our reward that it turns out to be best for us too."

Ian Hamilton.

A Measure of Munros: Graham Wilson, with illustrations by Gerry Dale (Millrace, hardback, 181pp., ISBN 1-902173-18-X. £13.95.)

The OED gives no fewer than 23 different definitions of the noun 'measure' and this book incorporates a number of these in dealing with the Munros. There is something on the history of Sir Hugh's action in preparing his tables, leading to comment on the quantity ascertained. Further discussion of the tables and their revision involves forming an opinion and also involves 'Munro' as a unit of denomination and whether or not it is a standard denomination. How various Munroists have approached their odyssey gives rise to a plan or course of action – and so on.

As a consequence, the broad-brush approach does not fit easily into the normal categories of books about Munros. It is neither a guide book nor a detailed account of the author's peregrinations among the Scottish hills, though these are touched on. Rather it is a *tour d'horizon,* laced with reminiscences, which acknowledges many of the matters which are of concern and interest to the ever-growing cohort of those who climb Munros. While there are no strikingly novel topics or insights, the text bounces along in a slightly jokey way which entertains without being demanding. Such an oversight of the Munro scene is useful, particularly so as the author is concerned with a Scotland-based activity but from an England-based perspective. Wilson's acquaintanceship with Scotland clearly goes back some time with a first introduction during a wet sojourn in Glen Brittle. It is implicit in the text that his mountain experience is in no way confined to the Highlands, but clearly his regard for them has been enduring and he makes a pleasant companion during his tour.

The book though hardback is smaller than a normal paperback and at 181 pages is not long. The small format detracts from Gerry Dale's drawings which are all less than a page in size and at times difficult to identify with the given title. There are also some minor errors – the 'Whitbread Wilderness' was not in Knoydart – but these tend to keep one alert rather than annoy. As a succinct and readable review of 'Munro Matters' Wilson's book has much to recommend it.

Iain A. Robertson.

Millican Dalton – A search for Romance and Freedom (The Life and Times of a Borrowdale Caveman) M. D. Entwistle (Mountainmere Research, 2004, Paperback, £8.99.

Anyone who has ever visited a pub in Keswick will have likely noticed an old monochrome photo on the wall of a strange lanky bearded figure in shorts and a 'Robin Hood' hat piloting an even stranger looking craft, a raft made of sticks and old junk equipped with a tattered sail, close to the shore of a lake (it matters not which pub, there is one in nearly all of them). Inquiry with the barman will reveal that the subject of the photo was Millican Dalton and that, "before the War", he lived in a cave and gave climbing lessons to tourists. And that, quite probably is the extent of the barman's, and indeed most other Keswickian's knowledge, but now Mathew Entwhistle has gathered together what flesh he can to pad out those bare bones and produce this small biography of Borrowdale's self-styled 'Professor of Adventure'.

Dalton was born in Nenthead, near Alston, Cumbria in 1867, where his father worked at a lead mine. However, with the early death of his father, and the decline of the lead industry, the family moved to London when he was 13 years old. From his early days he had an adventurous spirit, and by his late teens was visiting the Lake District and North Wales for walking holidays accompanied by his brothers and other friends. He was by now working in an office but felt "stifled" and in 1901, quit his job to live on a plot of land he had bought in rural Essex, and pursue his dreams of "romance freedom and escapism" and of becoming a mountain-guide. In fact, Dalton soon became what would now be called a multi-activity instructor, offering the chance not only to walk and climb, but also, as he advertised, 'Camping Holidays, Mountain Rapid Shooting, Rafting, Hairbreadth Escapes', and he operated in the Alps, as well as in Snowdonia, the Scottish Highlands, and the Lake District. It was the latter that became his main centre, and he was soon pitching camp all summer at High Lodore Farm (at the foot of Shepherd's Crag), from where he ran his courses.

He continued to run them for almost half-a-century, though quickly adopted a cave on Castle Crag in the Jaws of Borrowdale as a more weather-proof summer residence. He died, at the age of 79, in the hard winter of 1947, and had been still active guiding in the summer before his death. Sadly, his ongoing and unfinished work *Philosophy of Life* has vanished, but can probably best be summed up with his quote: "The simplest life is the happiest." It is safe to say that Dalton was neither a great, nor a notorious man (the more usual subjects of biographies), but he was one of the most picturesque characters that climbing has produced.

In addition to his guiding activities, he was a notable expert on the manufacture of lightweight camping equipment and clothes (he used to make all his own), and despite his lack of hygiene (it was apparently wise to stay downwind of him!) he was popular with the ladies and became a good friend of the noted Lakeland climber Mabel Barker. He was too old to fight in the Great War, but as a dedicated pacifist, he would almost certainly have refused anyway. His greatest achievement though, is that he did what so many of us long to do but dare not, he quit his job and lived a life of freedom. That old monochrome photo on the pub wall hangs today, a monument and a niggling reminder to us all that it can be done.

Entwistle has done the climbing community a great service in researching and gathering together what he can about a man who left no written records – never the easiest of tasks, and taking the gamble of publishing it himself. His account is workmanlike, rather than a masterpiece of modern literature, but it is readable enough, and is enlivened by many of the photographs of Dalton that have survived. Further information is available at his website www.professor-of-adventure.com.

Stephen Reid.

Breaking Trail: Arlene Blum (Simon and Schuster,2005, Hardback, 336pp., ISBN 978– 0743258463, £18.99.)

Arlene Blum writes a gripping autobiography of her life among the enchantingly beautiful, but dangerous high-altitude peaks. She tells a short poignant or humorous story of an aspect of her difficult childhood at the start of each chapter and we learn how this fuelled her determination to succeed in life. This is the determination she displays in her climbing and it enables her to be a successful leader of world-class expeditions, the first American ascent of Annapurna and the first all women ascent of Mount McKinley to name but two. It also results in a highly-successful career in bio-chemical research and in parenting.

A book as well suited for the climber as non–climber for it's powerful and interesting insight into this amazingly accomplished and fascinating life. It is intensely personal at times. We are given a humorous insight into the characters of the climbers she spends time with on her expeditions. She shares both the good and bad times, including the loss of life as a result of the vagaries of avalanche, an ever-present threat on the high mountains she conquers. She also covers extremely well the sex discrimination of the 1970s, when men would not allow women to achieve the same successes on the hill as themselves, nor recognise female achievements, as equals in climbing, when they occurred.

I endorse the foreword by no less a mountaineer than Chris Bonnington: "The book is a compelling narrative on many levels – it is a warm and intimate memoir, an important account of the development of women's mountaineering and a dramatic adventure story."

Ann Macdonald.

Todhra: Dennis Gray, (The Flux Gallery Press, Leeds, 2005, 179pp., ISBN 0-9550158-1-2).

Works of fiction are rare in the world of climbing literature. Invented adventures are simply not as vivid or believable as real life, and fiction best deals with relationships and feelings, things with which climbers are not always comfortable. Dennis Gray's 'coming out' novel of how a climber and his circle of friends come to terms with his being gay proves both points.

The subject matter is in part autobiographical, but would have been too raw and painful to deal with in this form. The settings are all very familiar, Ben Nevis, the Alps, well known cliffs and climbs. A remarkable fictional climbing career is portrayed, with the protagonist achieving new routes on the Orion Face, the Grandes Jorasses and Nanga Parbat in quick succession, with the odd climbing competition win thrown in for good measure. None of this comes over as very credible, and contrasts with the intense and even traumatic personal experiences the main character has to deal with alongside his climbing triumphs. These are described candidly and much more convincingly than the cliched and prosaic climbing action.

The title, *Todhra*, is taken from a desert gorge in Morocco, but the front cover features an icy Karakoram spire. This confusion of images reflects a similar contradiction between the dry action sequences on the climbs and the uncomfortable but powerful emotions described in the intervening pages. The main character is real and vulnerable enough, at least when not on the rocks, though secondary characterisation is rather more limited. Gray's style (despite the efforts of an editor) is perhaps more suited to a magazine article, and the plot stretches credibility farther than a nylon rope, but none of this should detract from an honest attempt to tackle a difficult and largely unspoken subject.

Adam Kassyk.

The Lowland Outcrops, Edited by Tom Prentice (SMT, 460pp., ISBN 978–0907521846, £20).

The Cinderella of Scottish climbing goes to the ball. This, the latest in the SMC's gorgeously revamped series of guides, showcases that most neglected hinterland of Scotland's climbing empire – the Southern Lowlands and the Galloway hills. Often by-passed by Anglos intent on the lure of the Highlands, and only sporadically visited by north-centric Scots, vast areas of rock remain to be discovered by a mass audience. History suggests this traditional indifference is likely to continue, but this magnificently detailed and presented guidebook now means that ignorance is no excuse.

Its 460 pages encompass markedly contrasting and varied climbing terrain, from vast tracts of beautiful and peaceful terrain in Galloway and the Borders to the semi-industrial venues of the Central Belt quarries. The explosion of new routes all over this area, many of them of considerable quality, is a testament to the energy of a small band of exploratory enthusiasts over the last decade.

The 'modernisation' of Dumbarton Rock is comparatively well known (a climbing shot of the chief protoganist, Dave MacLeod, naturally takes pride of place on the front cover). But arguably, the most important function of the new guide for punters is in highlighting the development of places like the Galloway sea cliffs and exquisite roadside venues like Clifton in Dumfriesshire, as well as in detailing the thorough exploration of the: "least frequented climbing area in Britain", the Galloway Hills. (*The Lowland Outcrops* is a useful shorthand, but rather a misleading title in this regard.)

Even more surprising is the perhaps unlikely development of winter climbing in this part of the world, with neo-classic low and middle grade water ice routes such as *Dow Spout* and the wonderfully named *Spout of the Clints* which, climate change permitting, will surely join the ticklist of esoterica sought by cold climb aficionados.

The production standards are what we've come to expect from the SMC; quality binding, laminated cover, clean layout and a selection of often beautiful and well-reproduced colour photographs. Even the plethora of painfully punned route names on the theme of Goats in the Galloway section can't detract from the generally pleasing aesthetics of the guide.

For keen climbers based in northern England and southern Scotland, *The Lowland Outcrops* therefore represents a somewhat urgent addition to the library. For everyone else, it's an ideal source book of ideas for a trip away to somewhere different and often quite magical.

Colin Wells

Scottish Rock Climbs: Andy Nisbet, (SMT, 456pp., ISBN 978–0907521860, £21.)

Considering the sheer scale of mountainous and rocky terrain in Scotland, it is perhaps surprising there have been so few attempts to produce selective rock climbing guides. In the distant past this was due partly to a *de facto* embargo by the SMC on packaging detailed information in guidebook form; in order to write such a thing one had to be a well-informed insider, unconcerned by the pressure of peers, who desired to maintain the aura of mystery surrounding Scottish mountains.

Into the breach stepped brave Hamish McInnes with his two-volume Scottish Climbs (1971) which also covered winter climbs. Although it opened up Caledonia to the great unwashed and ruled the selected guide roost north of the Border for nearly two decades, MacInnes's work was only a partial success. Its eccentric descriptions, dependence on photo-topos and bizarrely unique grading system ensured it probably alienated as many visitors as it encouraged; hence its widely applied derisive moniker: "The MacInnes Bumper Book of

Lies." (As a consequence, there are still many who continue to regard rock-climbing north of the Border as a miasma of horrendous approach marches across midge-infested bogs, streaming cliffs in obscure corries, and cold mossy rock – an image which is only partly true).

It wasn't until the late 1980s that others felt confident enough to improve on this state of affairs. Ken Crocket and Steve Ashton's *100 Classic Climbs: Central and Southern Scotland* (1988) again felt the need to incorporate winter climbs and, excellent though it was, was comparatively limited in its compass and only covered the southern part of the Highlands (a projected northern companion volume sadly never materialised). The first attempt at a modern style rock-only greatest-hits compilation came in 1990 with Kevin Howett's *Rock Climbing in Scotland.* This, however, suffered from the inclusion of a disproportionate number of technically hard routes, with 30% being E3 or 6a or above. Given that the main purchasers of selective guides tend to be less-than obsessed recreational climbers, the inclusion of routes at E7 6c was probably regarded by the majority of users as aspirational fantasy decoration only (Crockett and Ashton's guide, for example, consciously rejected any climbs above E2).

So by the 21st century the world was still waiting for a modern, balanced guide to Scottish rock climbs that showcased the best routes at grades that most on-sighting visitors could cope with. And at last, here it is; ironically produced by the venerable club that did so much to keep the country's rocky jewels hidden through much of the previous century. But these days the SMC is a very different beast, a reformed character with respect to data protection and keen to show off its formidable knowledge. And as a major pioneer of routes in his own right, and a gifted communicator, there are few better people qualified to compile such a guidebook than Andy Nisbet.

His selection of climbs is grand, sampling the best rock from Orkney to Galloway, and from the Outer Hebrides to the Cairngorms. The mix of styles is equally eclectic, from 11-pitch Alpine scale climbs on Ben Nevis to eight-metre high outcrop routes by the road. Selective crag photo topos and diagrams are clear and crisp, while copious photographs illustrate the nature of many of the climbs. Packaged in the SMC's now established 'long thin' style, the guide remains relatively compact despite being packed with an astonishing 1200 routes – there's enough here to fill a lifetime of visits. The book is designed to last for this length of time too – sealed with a robust plastic-backed cover, this is also a guide which is likely to survive many outings in the dreichest of Scottish weather.

Best of all is Nisbet's concisely informative and occasionally lyrical text which exudes authority and wise advice about a boggling array of climbs using little textual h*ors d'ouvres* prior to clear pitch descriptions. It makes this more than a guidebook to take to the crag, but one to dip into at home for inspiration and to relive old adventures, something to lose yourself in over a dram or two by a roaring fire. Its spirit is best summed up by Nibet's wise words: "Don't let the pace of modern life dominate; make time for your climbing."

Colin Wells

On Thin Ice: Mick Fowler, (Baton Wicks, hardback, 224pp., ISBN 978–1898573586, £18.99).

The beauty of climbing really is that there is so much freedom to find your own wee 'brand' of experience within a broad sport, free of rules and, for some at least, a rebel of fashion. Just say the word 'Fowler' to any outdoor climber and they will smile and know exactly what kind of climbing is coming up next in the conversation. Mick Fowler's name is utterly synonymous with adventure – British style.

In his previous writing, Fowler (he likes to refer to himself and climbing peers by second name only, so I'll do the same) has gradually perfected the art of convincing us that he is nothing more than a keen bumbly just like you and me, tumbling on their remarkable adventure almost by chance. The image works well; it seems like anyone could get into these situations, and if Fowler can get into all these scrapes, and get out again, then maybe you or I could as well? Fowler talks to us on our level once again in *On Thin Ice*, relating the stories of more great Himalayan first ascents and other unusual adventures, from one adventurous soul to an adventurous audience who will believe that they could pull this sort of stuff off too.

The accessible (and therefore all the more inspiring) image is sealed by two more aspects of the Fowler demeanour; his easy writing style and constant reminders that he is a nine-to-five man just like the rest of us. There is no doubt it is quite fascinating to read how he has constructed this life of holding down a responsible job as a taxman, living a family life and getting his house featured in *Period Homes* magazine. Yet on the 'other side' he's planning audacious first ascents in little known corners of the world over a real ale down the local and then getting out there and making them happen with exceptional consistency. Real life versus climbing life is a constant battle back and forth, running round the heads of mountaineers trying to have their cake and eat it in life. Fowler not only seems to have found the secret to climbing–life plate spinning, but practises what he preaches with seemingly effortless ease. And now he has written the definitive book on it.

On Thin Ice can be either of two things for you; an entertaining, at times funny and captivating read about one man's adventures in beautiful places and an insight into his motivation and appreciation of the art of climbing, or it can be a one stop guide to being a world class mountaineer yet somehow never doing any training and doing it all within the bounds of the meagre yearly holiday allowance.

The highpoint of the first ascent stories is the dramatic and ultimately tragic ascent of Changabang in 1997 with Steve Sustad, Andy Cave and Brendan Murphy. Murphy was killed on the descent. After a few chapters of the familiar formula of sticky situations somehow turning out for the good, this epic cuts starkly back to the fact that the mountains have the last word, always. The Changabang story comes fairly early in the book and it takes several more chapters before its influence on you wears off and you begin to enjoy the new and positive climbing experiences Fowler gets up to. I guess that is a measure of the strength of this, the most powerful part of the book. Occasionally, I found the self-deprecating style a little overdone. We all know, including Fowler himself, that in truth he isn't really a bumbly at all, but this is his style of humour and it does entertain.

The lasting feeling I had from this work was that far away places and far flung adventures aren't really so far away – you just have to go forth and have them. You may find yourself questioning the logic of going to the Alps next summer – after all China is just another few hours away.

Dave MacLeod.

The Climbing Essays: Jim Perrin,(In Pinn, 2006, 336pp., ISBN 978–1903238479, £18.00).

I have to confess to a somewhat hypocritical dubiety. I've produced one (or two, if you include an accidental alias) book reviews for the SMCJ in the past and I'm still not sure what they are meant to achieve. They provide free publicity for the publishers, of course, but I doubt that anything I have to say will really influence your decision to read and/or buy this or any other book. In this sense, I suppose, it bears comparison with a rock or ice-climb.

I can tell you where it goes, give you a more-or-less objective appraisal of its features, but I can't tell you how it will make you feel. Only afterwards, when we've both done it, can we compare our exalted reflections, relive with animated air-gymnastics this or that move and, for a fleeting moment, possibly experience a resonant correlation. So, instead of using this as a guide, it might be better for you to read the book first, ruminate upon its impact on you and then, of secondary consequence, we can exchange our subjective views about the quality of its pitches.

Before I even opened the book, I was struck by the significance of the cover-design, which features powdery finger-ends tenuously gripping a rocky wrinkle, fixed in a Stygian night-sky. That's all you get – no snowy landscape or rocky spires to sell a fantasy – and it's all you need; just a climber's hand reaching out towards you. It's a simple image but a succinct visual metaphor, for this is also a writer's hand chalking its poignant messages of thought, observation, joy, loss and grief upon the slate. Whether the crafting of those words has any meaning, whether they echo around your mind, is as much about you as their composer. For me, they do, most of the time.

The better mountaineering writers can bring this unique reflection, an almost musical resonance, to their score but I know of few who can do it as consistently as Jim Perrin, other than our own master-wordsmith, Iain Smart, with his cardinal ability to capture your own memories and paste them to a page. Jim Perrin is a professional writer who makes his living from his craft, although this isn't to denigrate his motivation. However, there is, albeit rarely and perhaps quite naturally, a sense of superfluous and irritating and, dare I say, self-indulgent gobbledygook journalism about some of the work and this is where he loses my sympathy, although not necessarily my concord.

At its simplest, this book is a collection of Perrin's best climbing articles, written from 1967 to 2005 and most of them previously published, with a section of candid, often moving, autobiographical sketches by way of introduction. It is a kaleidoscopic and pensive look at climbers and climbing over nearly four decades of crucial changes in the sport, if such a word can accurately encompass this most enigmatic of activities. You might expect that a motley assemblage of 60 essays, such as this, would lack continuity, but form and harmony are provided by the way that they are grouped together in three sections – the Climbs, the Climbers, and Climbing itself.

Three themes and, within, a triple story of Jim's journey from Manchester's post-war, wasted streets, the promise of spaciousness offered by the Pennine horizon, then rock-climbing and its world, and his intelligent, penetrating probing of the hypocrisies and rewards of that world through his prose, a style which has evolved, like a vital hold on a classic climb, from the raw to the rounded. However, you might want to have a specialist dictionary to hand, for Jim often uses literary references and the full variety of vocabulary; this is no bad thing but it can be a distraction while you stop to delve. *Cathy Powell: A Character Rewritten,* for example, although superficially describing an atmospheric account of a solo ascent of Tryfan's *Grooved Arête*, only has a fuller, more-significant meaning if you've read Elizabeth Coxhead's novel, *One Green Bottle*. Nevertheless, this has its advantages, acting as a window or gateway, even, should you decide to follow these side-roads, and I now have a mental list of further reading to pursue, from Roberts' *A Ragged Schooling* to Shipton's *That Untravelled World.*

What is the significance of the choice of 60, I wonder? Although that number recurs several times – we have 60ft. of perfect gritstone climbing at Laddow in *The Way and The Outcrop* (2002), for example – I think the answer lies, more significantly, in a 'revelation' experienced on a wintry Beinn a` Chaorainn, and described, Murray-like, in a *Vision of Glory* (1993). Jim asks: "how many of us could count even 60 such?" Each essay, then, is perhaps chosen to reflect a beat of the tattoo, imprinted that day upon his consciousness as part of his essential 'heart-life', a tick of time as the hand goes full circle. I can feel for that pulse, can tell you that it's powerfully there and tap out a bit of the rhythm on my keyboard in a limited sort of way but, repeating myself, I cannot tell you if it will resonate with your own.

Last February snow fell, apparently a newsworthy event, in Birmingham and elsewhere in England, and schools were closed by a Health and Safety-conscious official, worried that children might slip and hurt themselves. In my bit of Scotland it was a miserable day, dusk came early by mid-afternoon, so I started to dip – the literary equivalent of snacking into the book with *Adventuring On The Lleyn,* (1991). On just such a day, at much the same time, Jim and his companion were tip-toeing on creaky, "scrotumtightening" sea-cliffs… "this may have been a mistake… but you carry on because to commit yourself to it brings into play a primal reliance on your own resources that's close to the essence of why we climb". I finished the page, the football results were in and I half-listened but, for Captivity v Release, there was no contest

Such is the attraction of the 'collection' format, you don't have to start at the beginning and my earlier analogy to a climb, I realise, isn't quite right, for that suggests a progression on the same cliff while, in reality, each piece stands alone as a single quality pitch on differing strata. Choose a topic to suit your mood, take your time, rest on a heathery ledge and contemplate…for you can't rush this book, there's just too much to think about – and isn't that what you want?

The "'how' as well as an enduring 'why' attached to our going into themountains …" are themes which appear, with constant questioning and probing, sometimes with light-hearted mockery, often with justified derision at the laughable vanity of it all. You might expect that there isn't much more to be thought, said or written about the mountaineering world that hasn't already been expressed in one way or another, but the one shining virtue of Perrin's work is its originality of thought and expression. In the distant past I used to travel to school by train and the route involved a long tunnel. Occasionally, light from the preceding carriage would illuminate the vague outline of a sentry-box set into the brickwork where rail-workers took shelter, inches from annihilation. I am not aware of ever having dredged this particular memory from its dusty niche but, after the death of his friend Al Harris, just the power of a few words in Jim's tribute – as "we crouch in our retreats and know your passing" – suddenly brought it back in all the dirty reality of smuts of soot and that unique reek of smoky steam-powered engines. He picks the right, rapier words at the right time, like the boxer that he aspired to be, that he would have been, not bludgeoning but striking where it scores, re-awakening distant memories and feelings.

You may remember a television series where 'celebrities' from the outdoor world were filmed as they walked and talked in remote places. I was disappointed that Perrin had boarded this particular gravy-train with McNappy, telescopic-poles all adangle in Dingle, but not surprised when, halfway through the coastal walk, he disappeared, to the consternation of the film-crew. Although the public excuse was that he had fallen asleep on a grassy shelf, it seemed pretty obvious that he had grown tired of the trite questions and absented himself, sensing their irrelevant intrusion on the grandeur of the scenery. He re-appeared at the end and recited a piece of poetry that he had just written, the only speck of gold in the verbal dross – his writing a mirror to the man.

Like W. H. Murray, who inspired him, Jim doesn't hide behind his words; he is not ashamed of honesty, to write what he feels, to point out hypocrisy and to let us see beyond his shield. This has left him, over the years, vulnerable to sniping but he has weathered the storm with dignity and there is no sense of rancour in his compositions. His life in pieces, he soloed *Coronation Street*, high on cocaine, and was vilified by the Establishment, but who would disagree with the basic principle "…that if you want to climb, this is the core experience?" He has moved through the rock-climbing world at the highest level and known some of its greatest protagonists – Tilman, Longland, Joe Brown, Steve Haston and more, and writes about them with great generosity of spirit. In *The Only Genuine Joe: A Tribute* (1998) the most significant sentence, for me, is: "The mark of a person is the way they are to those who have nothing to offer." Forget the climbs and hero-worship – this is a nugget for both its possession and recognition. It draws back to a more honourable time when "…images of joyful achievement and aspiring, of innocent mountain ambition" were our *raison d'etre*, before the day when an inconveniently dying man could be ignored and stepped around on an Everest summit bid.

Although I am reluctant to draw attention to the irrelevancies of boundaries, there is no doubt that Scottish climbing has a unique tradition and ethos, where the mountains still have the edge on mankind's reductive processes, something that Jim recognises in *The Ice Climbers* (1985) and their "…richly diverse and excellent" writings. "The simple common bond lies in their subject matter – Scottish winter-climbing – a sphere of action every bit as evocative, resonant, heroic and eventful as Arctic exploration, the Alpine Golden Age, Himalayan first ascents, or any of the other great sagas of adventure and elemental hardship.In this last is the key. It is easy enough to write gilded contemplations of sunny days on rock. But in the strange sub-Arctic of the Scottish mountains in winter, the climbers probing up in the half-light, sketchily belayed, uncertain as to route, conditions, or even possibility, the narrative takes on an intense thrust and urgency".

Although composed more than 20 years ago, the sentiment that it is for qualities beyond the mundane descriptions of events that we remember great mountain writers is still very apt, perhaps more-so as the twin-edged sword of 'development', while making climbing more comfortable, both physically and mentally, also lowers the risk, down-grades the adventure, and reduces the challenge – all topics which he takes to heart. We may curse the midges, the bogs, the rain, the long access – but we need them to help keep our particular shibboleth unassailable. In *Bogles and Bog-trots* (2004) there is a tribute to the "best and most esoteric long-walk crag of them all – the Meadow Face of Beinn Tarsuinn" and praise for its three long crack-lines, including *"The Bender*, a big corner groove… about which superlatives fail me". This is all written in praise of "one of the most sweeping and beautifully architectonic cliffs you've ever seen" and in recognition of one of the pioneers, Bill Skidmore, a typically noble gesture. Perrin is clearly a man who gets far more pleasure from the act of giving than receiving accolades, so that when he writes "… and I haven't yet been to Creag an Dubh Loch or Carnmore…" it is because he is content to admit to a default and not through any boastfulness.

The twin threads of mountaineering literature and history weave their ways through the text and, in conversation with *The Essential Jack Longland* (1988), we have a real connection as far back as the 19th century, where it all started, through Geoffrey Winthrop Young and Cecil Slingsby. You can sense, too, that unique 'Golden Era' vortex of climbing development in North Wales in the 1920-30s, in *John Hoyland – The Missing Dates* (1985) and I may even be able to add a little to the history. The Professor Turnbull who fell on Cloggy was none other than SMC ex-president Herbert Turnbull (and, for those who remember him, uncle of Oliver Turnbull). Herbert was often an external examiner at Bangor University and perhaps, imprudently, was tempted onto a climb that was beyond him. All of this isn't to say that I don't find some semi-pretentious molehills turned into mountains as, for example, in *That Old Thing About Grace* (2001) but you might like it.

So it goes. I wouldn't dare argue with Jim's assertion that Menlove Edwards was "climbing's greatest-ever prose-writer with the wry intelligence and visceral clarity he brings to recording the climbing experience" but it is only fair to say that Perrin carries on that tradition in very similar vein. This is mountain literature of the highest order – evocative, interesting, and thought-provoking.

Mike Jacob.

Mountain Rescue – Chamonix-Mont Blanc: Anne Sauvy. (Baton Wicks – London; 368pp.; illus; £14.99; ISBS1-898573-52-2).

I generally try to steer clear of anything to do with mountain rescue. I know rescuers do a great job, but reading about unfortunate climbers being carted off the hill is not for me. However, this book is about mountain rescue in Chamonix and anything to do with the Mont Blanc area grabs my interest.

Anne Sauvy spent the summer of 1997 at the Les Bois headquarters of the Peloton de Gendarmerie de Haute Montagne. (PGHM) observing the rescue activities of these skilled mountaineers.

After a month she nearly gave up the assignment – so disturbed she was by some of the events. Members of the PGHM, however, persuaded her to carry on so she could present their story accurately and counteract the sometimes ill-informed and stupid media reports.

Anne Sauvy gives a very moving account of the trials and tribulations experienced by the rescuers on the mountain and in the valley.

I know that these days the Chamonix area is a crazy place to go climbing, but I had not realised the extent of the insanity. Some of the stories in this book beggar belief. I'm glad Anne Sauvy didn't quit and carried on regardless to produce this excellent chronicle of life at the sharp end of mountain rescue.

Essential reading for our own rescue teams.

D.P.

OFFICE BEARERS 2006-2007

Honorary President: William. D. Brooker
Honorary Vice-Presidents: Douglas Scott, Gerry S. Peet
President: Paul V. Brian
Vice-Presidents: Brian R. Shackelton, Brian Findlay

Honorary Secretary: John R. R. Fowler, 4 Doune Terrace, Edinburgh, EH3 6DY.
Honorary Treasurer: John A. Wood, Spout Close, Millbeck, Underskiddaw,
Keswick, Cumbria CA12 4PS. **Honorary Editor:** Charles J. Orr, 28 Chesters
View, Bonnyrigg, Midlothian EH19 3PU. **Convener of the Publications Sub-
Committee:** Rab Anderson, 24 Paties Road, Edinburgh, EH141EE. **Honorary
Librarian:** John Hunter, 2 Lorraine Road, Dowanhill, Glasgow, G12 9NZ.
Honorary Custodian of Slides: David Stone, 30 Summerside Street, Edinburgh,
EH 6 4NU. **Honorary Archivist:** Robin N. Campbell, Glynside, by Fintry,
Stirlingshire, G63 0LW. **Convener of the Huts Sub-Committee:** William H.
Duncan, Kirktoun, East End, Lochwinnoch, Renfrewshire, PA12 4ER. **Custodian
of the CIC Hut:** Robin Clothier, 35 Broompark Drive, Newton Mearns, Glasgow,
G77 5DZ. **Custodian of Lagangarbh Hut:** Bernard M. Swan, 16 Knowes View,
Faifley, Clydebank, Dunbartonshire, G81 5AT. **Custodian of the Ling Hut:**
William Skidmore, 1 Kirkton Drive, Lochcarron, Wester Ross, IV54 8UD.
Custodian of the Raeburn Hut: Heather Morning, Duach Mills, Nethybridge,
Inverness-shire, PH253DH. **Custodian of the Naismith Hut:** William S.
McKerrow, Scotsburn House, Drummond Road, Inverness, IV2 4NA. **Committee:**
Ann Macdonald, David M. Nichols, Chris R. Ravey, Campbell Forrest, Gillian E.
Irvine, Clifford D. Smith, James Beaton, Peter J. Biggar, Andrew M. James.

SMC Internet Address – http://www.smc.org.uk SMC e-mail: smc@smc.org.uk

Journal Information

Editor:	Charles J. Orr, 28 Chesters View, Bonnyrigg, Midlothian EH193PU. (e-mail: charliejorr@hotmail.com).
New Routes Editor:	A. D. Nisbet, 20 Craigie Avenue, Boat of Garten, Inverness-shire PH24 3BL. (e-mail: anisbe@globalnet.co.uk).
Photos Editor:	A. Tibbs, Crown Cottage, 4 Crown Circus, Inverness, IV2 3NQ. (e-mail: teamtibbs@hotmail.com)
Distribution:	D. F. Lang, Hillfoot Hey, 580 Perth Road, Dundee, DD2 1PZ.

INSTRUCTIONS TO CONTRIBUTORS

Articles for the Journal should be submitted before the end of January for consideration for
the following issue. Lengthy contributions are preferably typed, double-spaced, on one side
only, and with ample margins (minimum 30mm). Articles may be accepted on floppy disk,
IBM compatible (contact Editor beforehand), or by e-mail. The Editor welcomes material
from both members and non-members, with priority being given to articles of Scottish
Mountaineering content. Photographs are also welcome, and should be good quality colour
slides. All textual material should be sent to the Editor, address and e-mail as above.
Photographic material should be sent direct to the Editor of Photographs, address as above.
Copyright.Textual matter appearing in the Miscellaneous section of the Journal, including
New Climbs, is copyright of the publishers. Copyright of articles in the main section of the
Journal is retained by individual authors.

i